The **C**omplete,

CROSS-REFERENCED GUIDE to the

Baby Buster
Generation's

Collective
Unconscious

The Complete,

CROSS-REFERENCED GUIDE to the

Baby Buster Generation's

Collective
Unconscious

Glenn Gaslin and Rick Porter

 Boulevard Books, New York

THE COMPLETE, CROSS-REFERENCED GUIDE TO THE BABY BUSTER GENERATION'S
COLLECTIVE UNCONSCIOUS

A Boulevard Book / published by arrangement with the authors.

PRINTING HISTORY
Boulevard trade paperback edition / January 1998

Photos reprinted by permission of Archive Photos.

"Mad Lib" is a trademark belonging
to Price Stern Sloan; "Mad Lib"
template used by permission.

The Putnam Berkley World Wide Web site address is
http://.berkley.com

ISBN: 1-57297-335-8

BOULEVARD
Boulevard Books are published by The Berkley Publishing Group,
a member of Penguin Putnam Inc., 200 Madison Avenue,
New York, New York 10016.
BOULEVARD and its logo are trademarks
belonging to Berkley Publishing Corporation.

PRINTED IN THE UNITED STATES OF AMERICA

10   9   8   7   6   5   4   3   2   1

THIS BOOK ISN'T ABOUT ANYTHING. Seriously. So don't go looking for a point. Don't fish around for a thesis statement or a grand unifying paragraph saying what this book is and why it exists and why you—and everybody you know—should buy it, read it, and keep it near where you sleep. There isn't one. There never will be one. There shouldn't be one. That's why it looks the way it does, with the content chopped up into little pithy blocks of knowledge and thrown in alphabetic order. There's no issue, item, statement, person, event, thought, non sequitur, dream, ad campaign, or point of view around which this stuff revolves, or to which it sticks. That's why the title's so long, why there's yet another title stripped across the top of the cover, and why, when you open it all up, you find a whole mess of pages explaining what this book is about, which, as we said earlier, just simply isn't anything.

So let us clarify that. This book, as you can tell, does *contain* things, while it is not necessarily *about* any of them. These pages speak of a great many things, in fact, things that (hopefully) you find familiar, things about which you might not have thought recently and that make you think of other things. Things. Thingsthingsthings. See? There you have it. The point. The thesis we said couldn't be found. *This book contains things!*

Now, with that out of the way, let's move on to the good stuff. All of you are surely asking, "Why does this book, which isn't about anything yet contains thousands of things, exist? Where did it come from? Why is the title so long? Who are these Glenn and Rick guys? Are they gay? Who am I? Why am I so confused about myself and my direction in life, and will this here book help me figure it all out?"

The answers, patient reader, will come.

First, we want you to help us illustrate a point. Open this book. Right, it's already open, we realize, but open it further. Flip to one of the pages in the middle. Read the first entry that catches your attention. Digest it. Laugh. Now, follow one of the cross-references at the end and read that entry, too. (Ideally, if you didn't have explicit instructions to come back and see us here in the "Introduction," you should just keep reading like that all day, flipping and flipping and saying, "Gosh, did they put *Gilligan's Planet* in here?" and looking that up, too.) So now, dear reader, you just witnessed the heart of this book, a few of the things about which we talked earlier, things that we (the authors) plucked, with the utmost of caution and care, from the entire history of mankind and placed in your hands today.

And, as you may or may not have noticed, the epicenter of all human knowledge, at least according to the criteria driving this book and the minds of your authors, is a decade in the last half of the 20th century, the late, great 1980s, more affectionately and commonly known as simply *the '80s*. In order for the things to make the cut for this book, they had to take place either in that magical decade or in its periphery. The reasons why will become evident. The 1970s, too, some would argue, had some effect on how the '80s shook out, hence their modest showing here. Other folks, however, would say that Reagan, with a handful of Jelly Bellies, started history anew in 1980, with what we call "morning in America." Those people should be shunned and jailed. Neither Reagan nor God (see entries for both in this book) have the power to reverse the impact of disco, *Good Times*, and Susan B. Anthony dollars, which, of course, have been diligently and masterfully immortalized in this book.

This obsessive, Hinckley-like focus on a particular decade may scare some of you. It may conjure images of other misled historical crusades, failed empires, or cheesy books on popular culture. But there is a method to this seemingly insane behavior: We (the authors) and you (the twentysomething consumers of today's America) grew up in the '80s. We grew up in the *same* '80s. No matter where we lived in this country, so many of us shared the same culture, the same massive volumes of art and wisdom being pumped out of Hollywood and into our homes through magic underground tubes called "cable." We bought the same clothes in the same stores while having nearly identical personal experiences in nearly identical malls. We think we're OK here in making the argument that, more so than in any time in history, the lives of America's youth were *exactly the same*. We may be the first class of youngsters ever to have no great and unifying event in the form of a war, who have no assassinations or Depression or even significant constitutional amendments.

In the absence of any terrific, horrible, life-affirming, epoch-staging, Great Society–building, paradigm-shifting, destiny-manifesting, clock-setting event, these are the things that define us: Pong and the Rubik's Cube, *The A-Team* and that Herb guy from the Burger King ads, Gorbachev's splotch and Imelda's shoes, Kajagoogoo and Duran Duran and Sigue Sigue Sputnik. Things. Lots and lots and lots of things. Things that we remember and might rather forget, cultural goo caught in our brains. Some of these things may have altered the course of mankind, sure, and some were merely blips of awful noise that passed in and out of the Top 40 without causing too much trouble. In this book, we treat them with fairly equal weight. They all inhabit similar pockets in our minds, synaptic divots filled during a few minutes in front of one medium or another, neurological nuggets that connect seamlessly with hundreds of others containing, as you may have guessed, more things.

And this brings us back to what will have to be called, for lack of a better word, the *point*. If you'll remember, we asked you to venture into the meat of this thick tome and examine a few entries. Let's say, for example, that you got lucky and opened to the paragraph on the aforementioned HERB, an elusive geek who had never eaten a Burger King Whopper yet was loved by his friends. And then you took a cross-referenced journey to our analysis of the '80s-centric cultural stereotype known as the NERD. And maybe from there you learned more about ANTHONY EDWARDS (star of *Revenge of the Nerds*) and then flipped to *Top Gun* (in which he played Goose) and from there checked out RONALD REAGAN and the IRAN-CONTRA THING and on and on. All these things, be they actual human beings, academic sociological concepts, or examples of advertising genius, carry equal weight in the collective unconscious. Or so we (the authors) would have you (the savvy, sassy, clued-in crowd of Young America) believe.

Indeed, if we were to continue onward with this Introduction, we might corner ourselves into writing some sort of unifying analysis, creating some fictional, logical model of the universe in which these things actually *mean* something. We would be forced to place some importance on the whole of this book, its contents, and, by parallel association, the stuff inside your head. Given enough time and paper, we could even convince ourselves that this book *does* have a purpose after all, that the things we know and you know form the core of knowledge necessary to speed the human race into the future, that these things are the key to Progress on Planet Earth, that we know them for *a reason*. But, realizing that

Our fearless leader.

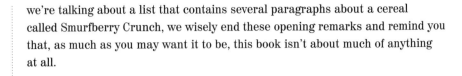

we're talking about a list that contains several paragraphs about a cereal called Smurfberry Crunch, we wisely end these opening remarks and remind you that, as much as you may want it to be, this book isn't about much of anything at all.

ABBA

The only things you need to remember about this campy, disco-era band are that they were 1) extremely popular around the turn of the decade, and 2) extremely Swedish. Every few years, they become sort of popular again. Erasure even did an entire album of ABBA remakes.

See also DISCO; ERASURE; SYNTH-POP

ABDUL, PAULA

Former Lakers cheerleader who wanted you to know that, "straight up," she was "forever your girl," except that you're a "cold-hearted" snake. Then she danced a lot and had a phenomenal string of No. 1 songs in the late '80s.

See also JACKSON, JANET; JOHNSON, EARVIN "MAGIC"

ACID WASH

Call it faded, relaxed, stonewashed, or acid-washed, but the look of denim changed forever. The decision was made in the mid-'80s. The proper authorities were notified, the designers commissioned, the sewing machines fired up, the ad writers instructed, and the Great Unwashed Masses of America informed: *Blue jeans shall not be considered cool unless they look like they have been worn mountain climbing in harsh weather every day for the past three years*. No longer could jeans look "new." A deep blue philosophy faded into a lighter-hued mindset. Harsh streaks of white swiped through the blue. Light overpowered dark. And iffy coloring defeated solids. You could even buy rocks and stonewash your own leg wear. As an organic and natural side effect to this, the bulletproof denim of Wranglers and Tuffskins was rendered hopelessly fashionless.

See also 501 BLUES; JEAN JACKETS; TWO-TONE JEANS

"ADDICTED TO LOVE" GIRLS, THE

These were the pale-faced, emotionless zombie-women standing behind Robert Palmer in his "Addicted to Love" video. They wore slinky black dresses and bright lipstick. They never smiled. They played instruments, looked vaguely robotic, and were widely regarded as being very sexy indeed. Some outspoken "Addicted to Love girls" opponents, however, decided that the ladies appeared to be mindless sex slaves, and that, as we all know, is a bad thing.

See also POWER STATION; BLU-BLOCKER GUY, THE

A big moment in our lifetimes

On January 20, 1981, after 444 days and one tragically botched rescue attempt, Iran releases the 52 American hostages it was holding at the U.S. embassy in Tehran. Newspapers trumpeted the event with 3-inch high banner headlines. Oh, and Ronald Reagan became president that day, too.

ADIDAS

This name brand stands for, as we all know, "all day I dream about sex."

See also NIKE; REEBOK; SALT II

ADVENTURE PEOPLE

A collection of Fisher-Price action figures depicting regular moes who simply enjoy outdoor sports. Sets included a recreational sky diver, a kayaker, a forest ranger, a prop-plane pilot, and a guy cruising with a big van, a parachute, and a motorbike. These were much sturdier than *Star Wars* figures and G.I. Joes, but had fewer bendable joints. They bridged the gap between doll-sized boy toys (like the old G.I. Joes) and masculine, gun-toting action figures.

See also G.I. JOE; MASTERS OF THE UNIVERSE; STAR WARS; STRAWBERRY SHORTCAKE

AEROBICS

A method of exercising based on the idea that jumping up and down is good for you, especially when set to the Go-Gos or Wham! Aerobics started filling gyms with bouncing women wearing leg warmers in the early '80s, and there is no way to tell if this was the cause or effect of millions of soft, white leather shoes being made by Reebok.

See also FONDA, JANE; JAZZERCISE; LEG WARMERS; REEBOK

AFGHANISTAN

The Soviet Union made a lot of blunders between 1917 and 1991, but invading this desert nation in 1979 just about topped the list. Didn't they have enough arid land already? This conquest did, however, provide a much-needed bridge between the Evil Empire and the Middle East, Reagan's two main adversaries. We suspect Sylvester Stallone was in on the Soviet decision-making.

See also KHOMEINI, AYATOLLAH RUHOLLAH; RAMBO; REAGAN, RONALD

AFTERMASH

Game but ultimately unsuccessful attempt at a spin-off from *M*A*S*H*, with Col. Potter running a small hospital with the help of Radar and Klinger. As spin-offs go it was OK, but there weren't enough of the central characters from the old show to hold our interest.

See also LAST EPISODE OF *M*A*S*H*

AIDS

The disease of our generation. We're too young to remember other massive outbreaks, like smallpox and influenza and the black plague. AIDS emerged in the early '80s, and we just don't need to get into all the details about the impact it's had on our sex lives.

See also HARING, KEITH; HUDSON, ROCK; PATIENT ZERO; WHITE, RYAN

AIDS RIBBON

A simple little red bow that most people started noticing when celebrities wore them to the Academy Awards in the late '80s, and has since

---

Movie lines we said a lot

"You dick!"

—A Spicoli line from *Fast Times at Ridgemont High* we used when mock outrage was called for. Particular attention to Spicoliesque inflection is called for to avoid merely sounding like a dick yourself.

become as synonymous with the AIDS cause as Keith Haring's art. The ribbon basically says that the wearer recognizes the problem of AIDS and would like you to, as well. A fine example of national logo recognition being used for something other than selling stuff.

See also AIDS; HARING, KEITH; YELLOW RIBBONS

AIRPLANE!

The funniest movie ever made. No film, before or since, has jammed so many sight gags, random parodies, and shameless puns into such an unapologetic tirade about the evils of '70s disaster flicks. It would be impossible to mention all the great lines ("It looks like I picked the wrong week to stop sniffing glue") and spoofs without just printing the screenplay. And stop calling me Shirley.

See also KENTUCKY FRIED MOVIE; SATURDAY NIGHT FEVER; SWARM, THE; ZUCKER BROTHERS

AIR SUPPLY

Barry Manilow times two. No, worse. Lionel Richie squared. Times Journey and plus Toto and Asia.

See also HALL & OATES; RICHIE, LIONEL

AIRWOLF

CBS rip-off of the ABC rip-off of the 1984 combat chopper movie *Blue Thunder*. Jan-Michael Vincent starred as a renegade pilot on the trail of his long-lost brother, Sinjun, using a jet-powered, high-tech helicopter to track down the shadowy forces behind his disappearance. Ernest Borgnine costarred as Vincent's mentor and mechanic.

See also BLUE THUNDER; KNIGHT RIDER; SUPER FUZZ

A/K/A PABLO

Bad sitcom starring comic Paul Rodriguez as a comic who had a just-plain-*loco* family and made a lot of Mexican jokes. The show lasted about a month.

See also MAMA'S FAMILY

AKIRA

The only cartoon ballsy enough to nuke Tokyo. In 1987, this Japanese film and comic book series helped define the growing, dark world of cyberpunk. The motorcycles were cool, too.

See also BLADE RUNNER; CYBERPUNK; NEUROMANCER; STAR BLAZERS; WATCHMEN

ALASKA PIPELINE

This 800-mile stretch of pipe that runs the length of the 49th state didn't really mean much to you, me, or gas prices. But the way Exxon hyped it in TV ads when it was finished led us to believe that it was the greatest thing since toothpaste pumps, which hadn't even been invented yet.

See also EXXON VALDEZ; PUMP TOOTHPASTE

ALBANO, CAPT. LOU

With rubber bands stuck to his facial hair and Cyndi Lauper on his arm, he led the charge of the World Wrestling Federation into the world of mainstream entertainment. Other early key players included "Macho Man" Randy Savage, Jesse "The Body" Ventura, "Rowdy" Roddy Piper, Hulk Hogan, Andre the Giant (may he rest in peace), and Mean Gene Okerlund.

See also Hogan, Hulk; Lauper, Cyndi

AL CAPONE'S VAULT

Empty.

See also Gotti, John; Rivera, Geraldo

ALF

A wisecracking alien who lived secretly with the Tanners (another '80s prime-time NBC nuclear family) after crash-landing in their garage. He came from the planet Melmac, spoke English, and looked *a lot* like Fozzie Bear. Everybody called him Alf (Get it? Alien Life Form?), even though his name was Gordon Shumway. The plot to almost every episode involved somebody outside the family *almost* finding out about Alf. Sort of like *Gilligan's Island*, where they *almost* get off the island every week—except not so funny. And *Gilligan's Island* wasn't that funny.

See also Alf Cartoon; Cosby Show, The; Family Ties; Gilligan's Planet; Growing Pains; Hogans, The

ALF CARTOON

Saturday morning series about Alf (aka Gordon Shumway) hanging out on his home planet of Melmac. Much funnier than the prime-time show.

See also Alf; Punky Brewster; Fonzie Cartoon; Gilligan's Planet; Mr. T and the T Force

That's Gordon Shumway to you.

ALICE

Sitcom about the staff of Mel's Diner that ran just about forever ('76 to '85), so, during its height, we could watch reruns in the afternoon and then new episodes at night until we were so sick of Alice (Linda Lavin), Tommy (Philip McKeon), Mel (Vic Tayback), Vera (Beth Howland), and Flo (Polly Holiday) that we wanted to tell them all to "Kiss my grits!"

BONUS FACT: This was based on the Martin Scorsese movie *Alice Doesn't Live Here Anymore*, which wasn't quite so funny.

See also Flo; It's a Living; Waitresses, The

ALIEN

One of the first truly scary movies we were allowed to see, usually on cable. The best part was when the baby alien comes out of that guy's stomach.

See also Scott, Ridley; Spaceballs; V.; Weaver, Sigourney

AMADEUS

It was an Academy Award–winning

movie starring F. Murray Abraham and Tom Hulce that came out two years before a lame techno-pop song by some guy named Falco.

See also Falco

AMAZING STORIES

Steven Spielberg's first attempt at television. This science fiction/ mystery/comedy was pretty cool with a lot of gee-whiz appeal, but it failed in the ratings. Memorable episodes included one about a WWII gunner (Casey Siemaszko) who drew cartoon landing gear for his disabled plane (the crew also included then-obscure Kevin Costner and Kiefer Sutherland) and one where a jock guy and a nerd girl were made magnetic—literally— and stuck to each other. It ran with the new *Alfred Hitchcock Presents* on NBC in 1985.

See also Costner, Kevin; Spielberg, Steven; *Three O'Clock High*; *Young Guns*

AMAZON WOMEN ON THE MOON

An obscure-but-hilarious collection of movie and commercial parodies. Also a pseudo-sequel to 1977's *Kentucky Fried Movie*. John Landis directed both movies (with a little help the second time from the likes of Joe *Gremlins* Dante), but *KFM* was written by the Zucker-Abrahams-Zucker comedy think tank. *Amazon Women* featured Rosanna Arquette, Steve Guttenberg, Arsenio Hall, and David Alan Grier in 1987. Neither movie did well in theaters, but both are VCR cult classics.

Bonus clarification: *Amazon Women on the Moon* is often confused with several soft-core porn and horror films with similar titles, including: *Cannibal Women in the Avocado Jungle of Death*, *Sorority Babes in the Slimeball Bowl-O-Rama*, and *Killer Klowns from Outer Space*.

See also Guttenberg, Steve; Hall, Arsenio; Landis, John; Zucker Brothers

AMERICAN WEREWOLF IN LONDON, AN

A rarity among 1980s horror films: it was good. This masterpiece from John Landis was scary without the excessive gore of your standard slasher flick, was very well written and genuinely funny, and didn't insult the intelligence of viewers. Plus the transformation scene was amazing.

See also Landis, John; *Thriller*

AMERICATHON

The first motion picture brave enough to give top billing to John Ritter, and the only one to let him play the President of the United States. In the future, according to this unwatchable 1979 mess, our great nation runs out of money and Ritter hosts a fundraising telethon, selling off parts of California to Mexico, etc. Also starred George Carlin, Elvis Costello, and Meat Loaf.

See also "Paradise by the Dashboard Light"; *Three's Company*

AMERIKA

This is how the world ends, not with a bang but with a grueling 18-hour miniseries. Our fear of an invasion by the Evil Empire climaxed and fizzled with this much-hyped Kris Kristofferson vehicle, which was as dull as Nebraska and aired in 1987, when *glasnost* had already become part of our vocabulary. The only cool parts were the uniforms that made Soviet soldiers look like storm troopers.

BONUS FACT: The regions into which the Soviets divided the country just happened to correspond with the spheres of influence of the Baby Bells, and if you look real close, you will see that the Midwest region was actually called "Ameritech."

See also EVIL EMPIRE; GLASNOST; GORBACHEV, MIKHAIL S.; *INVASION USA*; MINISERIES; *RED DAWN*

AMNESTY INTERNATIONAL

The first political organization that many of us who grew up in the '80s joined. Before environmental groups took advantage of liberal leanings in youngsters, Amnesty International invaded high schools and held meetings and staged mass letter-writing campaigns, trying to free somebody from a foreign prison somewhere. The group also focused attention on the evil of apartheid in South Africa. Free Mandela and all that.

See also APARTHEID; CD LONGBOXES; FREE JAMES BROWN; IRANIAN HOSTAGE CRISIS; TIANANMEN SQUARE

ANDREWS, V.C.

Mysterious author of creepy books that, for some reason, teenage girls loved. A series of her paperbacks included *Flowers in the Attic* and *Petals on the Wind*, which had something to do with incest and kids locked in an attic, and widespread reports of the author's nonexistence/death made the whole thing that much weirder. Also, the book covers had holes in them through which you could see a painting of a freaky, pale-faced teen, which was part of a larger image on the inside flap.

See also BLUME, JUDY; DREW, NANCY

ANDROPOV, YURI

Soviet leader who died in 1984.

See also CHERNENKO, KONSTANTIN

ANGEL HEART

A 1987 film starring Mickey Rourke that would be totally forgotten had it not featured a torrid, bloody love scene between Rourke and Lisa Bonet, star of the squeaky-clean *The Cosby Show*. The filmmakers eventually cut part of the scene to avoid an X rating, but our image of Denise Huxtable was tarnished forever.

See also COSBY SHOW, THE; ROURKE, MICKEY; THURSDAY NIGHT LINEUP

ANNIE

The world went gaga over the little orphan girl with the empty eyes around 1980, when the classic radio show and comic strip became a big Broadway show, featuring the song

"Tomorrow" and Sarah Jessica Parker as Annie in the touring version. It was then made into a movie, starring Aileen Quinn and directed by John Huston. *Annie* was so big, in fact, that there was a "Bloom County" parody of it.

See also **"Bloom County"**

ANSWERING MACHINES

Remember how you used to get annoyed when somebody had one?

See also **Compact discs; Microwaves; VCRs; Walkman**

ANYTHING BOX

British synth band that emerged and vanished in 1989 with the song "Living in Oblivion," now the title of a series of albums chronicling the best (?) music of the '80s.

See also **Living in a Box**

APARTHEID

In the vacuum of serious, definable social crises at home, the political-minded youth of the '80s turned to South Africa for a cause. The pure, unfiltered racism of apartheid made it hard to defend, but debate did erupt around fuzzier issues, like whether U.S. companies should leave the country. Many people refused to drink Coca-Cola because the company kept making and selling fluids in South Africa long after Pepsi and other huge American corporations left. (This was part of a massive boycott-mania that gripped mid-'80s activists.) But opponents said that capitalism had to thrive in order for the revolution to take place, so everyone, please, have a Coke and support the cause of change in the tip of a faraway continent.

See also **Amnesty International; Mandela, Nelson; New Coke; *Roots***

APOCALYPSE NOW

First, most symbolic, and weirdest of all the big Vietnam movies, loosely based on Joseph Conrad's *Heart of Darkness*. It starred Martin Sheen as an Army intelligence guy sent to find Col. Kurtz (Marlon Brando), who had gone nuts and surrounded himself with natives who worshipped him and killed for him. Dennis Hopper was also in there. And anyone who says they love the smell of napalm in the morning gets it from this film.

See also **Blue Velvet; Full Metal Jacket; Platoon**

APPLE IIE

The classroom computer of choice during our formative years, the one on which we played Oregon Trail and Summer Games II. This beige monster boasted bright green type on the monitor, a loud clack from the keyboard, and an even louder whir from the disk drive. Also a popular first home computer.

See also **Atari; Big Brother Ad; Commodore 64; Jobs, Steve; TRS 80**

AQUAFRESH

Toothpaste that, when introduced, caused a bit of a stir, mixing gel and paste into a single stream of goo as it did. Many of us who tried this new, supposedly "fun," dental care sustance were disappointed that we couldn't get the stuff to come out neatly swirled, like on the commercials. Instead, it emerged from the tube all mushed up, like any other toothpaste.

See also GEL; GINGIVITIS; PLAQUE; PUMP TOOTHPASTE; TARTAR

ARCADIA

One of two groups spun from Duran Duran. Simon LeBon, Nick Rhodes, and Roger Taylor looked slick and sounded fairly, shall we say, techno. Their big song, "Election Day," also featured gigantic actress/alien Grace Jones.

See also DURAN DURAN; JONES, GRACE; POWER STATION

ARMSTRONG, CURTIS

The quintessential scuzzy loser '80s actor. He played scuzzy loser Booger in *Revenge of the Nerds*, scuzzy loser Herbert Viola in *Moonlighting*, a scuzzy snow-snorting loser in *Better Off Dead,* and a scuzzy hooker-summoning loser in *Risky Business*.

See also BETTER OFF DEAD; EDWARDS, ANTHONY; FOX, MICHAEL J.; HALL, ANTHONY MICHAEL; MOONLIGHTING; REVENGE OF THE NERDS

ART OF BEING NICK, THE

A *Family Ties* spin-off about Nick (Mallory Keaton's boyfriend, the talented garbage sculptor) trying to make it as an artist in The Big City. This lasted one—count 'em, one—episode.

See also ENOS; FAMILY TIES

ART OF NOISE

Not just another British synth-pop band. They mixed everyday sounds (like car ignitions and plumbing creaks) into some of the weirdest music of the '80s. They foreshadowed the house and ambient music of the next decade, and had minor hits with remakes of the "Peter Gunn" theme (with '60s twangster Duanne Eddy) and Prince's "Kiss" (with croonster Tom Jones). Also, torso-free sensation Max Headroom starred in the group's "Paranoimia" video.

See also HEADROOM, MAX; JONES, TOM; PRINCE; SYNTH-POP

ASIA

Once only a continent, in 1982 it also became a sorry power-pop band whose 13.5 minutes of fame forced us to endure such songs as "Heat of the Moment" and "Only Time Will Tell."

See also NIGHT RANGER

ASTEROIDS

So, how many times could you "flip" the score-counter on the home version of this pioneer game?

See also ATARI

ATARI

The company credited with inventing the first video game, Pong. A few years later, the Atari 2600 machine, with its tiny control levers and fragile joysticks, became the most socially significant technology of the past two decades. The home video game craze also included the Atari 5200, Atari 7200, Intellivision, and Colecovision. The word "Atari" was, for almost 10 years, the generic term for a home video game system. And then along came Nintendo.

See also ASTEROIDS; ATARI 400; BUCKNER AND GARCIA; BUMP AND JUMP; BURGER TIME; CENTIPEDE; CHOPLIFTER; COLECOVISION; COMMODORE 64; DEFENDER; DIG DUG; DONKEY KONG; DRAGON'S LAIR; FOOD FIGHT; FROGGER; GALAGA/GALAXIAN/GORF; GAUNTLET; INTELLIVISION; KICK!; M.A.C.H. 3; MISSILE COMMAND; MR. DO; NEXT; PAC-MAN; POLE POSITION; PONG; PUNCH-OUT; Q-BERT; RAMPAGE; SATURDAY SUPERCADE; SPACE INVADERS; SPY HUNTER; STARCADE; SUMMER GAMES; TEMPEST; TRACK AND FIELD; TRON (THE VIDEO GAME); TURBO; WINTER GAMES; ZAXXON; ZORK

ATARI 400

Another video game machine posing as one of the first home computers. The games were better than anything else on the market in the early '80s, but the flat "membrane keyboard" hurt your fingers and the tape drive took forever to load games or programs you wrote in Basic.

See also APPLE IIE; ATARI; COMMODORE 64; VIC 20

A-TEAM, THE

One of the most violent shows in the history of mankind. The funny thing is that no one ever died. The cast was George Peppard as Capt. John "Hannibal" Smith, Dwight Schultz as "Howling Mad" Murdoch, Dirk Bene-dict as Faceman, and Mr. T (fresh from *Rocky III*) as Sgt. Bosco "B.A." Baracus. The characters, all former federal employees and all "legally dead," banded together to step into sticky situations for a little vigilante justice. How innocent folks-in-need got hold of the reclusive and underground A-Team remains a mystery. Most episodes during the 1983–87 run on NBC had two highlights: 1) the musical montage during which B.A. and Murdoch souped up trucks or built a fort or put tank armor on a car or something, and 2) the final scene in which Hannibal said, "I love it when a plan comes together."

See also CANNELL, STEPHEN J.; MR. T CEREAL

ATHENS, GA.

The first city in our time to be judged center of all that is cool in the musical universe. In the late '70s and early '80s, a scene developed there, influenced by an odd combination of post-punk, pop, folk, and maybe even country music. From it arose such megastars as R.E.M. and the B-52s, as well as scores of other bands, like Guadalcanal Diary, Pylon, and Love Tractor.

See also R.E.M.; "ROCK LOBSTER"; TEXAS

ATKINS, CHRISTOPHER

Brooke's loinclothed beau in *The Blue Lagoon*. Last seen guesting on *Dallas* in its later seasons.

See also DALLAS; SHIELDS, BROOKE

AUSSIEMANIA

First *Mad Max* came zooming down the highway in 1979. Then in 1983, Men at Work pulled up in their fried-out combie, talking of vegemite sandwiches and chundering, and pretty soon, everyone was walking around saying "G'dye, mate" and putting some shrimp on the "barbie." Then Yahoo Serious came along, and that was the end of that.

See also HOGAN, PAUL; INXS; JOCKO; *MAD MAX*; MEN AT WORK; NEWTON-JOHN, OLIVIA

AUSTIN, TRACY

Teen tennis sensation of the late 1970s who dethroned Chris Evert from her place at the top of the women's circuit, pigtails flying all the while.

See also RETTON, MARY LOU

AUTOMAN

A 1983 show about a guy who glowed in the dark and could turn into a car. Starred Desi Arnaz, Jr., and was part of the stupid sci-fi show boom of the era.

See also MANIMAL

AWACS

Expensive, goofy-looking radar surveillance planes that the Saudis wanted really bad round about 1982.

See also STEALTH

B

BABY FAE

Little girl that all of America watched in November 1984, when she received a transplant of a baboon's heart shortly after her birth. The experiment didn't work.

See also BABY JESSICA; BABY M; CLARK, BARNEY

BABY JESSICA

The little girl who fell down the well in Texas. For once, people didn't rail against the mother for being a bad parent and letting her kid out of sight for a moment. We just watched and waited for 36 hours or so until firefighters rescued her. The image of the one guy, still in helmet and yellow fireman's gear, carrying her across the field was used for several years to tout network news coverage. It goes without saying that there was eventually a TV movie.

See also BABY FAE; BABY M

BABY M

Third in the triumvirate of babies without last names who made big news in the late '80s. Little M was the subject of a bitter, hugely publicized custody battle between the surrogate mother who bore her and the parents who paid said surrogate to carry the child. It made for great TV.

See also BABY FAE; BABY JESSICA; TEST-TUBE BABY

BABY ON BOARD

Ubiquitous car accessory of the mid-'80s that emerged when Baby Boomers started having kids and wanted everyone to know it. Endless fodder for comedians and smart-asses around the world. The most popular derivation of the sign was "Baby (or Ex-Wife or Ex-Husband) in Trunk."

See also SHIT HAPPENS; SUCTION-CUP GARFIELD; VISUALIZE WHIRLED PEAS

BABYSITTER'S CLUB, THE

Best-selling series of books about a group of junior high school girls who baby-sat and cooked up a bunch of schemes together. Sort of a younger Sweet Valley High with a Nancy Drew edge.

See also BROWN, ENCYCLOPEDIA; DREW, NANCY; HARDY BOYS, THE; *NIGHT OF THE COMET*; SWEET VALLEY HIGH

BACKLESS CHAIRS

Odd, twisted pieces of metal covered with cylindrical pads that you were supposed to *sit on* while typing on that new computer. You put your knees on one bar and your butt on a higher bar, and you kept your back straight. These became popular shortly after home computers and were supposed to be good for posture, but they never really caught on. A few still exist in suburban basement computer rooms with old Commodore 64s and dot matrix printers.

See also COMMODORE 64

BACK TO THE FUTURE

If '80s culture could be summed up with one movie, this might be it. It's a high-school-kids-can-do-anything adventure! It's got Michael J. Fox on a skateboard! It's got a bunch of Huey Lewis songs! It's got Spielberg's name on it!

And Marty McFly nicely accentuates the details of the '80s as "the future" when he travels to 1955. Like, for example, when he orders a Tab and a Pepsi Free at a soda fountain.

See also DELOREAN; FOX, MICHAEL J.; HEADROOM, MAX; *NIGHT OF THE COMET*; PEPSI FREE; PEPSI LITE; SPIELBERG, STEVEN; *WARGAMES*

BACKWARD BASEBALL HATS

Somebody, somewhere, decided this was a good idea. No one knows where this started, but the habit seems unavoidably associated with our generation. Youngsters from previous decades never had this problem. Or if they did, they were the geeky neighbor kids in SitcomLand and mostly wore their hats sideways.

See also DUDE

BACON, KEVIN

His career began inauspiciously: First he was whacked on the ass in *Animal House* (Key line: "Thank you, sir. May I have another?") and stabbed through the throat while lying in bed in *Friday the 13th*. But then he did a nice job in *Diner*, and a couple years later, he was in a little movie called *Footloose*, and by then the world couldn't get enough of this man named after a pork product.

See also DINER; FOOTLOOSE; FRIDAY THE 13TH

BAD NEWS BEARS, THE

First a movie, then a couple of sequels, and then a TV show. The original film starred Walter Matthau as the boozing manager of a team of Little League misfits, galvanized around a star girl pitcher (Tatum O'Neal) and a rebel kid with a dirt bike who just happens to be a great player. But the real cool thing was getting to hear kids our age cuss on screen.

BONUS MUSICAL NOTE: For many of us, this was our first exposure to kick-ass classical music on the soundtrack, such as the "1812 Overture" and "March of the Toreadors" (from *Carmen*).

See also MIRACLE ON ICE; O'NEAL, TATUM

BAIO, SCOTT

You know, Chachi. The Fonz, only smaller. The teen hunk ready-made for consumption by preadolescent girls via *Tiger Beat*, *Teen Dream*, *et al.* Of course, then he got older and had to do *Charles in Charge*.

See also CHARLES IN CHARGE; JOANIE LOVES CHACHI; ZAPPED!

BAKKER, TAMMY FAYE

Wife of humiliated TV superpreacher Jim Bakker and target of many, many mascara jokes.

See also HAHN, JESSICA

BALTIMORA

New Wave band who scored a minor hit in 1986 with the song "Tarzan Boy," which later showed up in Listerine commercials.

See also ANYTHING BOX; BOYS DON'T CRY; CUTTING CREW; DAVID AND DAVID; DR. AND THE MEDICS; DREAM ACADEMY; ESCAPE CLUB; FALCO; FLOCK OF SEAGULLS, A; FOX, SAMANTHA; GLASS TIGER; GRANT, EDDY; JONES, ORAN "JUICE"; JUMP 'N THE SADDLE BAND; LAID BACK; LIVING IN A BOX; LONE JUSTICE; M.A.R.R.S.; NENA; NÜ SHOOZ; POINDEXTER, BUSTER; ROCKWELL; SIGUE SIGUE SPUTNIK; TACO; TIMBUK 3; TIMELORDS; ULLMAN, TRACY; WALL OF VOODOO; WHEN IN ROME; YELLO

BAMBI VS. GODZILLA

A film that consists only of beginning credits and then a cartoon deer getting squished by a giant reptilian foot. That's it. Seen at animation festivals or before other cult movies.

See also DARK STAR; HARDWARE WARS

BANANA CLIPS

Giant hair accessories for girls, so named because of their shape. Cute enough for those under 16, but they had the potential of making your hair look like a horse's mane or the top of a Roman centurion's helmet.

See also BUTTERFLY CLIPS; COLORED HAIR SPRAY

BANANARAMA

Saucy English divas who vamped it up in their 1986 cover of Shocking Blue's "Venus," and walked all over MTV for many months, proving that yeah, baby, they did have it.

See also BANGLES, THE; *KARATE KID, THE*

BAND AID

The first in a rash of huge pop events trying to focus attention on people starving in the Ethiopian desert. This European supergroup was put together by Bob Geldof (lead singer of the Boomtown Rats and also the guy who shaved off his eyebrows in *The Wall*) a year before he organized Live Aid. Band Aid included Sting, Boy George, Phil Collins, George Michael, Paul Young, Duran Duran, and some people from U2 and Ultravox. Their song was "Do They Know It's Christmas," and it included the lyric, "There won't be snow in Africa this Christmas," which was kind of hard to believe. Africa's a pretty big place.

See also FARM AID; HEAR'N AID; LIVE AID; NORTHERN LIGHTS; USA FOR AFRICA

BANDANNAS

Hype fashion accessory for the breakdance set around 1984, when it was especially good if you could tie a pink or purple one around the leg of your parachute pants. The versatile cowboy face covering soon crossed over into the skate-punk movement, helped along by the fact that the singer of Suicidal Tendencies often wore one that obscured part of his eyes as well as his entire forehead. Later, after the premiere of *Colors*, the bandanna was often seen worn over the entire head and referred to as a "do rag." Their association with gangs caused some schools to ban them.

See also BREAKDANCING; *COLORS*; PARACHUTE PANTS; SKATEBOARDING

BANGLES

Decent all-female rock band from the mid-'80s that put out one album loaded with hits ("Manic Monday," "Walk Like an Egyptian," and "Eternal Flame"), did a remake of Simon & Garfunkel's "Hazy Shade of Winter" (for the *Less than Zero* soundtrack), and then disappeared. Lead singer Susanna Hoffs starred in a beach movie called *The Allnighter*, which sucked like an Egyptian.

See also GO-GOS; *LESS THAN ZERO*

BAN THE BOX

The ultimate in '80s activism and boycott-mania, and also an unintentional parody of it all. This group, supported by superstars like Sting, violently advocated getting rid of CD longboxes, which were making the planet uninhabitable.

See also APARTHEID; CD LONGBOXES; FREE JAMES BROWN; STING; USA FOR AFRICA

BANZAI, BUCKAROO

Neurosurgeon, rock star, physicist, rocket pilot, and government troubleshooter, Banzai traveled across the Eighth Dimension to find out that Orson Welles' "War of the Worlds" broadcast was, in fact, for real. The aliens were all named John and residing in New Jersey. Played in the 1984 film *The Adventures of Buckaroo Banzai Across the Eighth Dimension* by Peter *Robocop* Weller.

See also ROBOCOP

BARBARA MANDRELL & THE MANDRELL SISTERS

Inexplicable early-'80s prime-time variety show that consisted mostly of Barbara, Irene, and Louise plucking some down-homey music and playing up their sisterly tiffs. The show maintained a very surreal edge, however, with a house band called Truck Shackley & the Texas Critters, which consisted of five human-sized Krofft puppets (one of whom looked like John Denver) and their dog.

See also KROFFT SUPERSHOW; LAND OF THE LOST

BARBIE

For ours and most generations still in existence, this has been the doll by which all others are judged. By chasing the hot styles and by setting her own, Barbie dominated the playtime scene of our childhood in her pink Corvette and on her white unicorn. Sure, by being tall and blond (usually) and perfectly proportioned, she sets a hard biological example for young girls to follow and has been blamed for creating self-esteem problems. But most women eventually realize that being 12 inches tall and weighing 8 ounces isn't *that* sexy.

See also BRINKLEY, CHRISTIE; CABBAGE PATCH KIDS; G.I. JOE; MAKEOVER BARBIE; STRAWBERRY SHORTCAKE

BARRYMORE, DREW

One minute she's the adorable little sister in *E.T.* and the adorable telekinetic pyromaniac in *Firestarter*, then you turn around and she's in drug rehab before she can drive. Shirley Temple she wasn't.

See also CHILD STARS GONE BAD; *E.T.*; KING, STEPHEN

BARTLES & JAYMES GUYS

Charming, down-home advertising icons who used to sell alcohol in the late '80s. These two old Mayberry types sat in porch-front rocking chairs, and one of them told the television audience about the taste benefits of these new fruity "wine cooler" things from Bartles & Jaymes, and the other just rocked silently. Then they'd thank us for our support. Of course, neither of them was named Bartles and neither of them was named Jaymes.

See also BEERLAND; MACKENZIE, SPUDS; RETURN OF BRUNO, THE

BARYSHNIKOV, MIKHAIL

When being Russian and defecting to America was cool, this springy ballet stud pulled the stuffy and artsy crowd into the anti-commie craze. Also, he's the only ballet dancer that most of us can name.

See also KINKSI, NASTASSJA; SMIRNOFF, YAKOV; *WHITE NIGHTS*

BASIL, TONI

She thought Mickey was so fine and dressed up like a cheerleader in the video to prove it.

See also BALTIMORA; MTV; YANKOVIC, "WEIRD" AL

BATMANIA

The unprecedented and unexplained hype and public adoration given to one of the strangest movies ever: *Batman*. As directed by well-documented weirdo Tim Burton, this blockbuster more closely resembled *Blue Velvet* than *Superman*. Traditional fans of the comic books or the '60s Adam West TV show were baffled by all this attention and the casting of Michael "*Mr. Mom*" Keaton as the Dark Knight. Among the movie's notable oddities include a career highlight of a performance by Jack Nicholson and a supplemental soundtrack by another undisputed freak, Prince.

See also AKIRA; *BEETLEJUICE*; DARK KNIGHT RETURNS, THE; *INCREDIBLE HULK, THE*; PEE-WEE HERMAN; PRINCE; TEENAGE MUTANT NINJA TURTLES

BATTLE OF THE NETWORK STARS

Made-for-TV athletic competition in which stars of shows on the three big networks did such things as play flag football, kayak across a swimming

*Galactic freedom fighters
Starbuck and Apollo.*

**Another big moment
in our lifetimes**

On March 30, 1981, in a
twisted attempt to
impress/express his love
for actress Jodie Foster,
John Hinckley, Jr., shoots
President Reagan.

---

pool, and run obstacle courses. A staple during sweeps month.

SEE ALSO AMERICATHON; THAT'S INCREDIBLE!

BATTLESTAR GALACTICA

A TV show that capitalized on the success of *Star Wars* by using the same
formula: Undermanned and underpow-
ered freedom fighters (the two main
hunks were Richard Hatch as Apollo
and Dirk Benedict as Starbuck) fighting against the evil overlords and their
faceless soldiers, in this case the
Cylons. Lorne Greene played the wise
commander of the good guys.

*See also STAR WARS; THUNDARR THE
BARBARIAN*

BE ALL YOU CAN BE

You know, join the Army, so you can do
more before 9 a.m. than most people
do all day, earn money for college, and
learn the skills 9 of 10 employers look
for when they're hiring.

See also TOP GUN

BEALS, JENNIFER

Star of *Flashdance*, the film that
launched a million ripped sweatshirts.

*See also FLASHDANCE; LEG WARMERS;
RIPPED SWEATSHIRTS*

BEASTIE BOYS

The first white guys to have a hit rap
album, if you can call what they did
on *Licensed to Ill* rap. The album
was obnoxious, crude, and sopho-
moric. The beats were cribbed from
rock songs, the rhyming was not that

sophisticated, and the videos were
campy. In other words, it was the perfect mix to introduce a large white
audience to rap. And who didn't know
the lyrics to "Paul Revere"?

*See also RAP; RUBIN, RICK; RUN-D.M.C.;
TOGETHER FOREVER TOUR*

BEATBOXING

Method by which an MC or DJ makes
noises with his mouth and throat so
as to approximate the sound of drums
or scratching. Noted practitioners of
this rap dialect were Doug E. Fresh,
The Human Beatbox (of The Fat
Boys), and DJ Run of Run-D.M.C.

BONUS FACT: The kinda cool English band Big Audio Dynamite did a
song called "C'mon Every Beatbox" on
their album *No. 10 Upping Street*, but
it was, in fact, about the things we call
boom boxes. Just another one of those
little Brit language quirks, you see.

*See also CLASH, THE; FAT BOYS, THE; RAP;
RUN-D.M.C.*

BEAUTY AND THE BEAST

A prime-time TV show about a big hairy
mutant who lived in the sewers and
captured the hearts of viewers everywhere. Starred Linda Hamilton, who
was between Terminators at the time.

*See also MANIMAL; MR. SMITH;
TERMINATOR, THE*

BEDTIME FOR BONZO

When asked to name Ronald Reagan
movies, most people would list this
first. And last. The film came out in
1951 and tells (in stunning black-and-

white) of a college professor proving things about human nature using a chimpanzee, and it forever pegged the president as "a guy who acted with a monkey."

See also MONKEYMANIA; REAGAN, RONALD

BEERLAND

The magical world where beer commercials take place, a world where it's OK for both men and the laws of physics to misbehave. In Beerland, ordinary guys with no money, no personality, and no looks can drink the right brand of beer and get mobbed by big-breasted, thong-wearing hyperwomen who feed on a diet of pure beer and sex. Nobody has a job in Beerland. In fact, everybody is in a constant state of *just getting off from work*, perhaps the most euphoric feeling known to man.

The basic principles of science have also been altered in Beerland. Beer trucks can drive up the sides of buildings, and partyers can ski down them. Snow never deters the wearing of bikinis. Opening beer bottles can alter the climate, summoning a snowstorm in July, for example. The average sports fan can play with the pros. The burgers are never quite finished at barbecues, so the pre-meal drinking keeps going on and on and on. And a soundtrack of "classic rock" favorites loops constantly in the air of Beerland. The works of Bachman-Turner Overdrive, Joe Cocker, Boston, and Eric Clapton will not be forgotten here.

See also 501 BLUES; QUEEN

BEETLEJUICE

Ladies and gentlemen, meet Winona Ryder. This film from director/very strange guy Tim Burton introduced many of us to our lovely peer, here a grave, pale preteen who could make Michael Keaton materialize by saying "Beetlejuice. Beetlejuice. Beetlejuice!"

See also BATMANIA; DAVIS, GEENA; *GUNG HO*; HEATHERS; *LUCAS*; PEE-WEE HERMAN

BELIEVE IT . . . OR NOT

When Jack Palance breathily intoned these words on the *Ripley's* TV show about freaks and monsters and other mysterious stuff, which aired Sunday evenings in the early 1980s, well, we don't know about you, but we were inclined to believe it.

See also REAL PEOPLE; THAT'S INCREDIBLE!

BELUSHI, JOHN

The last man who could play the out-of-control lunatic/speed freak/drunk for laughs. He was brilliant on *Saturday Night Live* and in movies like *Animal House* and *The Blues Brothers*, but his death made us realize that experimenting with drugs maybe wasn't so funny. And that's one to grow on.

See also Animal House; Blues Brothers, The; Saturday Night Live

BENETAR, PAT

One of the first women to be big in rock 'n' roll without singing R&B tunes or fronting a male group. She had a whole bunch of hits in the first half of the 1980s, from the harsh "Heartbreaker" to "We Belong," a big ballad complete

November 1989: The Wall falls.

with choir. She was also something of a fashion plate, making short, spiky hair and garishly applied makeup the norm for all sorts of aspiring New Wavers.

See also JETT, JOAN

BERLIN WALL

Having a chunk of this is kind of our equivalent to saying, "I was at Woodstock." The fall of this structure was a masterpiece of symbolism. Leo Tolstoy couldn't have written a better metaphor for the fate of communism than a crumbling wall with Tom Brokaw standing on top.

See also GORBACHEV, MIKHAIL S.

BERT AND ERNIE

The stars of *Sesame Street*, these two guys are like the Abbott and Costello of the puppet world. Bert, the straight man, was always playing the fool to Ernie's jokes, punctuated by the lat-

ter's wheezy laugh. Favorite topics between the two include pigeons, bottle caps, and Ernie's rubber duckie. And we won't even have to mention the "longtime companion" rumors about the two roommates.

See also SESAME STREET

BERTINELLI, VALERIE

When *One Day at a Time* premiered, she was just cute. Then she started to grow up and get sexy, becoming the object of many an adolescent boy's, um, affection. Now, of course, we know her as Mrs. Edward Van Halen.

See also SCHNEIDER; VAN HALEN

BETAMAX

The ill-fated videocassette size that never caught on, largely because the inventors over at Sony wouldn't let anybody else make any. So now we all watch VHS tapes, even though they're bigger and clumsier than Betas.

See also DAT; VCR

BETTER OFF DEAD

Savage Steve Holland's classic portrait of a teenager (John Cusack) having a bad year. Also noted for its wild ski scenes and costar Curtis "Booger" Armstrong. Hardly anyone noticed it while it was in theaters, but it's huge on video, even to this day.

See also ARMSTRONG, CURTIS; *HEATHERS*; *SAY ANYTHING . . .*

BIG

Movie about a 12-year-old kid who

makes a wish to be "big" on an old carnival machine called Zoltar on Coney Island, then wakes up the next morning to find he's Tom Hanks. A good movie because you can believe Tom Hanks really is a kid.

See also FREAKY FRIDAY; LIKE FATHER, LIKE SON; SWITCHAROOMANIA; VICE VERSA

BIG BLUE MARBLE

If we happened to wake up on Saturday mornings before the cartoons started, we watched this kid-narrated PBS show about various places on our little planet.

See also 3-2-1 CONTACT

BIG BROTHER AD

This infamous TV spot, shown only once (during the 1984 Super Bowl halftime), introduced the world to the Macintosh computer while mocking Orwellian paranoia and IBM. A beautiful piece of work, mentioned almost every year in newspaper stories on how expensive it is to buy ad time during the Super Bowl.

See also APPLE IIE; JOBS, STEVE; ORWELL, GEORGE

BIG COMBS

These were between 6 and 8 inches long (even longer if you favored the kind with a handle), the teeth were huge, they came in bright colors, and *Seventeen* magazine said in May 1980 what most of us already knew—they were an essential fashion accessory.

See also BUTTERFLY CLIPS

BIG GULP

A fountain beverage size that didn't exist before 1981. But 7-Eleven's introduction of this 32-ounce cup set a new standard for the "large" drink, which was expanded again and again with the 44-ounce Super Big Gulp and 64-ounce (that's a half gallon to you and me) Double Gulp.

Unlike the leisurely sit-down soda fountains seen in *Leave It to Beaver*, 7-Eleven had to deliver fluids to the kids of America in one portable, shove-it-between-the-legs-while-you-drive shot. No refills. Hence the need for Big Gulps and beyond.

See also METRIC SYSTEM; MOUNTAIN DEW; NEW COKE; SUICIDE SLURPEES

BIG LEAGUE CHEW

Shredded bubble gum that came in a pouch. Little Leaguers could act like professional, tobacco-chewing ball players without getting mouth cancer or having to spit every five seconds. The gum formed a rock-hard ball you could stick in your cheek 10 minutes after you put it in your mouth.

See also FUN DIP

BIG WHEEL

Badass plastic tricycle-type thing that you could pedal low to the ground and, if you were lucky enough to have an earlier model, do fishtails with courtesy of the spinout lever, a hand brake on one of the two back wheels that caused you to careen sideways. Of course, these were removed after some parents raised concerns about the safety of the lever. But even if you did fall off, you weren't traveling more than 12 inches before you hit the ground. Stupid grown-ups.

See also GREEN MACHINE; INCHWORM

BILL AND TED'S EXCELLENT ADVENTURE

You could make the argument that this movie begat the current dumb industry in Hollywood. It was also mass America's introduction to Keanu Reeves (he's never quite shaken the image) and inspired lots of kids to use words they didn't really comprehend.

See also BACKWARD BASEBALL HATS; BILL&TEDSPEAK; DUDE

BILL&TEDSPEAK

A variety of slang that sounds more intelligent than it actually is. The key is to use big words ("excellent" or "bodacious" instead of "cool"; "heinous" and "egregious" instead of "gross"), use adverbs ("most definitely"), and to sound sort of aristocratic, as in: "Something most unusual is afoot at the Circle K." The dialect was inspired by the Bill and Ted movies and borrowed from Valley and surfer slang.

See also LIKE; RAD; TOTALLY; *VALLEY GIRL DICTIONARY*

BILLINGSLEY, PETER

For years, he was the adorable blond kid to beat all adorable blond kids. We know him as the embattled protagonist in *A Christmas Story*, the smarter-than-Skip-Stephenson correspondent on *Real People*, and as Messy Marvin from the Hershey's commercials. He also did some pretty lame movies, like *The Dirt Bike Kid* and *Russkies*, but we won't hold that against him.

See also CHRISTMAS STORY, A; MESSY MARVIN; REAL PEOPLE; RUSSKIES

BILLY AND THE BOINGERS

Fictional punk band that satirized the '80s music scene, featuring Bill the Cat on tongue, Opus the penguin on tuba, and Steve Dallas the lawyer as manager. They had a minor hit with "U Stink But I Luv U."

See also BILLY VERA AND THE BEATERS; "BLOOM COUNTY"

BILLY VERA AND THE BEATERS

Balding crooner (and band) whose sappy ballad, "At This Moment," hit No. 1 six years after its 1981 release because it figured as the love theme between Alex P. Keaton and his girlfriend on *Family Ties*. Also a slow-dance staple at high-school dances across America.

See also BILLY AND THE BOINGERS; COX, COURTENEY; *FAMILY TIES*

BIRD, LARRY

The man who proved that athletic ability does not count for everything in the world of professional sports. He was ugly and slow and white and couldn't jump, but his amazing shooting and passing led the Boston Celtics to three NBA championships in the 1980s and gave hope to gym rats everywhere. He was also involved in one of the last great man-to-man rivalries in sports with Magic Johnson, with whom he entered the league and battled for several titles.

See also JOHNSON, EARVIN "MAGIC"

BLACK CAULDRON, THE

A little-appreciated, full-length animated Disney movie about a couple of medieval kids taking on the forces of evil—*all by themselves*. Actually, they had the help of a fuzzy magical creature called Gurgi (not to be confused with Glomer, the fuzzy magical creature from the *Punky Brewster* cartoon) and a clairvoyant pig. But this 1985 movie (based on the Chronicles of Prydain kid fantasy books by Lloyd Alexander) was so dark, disturbing, and unpopular that Disney has pretty much disowned it. You probably won't ever see this released from the vaults and onto video.

See also CHRONICLES OF NARNIA, THE; NIGHT OF THE COMET

BLACK HOLE, THE

Disney's attempt to create a sci-fi franchise (made after the success of *Star Wars* and *Star Trek: The Motion Picture*) could well have been titled *20,000 Leagues in Space*, for its plot resembled that of the undersea classic: Marooned explorers come across a madman in an amazing ship who wants to do something that will result in almost certain death (he wants to dive into a black hole to see what's on the other side). Despite special effects and some lovable robots, it didn't quite work, perhaps because we felt like we'd seen most of it before.

See also COSMOS; HAWKING, STEPHEN; STAR TREK II: THE WRATH OF KAHN; STAR WARS

BLACK STALLION, THE

A series of books about a horse, written by Walter Farley, that young boys weren't ashamed to read. The first two books in the series were made into movies starring Mickey Rooney as the trainer and Kelly Reno as the kid.

See also HARDY BOYS; PHANTOM TOLLBOOTH, THE

BLADE RUNNER

In 1982, Ridley Scott's vision of Los Angeles A.D. 2019 set the visual stage for the science fiction subgenre of cyberpunk, which dwells in the seedy, techno-laden underside of the near-future. It's a place where drugs and guns rule. The smartest kids become criminals. Popular booty includes organic and cybernetic body parts, information, and any kind of fresh technology. A Philip K. Dick novel inspired this movie, but William Gibson and Bruce Sterling can claim titles as the creative movement's architects. An even better director's cut of *Blade Runner* came out nine years later.

See also AKIRA; FORD, HARRISON; HEADROOM, MAX; NEUROMANCER; SCOTT, RIDLEY

BLOCKBUSTER VIDEO

Giant entertainment chain that came to power in the late '80s by stocking a whole lot more movies than did the then-omnipresent neighborhood video stores. Blockbuster also gobbled up many of the mall music stores we remember, like Sound Warehouse and Record Bar.

See also BETAMAX; VCR

"BLOOM COUNTY"

Perhaps the most consistently funny comic strip of our time. Berke Breathed created a cast of characters (Milo, Binkley, Opus, Oliver Wendell Jones, Bill the Cat, Bobbi Harlow, Steve Dallas, Rosebud the Basselope) that skewered just about every '80s political and societal target you could imagine.

See also "CALVIN AND HOBBES"

BLOOPERMANIA

Over the last 15 years, there have been two things television viewers could count on during sweeps months: epic miniseries and behind-the-scenes blooper shows that, as the hosts put it, "show that these actors make mistakes just like you and me." The acknowledged masters of the genre are Dick Clark and Ed McMahon, who for several seasons hosted *TV's Bloopers and Practical Jokes* on NBC. Of course, ABC produced a lower-class twin, *Foul-Ups, Bleeps & Blunders*, hosted by Don Rickles and Steve Lawrence. You could also argue that the trend gave rise to shows like *America's Funniest Home Videos*.

See also REAL PEOPLE

BLU-BLOCKERS GUY, THE

A guy you may recognize from one of the first infomercials to creep onto late-night TV. He stood on a busy street corner, wore a big goofy hat, and rapped the praises of Blu-Blockers, the amazing sunglasses that, thanks to a major scientific breakthrough, look too big on everybody. Now the guy is so famous he's in this book.

See also GUY WHO TALKS REALLY FAST, THE; IZUSU, JOE; THAT "HEY VERN" GUY

BLUE FALCON AND DYNOMUTT

A slapstick takeoff on both the live-action and animated Batman shows of the 1960s and '70s.

See also BATMANIA; DARK KNIGHT RETURNS, THE

BLUE LIGHT SPECIAL

Three little words that meant big savings at your neighborhood Kmart.

See also MALLS

BLUES BROTHERS, THE

That would be Elwood and Jake. Or the title of the saga chronicling their "mission from God" to save the South Side orphanage in which they grew up, evading along the way Illinois Nazis (whom they hated), the state police, hut-hut-hutting SWAT troopers, the National Guard, and Steven Spielberg (he was the clerk at the assessor's office at the end of the movie).

See also Belushi, John; SPEEDBALL; SPIELBERG, STEVEN

BLUE THUNDER

TV action series spun off from the Roy Scheider film of the same name. Bubba Smith and Dick Butkus starred as two cops who piloted a superfast, superbad helicopter that could do just about everything but cook breakfast. A young Dana Carvey was also a regular. It competed with other era man-machine shows like *Knight Rider* and *Airwolf.*

See also AIRWOLF; AUTOMAN; KNIGHT RIDER

BLUE VELVET

A surreal David Lynch film that is Dennis Hopper's best work, as he demonstrates by so eloquently yelling that immortal line: "Baby wants to fuck!"

See also DUNE; ERASERHEAD; HOPPER, DENNIS

BLUME, JUDY

Children's author who was considered *dirty* because she wrote about things you're not supposed to talk about: masturbation, oral sex, regular sex, preteen angst, divorce, being fat, and menstruation. Reading *Are You There God? It's Me, Margaret* could make female puberty victims feel normal, while *Then Again, Maybe I Won't* did the same for males. But guys seen carrying *Margaret* around the elementary school looked like sexual deviants.

See also CLEARY, BEVERLY; FOREVER; PHANTOM TOLLBOOTH, THE; SUPERFUDGE

BMX

The cool kind of bike to have, even if you didn't take it to the dirt tracks and jump over three-foot mounds of dirt. Diamond Back and Mongoose were the preferred '80s brands.

See also BAD NEWS BEARS, THE; MOPEDS

BO

He knows.

See JACKSON, BO

BOBA FETT

A remorseless bounty hunter who, in his dinged-up and galaxy-worn green helmet, played only a small role in the *Star Wars* movies but emerged from the cult fandom perhaps the trilogy's most popular character. While most people who saw the films couldn't pick Boba Fett out of a line-up, fans can recite his few lines and many attractions, such as his silent mystery, his craftiness, his cool presence and his ability to capture, when commissioned by Darth Vader, that salty trader Han Solo.

See also STAR WARS; WEDGE

BOCHCO, STEVEN

Superproducer responsible for dramarific Thursday night fun on *Hill Street Blues* and *L.A. Law.* Out of respect, we won't even mention *Cop Rock.*

See also CANNELL, STEVEN J.; HILL STREET BLUES; L.A. LAW; TARTIKOFF, BRANDON

BODY HEAT

Another of those movies that made that one kid in your class instantly cool by virtue of his having seen it in the theater and being able to tell stories about steamy sex scenes. Of course, HBO rendered that status moot in the next few years, and it's a good thing, because that kid was usually a jerk anyway.

See also HBO

BOESKY, IVAN

He, Michael Milken, and Charles Keating were the three most notorious Wall Street crooks of the 1980s. Boesky bought and sold stock based on illegal inside information; Milken got rich on junk bonds, then watched it crumble around him; and Keating became the symbol of the S&L collapse and bought off five U.S. senators in the process. All served minimal time and are now back at it.

See also OCTOBER 19, 1987; WALL STREET

BONFIRE OF THE VANITIES, THE

A story widely regarded as an example of how to write a book and how *not* to make a movie. Tom *"The Right Stuff"* Wolfe's best-selling novel pretty much dissected American society of the 1980s, piling every ethnic, financial, and cultural problem onto a single man: Wall Street bond salesman Sherman McCoy, who, at one point, considered himself to be Master of the Universe.

And then director Brian De Palma's film masterfully miscast every character and avoided the book's crucial racial bits and did all sorts of things wrong. There was even a book (*The Devil's Candy* by Julie Salamon) about how much De Palma screwed up.

See also GREED; MASTERS OF THE UNIVERSE; RIGHT STUFF, THE

BON JOVI

Band that, along with Van Halen, helped open the Top-40 door for heavy metal acts at a time when New Wave and synth-pop were fading and pablum like Chicago and Whitney Houston and Phil Collins dominated the radio. In 1986, "You Give Love a Bad Name" was a No. 1 song. Soon after, the album *Slippery When Wet* became as huge as lead singer John Bon Jovi's hair, and he and guitarist Richie Sambora stole the hearts of many a jean jacket–wearing teenage girl.

BONUS CRITIQUE: Their two semi-acoustic, cowboy-themed songs, "Wanted Dead or Alive" and "Blaze of Glory," weren't that bad. OK. You're right. Yes they were.

See also GREAT WHITE; HEAVY METAL BOOM; MÖTLEY CRÜE; MOUSSE; POISON; QUIET RIOT; RATT; TWISTED SISTER; VAN HALEN; WARRANT

BOOM BOX

Portable stereo system that ran on about 10 D batteries and became extremely popular among '80s teens, despite a radical new technology called the Walkman. The big difference was that with a boom box, you could set up a breakdancing arena almost anywhere just by adding a big piece of cardboard and the *Krush Groove* soundtrack.

The boom box was also considered a threat to traditional society: a cheap, portable voice box through which the Youth of America could speak their mind. This allegory was demonstrated by a tragic character in Spike Lee's *Do the Right Thing* who carried a big boom box and got killed by cops. The more romantic side of boom boxes was seen in *say anything . . .*, as John Cusack stood outside Ione Skye's window, held a stereo system above his head, and blasted Peter Gabriel's "In Your Eyes." Aw.

See also Breakdancing; Ghetto blaster; say anything . . . ; Walkman

"BORDERLINE"

The bouncy, synth-pop single that launched the Madonna juggernaut. Soon we would see lace and useless wrist accessories on every street corner. It all seemed so innocent then, didn't it?

See also Madonna; Penn, Sean

BORK, ROBERT

The important thing to remember about this Supreme Court candidate—offered up by Reagan and incinerated by Congress—is his beard. While the chin-hugging strip of fuzz may not have been as radical as Surgeon General C. Everett Koop's, it spawned imitators all around the nation. High school kids struggled for months to grow enough hair for a "Bork." Business districts looked like Amish colonies. Even women got into the fad—HEY! WHOA, WAIT A SECOND! Just kidding. Really. Bork's beard had absolutely no effect on the fashion consciousness of the world. Take it easy. Never happened. Relax.

See also Koop, C. Everett; Reagan, Ronald

BORN IN THE USA

Was that really Bruce Springsteen's butt on the album cover?

See also John Cafferty and the Beaver Brown Band; Reagan, Ronald; Springsteen, Bruce

BOSOM BUDDIES

An early-'80s *Three's Company* mistaken-identity plot taken to the extreme, with two guys dressed up like women so they could live in an all-female hotel, The Susan B. Anthony. The cast included: Telma Hopkins, Tom Hanks, Peter Scolari, Donna Dixon, and Wendy Jo Sperber.

See also Big; Susan B. Anthony dollars; Three's Company

BOW WOW WOW

After the Sex Pistols disintegrated, Malcolm McLaren, perpetrator of *The Great Rock 'n' Roll Swindle*, needed to get himself a new band. So he found an exotic-looking fourteen-year-old singer, got some session musicians behind her, recorded the hit "I Want Kandy," and rode off into the sunset.

See also New Wave; Punk Rock

BOYS DON'T CRY

They sang that obtuse dance hit "I Wanna Be a Cowboy," and darned if most of us boys didn't when we heard that song. Also the name of a good Cure album.

See also Baltimora

BRANIFF AIRLINES

Though none of us ever flew on it, this outfit was the subject of much scrutiny and hand-wringing after it went belly-up in 1981. Why, we were too young to understand.

See also Eastern Airlines; Korean Airlines flight 007

Movie lines we said a lot

"All's I need is a cool buzz, some tasty waves, and I'm fine."

—This Spicoli line from *Fast Times at Ridgemont High* was used when we wanted to project the Spicoli-like image of not caring about much but getting high and surfing.

BRANIGAN, LAURA

Early '80s songstress who told us about the problems Gloria was having, and about her own ordeals with self-control.

See also CARNES, KIM

BRAT PACK, THE

A group of young stars that appeared in movies and painted the town together in the early 1980s, drawing very weak comparisons to the Rat Pack of Sinatra, Martin *et al.* The gang included Emilio Estevez, his brother Charlie Sheen, Judd Nelson, Anthony Michael Hall, Ally Sheedy, Demi Moore, Matt Dillon, James Spader, Andrew McCarthy, C. Thomas Howell, Molly Ringwald, Robert Downey, Jr., and Rob Lowe.

See also OUTSIDERS, THE; ST. ELMO'S FIRE

BRAZIL

A brilliant, if too cerebrally bizarre, movie parodying neo-Orwellian paranoia, bureaucracy, technology, and terrorism. This wasn't very popular in theaters during 1985 but picked up steam on video as it graced "best movies of the '80s" lists. Highlights include Robert DeNiro as a renegade heating-duct repairman and Kate Bush's version of the title song. Directed by Monty Python's Terry Gilliam, who did all those weird cartoons with old-fashioned-looking hands lifting open people's heads.

See also BIG BROTHER ad; *BLADE RUNNER*; AND ORWELL, GEORGE

BREAKDANCING

The dance craze of the early 1980s—all you needed was a tape of Kurtis Blow, Nucleus, or Herbie Hancock's "Rockit," and a big cardboard box to serve as your dance floor. Moves included the centipede, the backspin, the head spin, jellyman, and the ubiquitous moonwalk. No self-respecting breaker would be caught dead without his or her parachute pants, Vans, a fake-ripped sweatshirt with mesh at the neck, a jacket with lots of useless zippers, and a randomly placed pastel bandanna. *Breakin'*, *Breakin 2: Electric Boogaloo*, *Beat Street*, and *Krush Groove* brought the phenomenon into movie theaters, after which the trend pretty much died.

See also BEATBOXING; BOOM BOX; PARACHUTE PANTS; VANS (THE SHOES)

BREAKFAST CLUB, THE

Some would argue that this 1985 flick was the first movie forecasting the generally surly mood our generation would adopt in coming years. The story of five high-school kids from different backgrounds spending a Saturday detention together capsulized adolescent angst—caused by divorce, demanding parents, peer pressure, blah blah blah—and we ate it up.

See also BRAT PACK, THE; *HEATHERS*; HUGHES, JOHN; RINGWALD, MOLLY

BREZHNEV, LEONID

Soviet leader who ate it in 1982.

See also ANDROPOV, YURI

BRICKELL, EDIE

If she and her New Bohemians had released *Shooting Rubberbands at the Stars* in 1992 rather than 1987, it would have been an enormous hit and made her a big star. But as it stands, that album and the song "What I Am" is just another blip on our pop music screen, an erstwhile hippie trying to re-create that Summer of Love vibe.

See also NEW WAVE

BRIGHT LIGHTS, BIG CITY

Less than Zero in New York, basically. Based on a novel by Jay McInerney, who, along with Bret Easton Ellis, may be responsible for the glut of oversized glossy trade paperbacks (like this one) now dominating bookstores. This 1988 movie gave us our first look at Michael J. Fox as a "serious" actor, and also starred Phoebe Cates and Kiefer Sutherland as drifting, coke-eating, upper-class nippers.

See also FOX, MICHAEL J.; *LESS THAN ZERO*

BRING 'EM BACK ALIVE

One in a rash of shoddy *Raiders of the Lost Ark* rip-offs, this was on CBS in 1982. It used the same time period (pre-WWII) and the same exotic-like locales. Bruce Boxleitner (coming off of his role as Tron, but before *Scarecrow and Mrs. King*) starred as a poor man's Indy.

See also TALES OF THE GOLD MONKEY; TRON

BRINKLEY, CHRISTIE

A supermodel who managed to stay in the news after peaking, as models do in their early 20s. She did this by marrying somebody who was already famous, a Mr. Billy Joel. But the only real news to come out of the marriage was that Joel's music started to suck (remember "Uptown Girl"?).

See also FARRAH POSTER, THE; PORIZKOVA, PAULINA

BRITISH KNIGHTS

Sort-of cool fashion footwear that bore a diamond logo. The shoe took an image nose-dive when the company tried to enter the serious athletic shoe market at about the same time gangs incorporated them as "official" accessories, taking the BK logo to mean things like "blood killers."

See also COLORS; L.A. GEAR; REEBOK

BROOKE SHIELDS DOLL

The zenith of Brookemania.

See also ADVENTURE PEOPLE; MICHAEL JACKSON DOLL; SHIELDS, BROOKE

BROTHERS, DR. JOYCE

Psychologist who somehow got famous in the 1970s and dispensed advice whenever anyone put her in front of a camera. However, she deserves some commendation for being able to make fun of herself, as in her cameo in *The Naked Gun*.

See also WESTHEIMER, DR. RUTH

BROWN, ENCYCLOPEDIA

Whiz-kid superdetective who foiled small-time crookery in kids' books. Author Donald J. Sobol allowed the

---

Shows that should rerun every single night on Channel '80s

Manimal

Cheers

Family Ties

Webster

Knight Rider

Dallas

Max Headroom

The Cosby Show

Magnum, P.I.

The Facts of Life

Saved by the Bell

The A-Team

Remote Control

Voyagers!

Miami Vice

reader to try to solve the mystery before revealing the intricacies of the plot. Brown's foil was Bugs Meanie, leader of a local gang called the Tigers.

See also BLUME, JUDY; CLEARY, BEVERLY; WHIZ KIDS; *WRINKLE IN TIME, A*

BUCKNER AND GARCIA

These would-be minstrels of the Video Game Age recorded the song "Pac-Man Fever" in 1982 (in four different styles, including country 'n' western) and an entire album of other arcade songs, including "Do the Donkey Kong."

See also ATARI; PAC-MAN

BUELLER, FERRIS

A hero.

See also HUGHES, JOHN

BUGGLES

These guys would be just another irrelevant, early '80s synth-pop band had not their prophetic song "Video Killed the Radio Star" been the first video ever shown on MTV.

See also MTV

BUMP AND JUMP

A racing video game that appealed to the violent side that lurks in us. You raced along a disjointed course of several islands, jumping from one to the next to continue the race. And if some schmo got too close, you could bump him off the course, causing a crash.

See also ATARI; POLE POSITION

BUNDY, TED

Serial killer who, we were told, got to know his victims before he brutally raped and murdered them. He was handsome and appeared rational in interviews, and we heard stories about women sending him letters in prison and saying they wanted to marry him. Subject of the Jane's Addiction song "Ted, Just Admit It."

See also GACY, JOHN WAYNE; JANE'S ADDICTION; WILLIAMS, WAYNE

BURGER TIME

If nothing else, proof that people who make video games are not like you and me. You played a chef who ran around some huge superstructure holding the pieces of behemoth burgers. When you ran over them, they fell down a level, until everything was in its basket. But keep your saltshaker handy, because the evil fried egg and pickle chip are out to get you.

See also ATARI; FOOD FIGHT

BURTON, TIM

Brilliant. Weird but brilliant.

See also BATMANIA; BEETLEJUICE; PEE-WEE HERMAN

BUTTERFLY CLIPS

Multipurpose hair accessories that could hold ponytails, twists, and other configurations, and could be considered the female answer to the big comb.

See also BIG COMBS

C

CABBAGE PATCH KIDS

Ugly, pudgy dolls that caused a nationwide purchasing frenzy. Civilized parents ripped at each other's throats grabbing for the last Cabbage Patch Kid at the neighborhood Gold Circle or Kay-Bee or Toys "R" Us. They bought 10 at a time at sometimes $50 a head. These chubby, soft, sculptured-faced nippers were all-that-and-then-some for about two years in the mid-'80s and inspired plenty of rip-offs, including Rice Paddie Kids and Garbage Pail Kids. Each original Kid came with its own name, an adoption certificate, and the signature of inventor Xavier Roberts on its butt.

See also CARE BEARS; GARBAGE PAIL KIDS; SMURFS; STRAWBERRY SHORTCAKE

CABLE

A new form of TV reception that allowed us to see more channels with a better picture than the over-the-air, antenna-on-the-roof way. It exploded over the last decade, and some cable networks, like MTV, CNN, C-SPAN and ESPN, have revolutionized broadcasting (or, to be technical, cablecasting). But more programming did not always mean better programming, and the incessant replaying of syndicated television shows and B-grade movies is a big reason why so much of the stuff in this book is so permanently burned into our psyche.

See also CNN; HBO; MTV; YUPPIE PUPPIES

CADDYSHACK

One of those movies we quoted even before we saw it because some cool parent had let one of our friends go see it even though it was R-rated, and he came back with all these cool sayings like "Nnnnoonan!" and "Be the ball." Other favorite lines include any of Chevy Chase's throwaways ("People don't say that about you. Not as far as you know.") and Bill Murray's account of meeting the Dalai Lama.

See also FLETCH; MONTY PYTHON AND THE HOLY GRAIL

CAGNEY & LACEY

Buddy cop show where the buddies were two women. It never got over its reputation as a "chick show," but it really was good and lasted a lot longer than anyone thought it would.

BONUS FACT: Tyne Daly, who played Lacey, is the sister of Tim Daly, star of *Wings* and *Diner*.

See also DAYS AND NIGHTS OF MOLLY DODD, THE; DINER; STARSKY AND HUTCH

CALIFORNIA RAISINS

These Claymation marvels were the hottest thing in advertising in the mid-'80s . . . until everybody got sick of their version of "I Heard It through the Grapevine." Before the craze waned, these fictional fruits generated videos, a best-selling album, and a line of action figures.

See also BLU-BLOCKERS GUY, THE; NOID, THE

CALL TO GLORY

An underrated ABC show from the mid-'80s about an Air Force test pilot (Craig T. Nelson) and his family in the early '60s. Cindy Pickett was the wife who didn't particularly go for her man's line of work, Elisabeth Shue was the daughter who didn't like always being nice, and there was a son, too. The show's plotlines sometimes had to do with real things, like the U-2 plane being shot down over Russia, the Cuban missile crisis, and the death of JFK.

See also COCKTAIL; POLTERGEIST; RIGHT STUFF, THE; TOP GUN

"CALVIN AND HOBBES"

A comic strip about a philosophical, daydreaming six-year-old and his imaginary pet tiger raising hell. Sort of what we wish our childhood had been. If artist Bill Watterson had ever given in to the greedy impulse of licensing, Calvin hats and plush Hobbes dolls would have made us sick of this duo. But the only place we could get Calvin T-shirts (unauthorized, of course, and usually featuring a beer-swilling Calvin) was big fraternity parties.

See also "BLOOM COUNTY"; "GARFIELD"

CAMEO

Their '80s hit, after becoming one of the seminal funk bands of the '70s, was "Word Up." The lead singer had a deep, nasal voice and said "owww" a lot.

See also CHUNKY A

CAMERON, KIRK

Trendy hunk in the late '80s, when *Growing Pains* was hot and his character started dating. He made a couple of bad movies (*Like Father, Like Son* and *Listen to Me*) before disappearing from the pages of *Bop* magazine.

See also GROWING PAINS; SWITCHAROOMANIA

CAMP DAVID

Probably the first time any of us heard of this Maryland presidential hideout was when President Carter went there in 1978 and worked out a peace agreement with the leaders of Israel and Egypt, Menachem Begin and Anwar Sadat.

See also CARTER, BILLY; GIANT PEANUT WITH A BIG SMILE ON ITS SHELL; SALT II

CANNELL, STEPHEN J.

The brain behind formula adventure shows *The A-Team*, *The Greatest American Hero*, and *Riptide*.

See also A-TEAM, THE; GREATEST AMERICAN HERO, THE; RIPTIDE; SPELLING, AARON

CANNONBALL RUN, THE

Road movie made in 1981, shortly after Burt Reynolds' star began to fall. It covered the same territory, essentially, as the *Smokey and the Bandit* franchise, except this had more desperate attempts at humor, and "everybody" was in it (Roger Moore, Dean Martin, Farrah Fawcett, people like that). The sad thing is that Dom DeLuise carried the film.

See also FARRAH POSTER, THE; REYNOLDS, BURT; *SMOKEY AND THE BANDIT*

"CAN WE TALK?"

Joan Rivers' catchphrase.

See also "GO AHEAD, MAKE MY DAY"; "I'LL BE BACK"; "I PITY THE FOOL"; RIVERS, JOAN; "WHATCHOOTALKINBOUT?"

CAP'N CRUNCH

The standard against which all sugar cereals are judged.

See also C-3POS; G.I. JOE; MR. T CEREAL; NERDS CEREAL; OJS; SMURFBERRY CRUNCH; WAFFLE-OS

CAPRISUN

The beverage for anyone who wished they could drink from a bag instead of a can or cardboard box. This fruit drink (not actually juice, mind you) came in silver pods that stood up on the table. You had to stab the skin with a little blue pointed straw to get inside, but it was worth it. Violent yet delicious.

See also FRUIT ROLL-UPS; JUICE BOXES; MOUNTAIN DEW

CAPSELA

One of the more complex systems of plastic building toys from which we could choose during our developmental years. Each of our options was based around one basic shape: For Lego it was a rectangular box with a nub on top; for Lincoln logs a brown cylinder with two notches on either end; for Erector sets a flat rectangle of metal full of holes. Capsela centered around a clear plastic sphere affixed with six evenly spaced nubs, each of which connected to similar spheres. Some pieces contained motors, some contained gears, and a whole bunch of these could be connected to make some very weird-looking vehicles.

See also LEGO

CAPTAIN CAVEMAN

Large-footed, big-nosed blob of fur who traveled around cartoonland with three pretty girls, fighting crime with a prodigious yell and a jet-powered club that always gave out at the most inopportune times. Sort of a prehistoric *Scooby Doo*. Some episodes featured Schmoo.

See also CAVEMAN; FANGFACE; SCHMOO; SCOOBY DOO

CAPTAIN EO

Very short, 3-D sci-fi movie made by George Lucas and Francis Ford Coppola, starring Michael Jackson and seen only at Disney World and Disneyland.

See also EPCOT; JACKSON, MICHAEL; SPIELBERG, STEVEN; *STAR WARS*; 3-D MOVIES

CARA, IRENE

She secured her place in the People Who Wear Leg Warmers Hall of Fame by singing the theme songs from both *Fame* and *Flashdance*.

See also FAME; FLASHDANCE; LEG WARMERS; LOGGINS, KENNY

CARE BEARS

More intolerably cute gimmick toys with their paws in all the media. These teddy bears each had an icon on their chest explaining their emotional hang-ups (clouds, smiling suns, etc.). They had a TV series and a 1985 movie, in which they battled an evil being set on making everybody miserable. The music was by Carole King and ex-Lovin' Spoonful guy John Sebastian, who also did the theme song from *Welcome Back, Kotter*.

See also CABBAGE PATCH KIDS; SHIRT TALES, THE; STRAWBERRY SHORTCAKE; TEDDY RUXPIN; WELCOME BACK, KOTTER

CARLISLE, BELINDA

With the Go-Gos, she was a pioneer of the so-called New Wave established in the early '80s. She reinvented herself as a more mainstream soloist after a rumored bout with certain chemical addictions in 1986, becoming the object of many a teen boy's dreams and a favorite of David Letterman.

See also GO-GOS

CARMEL, CALIF.

Clint Eastwood was mayor of this filthy rich little town (actually called Carmel by the Sea) for two years in the '80s.

Locals sold T-shirts capitalizing on their leader's fame, including one with him done up in Western vigilante garb and the caption, "I *said,* curb your dog!" Of course, speculation about Sen. Eastwood (R-Calif.) and then President Eastwood followed.

BONUS FACT: Mayor Clint made everybody's day when he repealed a city ordinance that banned ice cream eating on public thoroughfares.

See also CITY HEAT; FIREFOX; "GO AHEAD, MAKE MY DAY"; REAGAN, RONALD

CARNES, KIM

She didn't have Bette Davis eyes her own self, but she sure did know a lot about them.

See also BALTIMORA; TYLER, BONNIE

CARPE DIEM

The phrase to utter among brooding, poetic types being oppressed by their comfortable suburban lifestyles—after they heard it uttered by moody prep-schoolers in *Dead Poets Society*. It's probably the only Latin phrase that any of us learned from a movie.

See also DEPECHE MODE; EXPLORERS

CARROT TRICK

This was perhaps our first exposure to blow jobs. Phoebe Cates teaches sexual newbie Jennifer Jason Leigh the art during the lunchroom sequence in *Fast Times at Ridgemont High*. This is the movie's second most famous scene, next to Jeff Spicoli (Sean Penn) ordering a pizza to Mr. Hand's U.S. history class.

The aforementioned pizza scene.

See also CROWE, CAMERON; *FAST TIMES AT RIDGEMONT HIGH*; *FOREVER*

CARS, THE

New Wave band from Boston that managed to make the jump to the regular pop charts and be successful with singles like "Let's Go" and "My Best Friend's Girl" and the album *Heartbeat City*. Incidentally, after marrying model Paulina Porizkova, goofy-looking lead singer Ric Ocasek was dubbed "The Luckiest Man Alive" by Dave Letterman.

See also BRINKLEY, CHRISTIE; LETTERMAN, DAVE; PORIZKOVA, PAULINA

CARTEL

Word only ever used to describe South American drug dealers.

See also COCAINE; ESCOBAR, PABLO; *MIAMI VICE*

CARTER, BILLY

Before Roger Clinton, there was this man, a perpetual embarrassment to President Jimmy Carter and basically an all-around lout. He tried his hand at business by making Billy Beer, but was about 12 years ahead of the microbrew trend.

See also GIANT PEANUT WITH A BIG SMILE ON ITS SHELL

CARTER, LYNDA

She played Wonder Woman on TV for a few seasons, bedeviling the bad guys with her skimpy costume, bullet-proof bracelets (made from a substance called feminum), and lasso that made everyone tell the truth. A lot of boys watched the show but were afraid to admit it.

See also LIVE-ACTION SUPERHERO SHOWS; *SUPERMAN: THE MOVIE*; *WONDER WOMAN*

CASUAL SEX?

Pretty silly movie about two women
(Lea Thompson and Victoria Jackson)
who get fed up with the singles scene
and head to a health resort to find
their true loves. There was some hype
surrounding this movie when it came
out, but for the life of us, we can't
remember why. Look for Andrew
"Dice" Clay as a sensitive dink.

See also CLAY, ANDREW "DICE"; HOWARD
THE DUCK; LAST TEMPTATION OF CHRIST, THE

CATTRALL, KIM

Actress who seems to have a knack
for turning up in randy sex farces and
"school" movies. Witness *Honeymoon Academy* and *Police Academy*. She's best known for her
performance as the title character in
Mannequin, an ancient Egyptian
princess inhabiting the body of a
store-window dummy.

See also MANNEQUIN; MATHESON, TIM

CAVEMAN

Lame 1981 spoof of prehistory movies
starring Ringo Starr, Dennis Quaid,
and Shelley Long as some *Homo
erectus* types who speak in grunts
and make a lot of fart jokes. An HBO
favorite during those long, early '80s
afternoons.

See also CANNONBALL RUN; CAPTAIN
CAVEMAN; CLAN OF THE CAVE BEAR; QUEST
FOR FIRE

CB RADIOS

Before there were cellular phones,
there was the citizens band, and with

the first great wave of country/
southern/truck-drivin' culture in the
'70s, a lot of us kids used phrases like
"breaker, breaker" and "10-4, good
buddy" when we talked to our friends.

See also DUKES OF HAZZARD, THE; SMOKEY
AND THE BANDIT

CD LONGBOXES

Long cardboard rectangles that, in
the olden days, housed new compact
discs. They were originally designed
so CDs could be displayed in shelves
built for vinyl records, but eventually
caused a storm of environmental
activism. Consumers protested,
rebellious artists like Sting and U2
sold discs without boxes, and a political group called Ban the Box
emerged. Their argument was that
excessive packaging of CDs causes
the world's life-giving rain forests to
disappear and become stamped with
pictures of people like Sting and
Bono. Eventually, longboxes vanished and the ecological balance of
planet Earth, once again, reached
equilibrium.

See also BAN THE BOX; COMPACT DISCS;
LEAD OR LEAVE; MINIDISCS

CENTIPEDE

The track-ball's finest hour came with
this arcade game. But what the hell
was your guy supposed to be, anyway?

See also ATARI

CENTRAL PARK JOGGER

An investment banker who had been
running at night in Central Park when

a pack of young thugs beat her with pipes and bricks and raped her. This was April 19, 1989, and people were already convinced that New York City was going to hell. This didn't help. We all heard about this woman's plight for months and knew her only as "the Central Park jogger." The media picked up the phrase "wilding" as a way to describe what those kids were up to that night.

See also BABY JESSICA; GOETZ, BERNIE; WILDING

CHALLENGER

Where were you when it blew up?

See McAULIFFE, CHRISTA

CHAOS

The trendiest esoteric science of the '80s, stuff that was cool to know about because you thought nobody else did. It's basically the study of randomness and the interconnectedness of all things, as in: the random or chaotic forces of the universe can be understood. The most common oversimplified example of chaos theory goes something like this: If you blow your nose somewhere in Minnesota, that has a tiny effect on the wind blowing near your head, which then triggers a larger shift in the overhead clouds, which redirects a low pressure system which . . . (insert snowballing effects on global weather patterns here) . . . and eventually this Minnesota snot is responsible for a typhoon that wipes out a village of perfectly nice Japanese folks. Thanks to quantum theory (the trendiest esoteric science of the '70s), the idea that

every event on Earth is connected and that nothing is a coincidence broke out from New Age philosophy and became a physical reality. Sort of. The ideas entered the pop science world with James Gleick's book, *Chaos*, and they eventually seeped into the rest of culture with a song called "Butterfly Wings" and Michael Crichton's *Jurassic Park*. As fodder for faux-intellectual semi-scientific banter, though, chaos was soon replaced by complexity theory, nanotechnology, and fuzzy logic.

See also COSMOS

CHAPMAN, MARK DAVID

The guy who shot John Lennon in 1980 and then quoted *Catcher in the Rye* as an excuse or something. In a truly weird twist, millions of Americans learned of this event from Howard Cosell, who interrupted *Monday Night Football* with the news.

See also HINCKLEY, JOHN; LENNON, JOHN

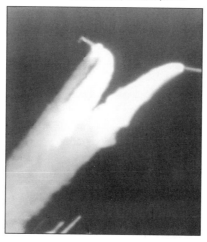

That they never made a movie-of-the-week out of this is indicative of just how deeply the nation was touched.

CHARIOTS OF FIRE

Movie about a bunch of British guys running a lot and wearing ugly socks that, inexplicably, was a huge hit and won some awards. The electronic/symphonic theme music by a hairy Greek guy named Vangelis was a No. 1 single, and is now synonymous with people running in slow motion.

See also BLADE RUNNER; OLYMPICS

CHARLES IN CHARGE

Boy did things get all topsy-turvy in 1984! If you believed network television, the men took over household chores and let the women work. In this show, Scott Baio and Willie Aames had to handle three kids and still look manly. And Tony Danza had to do much the same over on *Who's the Boss*.

See also BAIO, SCOTT; EIGHT IS ENOUGH; JOANIE LOVES CHACHI; WHO'S THE BOSS; ZAPPED!

CHARLIE'S ANGELS

Show done in the days when outright sexism was still profitable in Hollywood (1976–81). Exploiting themselves were Jaclyn Smith, Farrah Fawcett, Kate Jackson, Cheryl Ladd, Tanya Roberts, Shelley Hack, David Doyle, and the voice of John Forsythe.

See also FARRAH POSTER, THE; SPELLING, AARON

CHEERS

When *M*A*S*H* ended, the saga of the Boston bar where everybody knew everybody's name was entering its second season, and soon would take its place as the epochal sitcom of the 1980s. Sure, its Thursday night mate *The Cosby Show* got higher ratings, but *Cheers* captured us with its ongoing will they/won't they between Sam and Diane and its assorted bunch of regular people planted around the bar. In fact, thanks to them, *Cheers* was able to survive a major cast change when Shelley Long left, and though the show lost some of its spark in later years, it was still among the best things on TV. It also became one of the all-time syndication champions.

See also LAST EPISODE OF *M*A*S*H*; THURSDAY NIGHT LINEUP

CHERNENKO, KONSTANTIN

Soviet leader who uttered his final "*nyet*" in 1985.

See also GORBACHEV, MIKHAIL S.

CHERNOBYL

Just another unknown Soviet city until 1986, when the nuclear plant there melted down, killing workers and residents, and spewing radioactive clouds into the rest of Europe. It then became the topic of sick jokes and stand-up routines for years.

See also GORBACHEV, MIKHAIL S.; STAND-UP BOOM; THREE-MILE ISLAND

CHIC

At the height of the designer-jeans craze, these denims claimed to be friend to all women, being available as they were in 27 sizes. So how come the name is pronounced "chick"?

See also KLEIN, CALVIN; TWO-TONE JEANS

CHICKEN MCNUGGETS

Perhaps the only truly significant fast-food innovation of our lives. In the early '80s, McDonald's introduced these little deep-fried, batter-covered hunks of mushed-together chicken pieces and declared a new era in convenience dining, which, a decade later, had filled drive-through menus with chicken this and chicken that. The original McNuggets came in 6-, 9-, and 20-packs, included a variety of sauces; and tasted pretty good so you didn't even think about which part of the chicken the "nugget" came from.

See also MC-; MCDLT; PARTS IS PARTS

CHILD STARS GONE BAD

Seems you couldn't swing a dead cat in the 1980s without hitting some formerly beloved kid actor or actress who, having grown up and stopped being adorable, found him- or herself in a lineup somewhere. Look, there's Dana Plato posing for *Playboy*. Hey, there's Drew Barrymore, strung out at 14. Say, isn't that Todd Bridges getting busted on a drug charge? Wow, Danny Bonaduce's beating up a transvestite prostitute. Oh, and that's sweet little Susan Olsen doing a porno flick. Such a shame, really.

See also BARRYMORE, DREW; *DIFF'RENT STROKES*

CHINESE JUMP ROPE

A game that only *looked* complicated. Two people stood inside a big rubber band while somebody else jumped on it in a predetermined pattern (i.e.: in-out-on-out-twist). This was popular in schoolyards in the early '80s, before double dutch made a big comeback.

See also MISS LUCY

CHIPS

Erik Estrada forged his 15 minutes of fame with six years on this NBC cop drama, a spin-off of the fireman show *Emergency.* Larry Wilcox played Jon to Estrada's Ponch. The two played motorcycle cops patrolling (P) the California (C) highways (H) in search of love, adventure, and whatever the little "i" and "s" stood for.

See also STARSKY AND HUTCH

CHOOSE YOUR OWN ADVENTURE

R. L. Montgomery and Edward Packard (if those were their real names) created the books that allowed us to make up the story as we went along. If we died, we could go back and choose the other option. Popular titles were *Your Code Name Is Jonah* and *Who Killed Harlowe Thrombie?* This franchise began a publishing explosion of choose-your-own-whatever books, including a Dungeons & Dragons series and some time travel stuff. The creative edge of these skinny books has since been made obsolete by CD-ROMs and hypertext.

See also BROWN, ENCYCLOPEDIA; HARDY BOYS; HYPER-

CHOPLIFTER

You have to rescue a bunch of tiny people from barracks being blown away by enemy tanks. The gruesome part of this game is that you could (and many kids did) spend hours just picking away the helpless civilians instead of battling the bad guys.

See also ATARI

CHRIST, JESUS

A man widely believed to be the son of God and who is expected to visit Earth sometime to end history and all that. According to centuries of popular European aesthetics, he wore his hair long and had a beard. But so far as we've seen on TV and in the movies, he looks a lot like Willem Dafoe and Ted Neeley.

See also BAKKER, TAMMY FAE; DOBBS, J.R. "BOB"; FALWELL, JERRY; GOD; HAHN, JESSICA; LAST TEMPTATION OF CHRIST, THE

CHRISTMAS STORY, A

Perhaps the only movie of our time to become a *bona fide* "Christmas classic" (unless you count *Home Alone*, which we don't). Although the geeky hero (Peter Billingsley) grew up in the '40s, we could identify with his trials of bullies and girls and weird parents. Key moments involve his friend Flick sticking his tongue on a frozen pole, him dressed in a pink bunny suit, and his father ogling a glowing lamp shaped like a female leg. And, of course, there was the line everybody gave the kid when he talked about the Red Ryder air rifle he wanted for Christmas: "You'll shoot your eye out!"

See also BILLINGSLEY, PETER

CHRONICLES OF NARNIA, THE

Although the seven books in this series by superChristian C. S. Lewis were published in the 1950s, many of us know all about the adventures of kids Peter, Susan, Edmund, and Lucy in the magical, vaguely medieval land of Narnia. Of course, we probably learned more from watching the 1979 BBC TV shows than reading the volumes between *The Lion, the Witch and the Wardrobe* and *The Last Battle*.

See also BLACK CAULDRON, THE; CHRIST, JESUS; PHANTOM TOLLBOOTH, THE; WRINKLE IN TIME, A

CHUCK E. CHEESE

Rival to Show Biz Pizza Theater that featured similar mediocre pies, astounding game rooms, and silly animatronic characters. The two competitors eventually joined forces, keeping the Chuck banner.

See also SHOW BIZ PIZZA THEATER

CHUNKY A

An Arsenio Hall alter ego who had some people confused. He dressed up in fat-guy pads and gold chains, but some thought he really *was* Heavy D or Cameo or any number of the mid-'80s rap posse. They thought his parody album *Large and In Charge* was legit, and they made the single "Makes Me Go Owww!" a hit.

See also CAMEO; HALL, ARSENIO; RAP; YANKOVIC, "WEIRD" AL

CINCINNATI GARDENS

Site of the tragic Aug. 1, 1981, Who concert, in which festival seating and not enough open entrances led to the deaths of 13 people as the crowd stampeded in to get the best seats. Led to a ban on festival seating in many venues.

See also QUEEN

CINDERELLA

More crappy, late '80s metal boys who we feel we have to mention because they're so easily confused with all the other era bands with the same hair and sound and Spandex pants.

See also POISON; SCORPIONS; SKID ROW; WARRANT

CINNAMON TOAST CRUNCH

Basically, Golden Grahams with cinnamon on them instead of honey. Another in the line of cereals that tried to look or taste like other foods.

See also CAP'N CRUNCH; COOKIE CRISP; WAFFLE-OS

CITY HEAT

Cop movie spoof notable for two reasons: 1) It starred Clint Eastwood and Burt Reynolds, and 2) it helped proliferate a trend of cop movie names that continued with *Red Heat* (about Russians), *Dead Heat* (about the undead), and *Outer Heat* (an early working title for *Alien Nation*, which, you see, is about aliens).

See also CARMEL, CALIF.; *POLICE ACADEMY*; *RED HEAT*; *SMOKEY AND THE BANDIT*

CLANCY, TOM

Writer who achieved superstardom by exploiting one of the '80s most promi-

nent social pastimes: distaste for all things communist. Of course, it's a little more complicated than that. He threw in fascination with mechanical objects, some sympathetic Russians, plus a distaste for drug lords and shifty U.S. policy makers. Those of us who read his thick, thorough thrillers learned more about the workings of the U.S. government, world politics, and tanks than any social studies/ poli sci class could teach.

See also GORBACHEV, MIKHAIL S.; IRAN-CONTRA THING; KING, STEPHEN; NORTH, OLIVER; REAGAN, RONALD; RED OCTOBER

CLAN OF THE CAVE BEAR

It wasn't intended to be funny and, in fact, was based on a fairly serious, kinda scholarly book. But Daryl Hannah as a Neanderthal? What were they thinking?

See also QUEST FOR FIRE

CLARK, BARNEY

In 1982, this retired doctor from Utah became the first recipient of the Jarvik-7, an artificial heart. He died a few weeks later, but a major advance in medical science was made.

See also BABY FAE; TEST-TUBE BABY

CLASH, THE

The only punk band to have any kind of impact on the charts in America, thanks mostly to their album *Combat Rock*. Those partial to the band said they had a better understanding of music than most punkers; detractors said they were just sellouts for trying to reach a wider audience and making videos (and by the way, the video for "Rock the Casbah," featuring an armadillo, was pretty cool). Those who cried sellout were partially validated a few years after the band broke up, when Mick Jones formed the poppy Big Audio Dynamite.

See also BEATBOXING; PUNK ROCK

CLAY, ANDREW "DICE"

The stand-up comedy boom of the 1980s hit its nadir when this guy made it big with an assortment of jokes that most fourth-grade boys would be ashamed to tell.

See also KINISON, SAM; STAND-UP BOOM; TRULY TASTELESS JOKES

CLEARY, BEVERLY

Children's author for those who wanted something a little lighter than the angst and hormones of Judy Blume stories. Her books chronicled the neighborhood of Ramona and Beatrice Quimby, Henry Huggins and his dog Ribsy. She also wrote the Mouse and the Motorcycle books.

See also BLUME, JUDY; *WRINKLE IN TIME, A*

CLINTON, GEORGE

Master purveyor of the funk in the 1970s without whose songs, you could argue, rap as we know it would not exist. Practically every major rap artist, from Ice Cube to Gerardo, in the last 10 years has sampled a P-Funk jam at one time or another.

See also RAP; SAMPLING; WOO-YEAH SAMPLE

CLOAK AND DAGGER

A movie that could only have happened in the '80s, when kids could do anything. A regular preteener (Henry Thomas from *E.T.*) gets wrapped up in an international spy ring or something after buying an Atari game cartridge containing secret information. So the bad guys are after him, and he turns to his imaginary spy buddy (Dabney Coleman) and a bunch of computer geeks for help. Good prevails.

See also ATARI; COLEMAN, DABNEY; *E.T.*; *NIGHT OF THE COMET*; *WARGAMES*

CLOVE CIGARETTES

Carcinogen of choice among the darker, more brooding souls in our high schools, the kids who had "Love Kills" stickers on their backpacks and listened to lots of goth rock.

See also CURE, THE; SMITHS, THE

CLUE CLUB

Cool '70s cartoon show featuring a band of crime-solving kids and their two talking basset hounds (one of whom wore a Sherlock Holmes hat). They rode around in a dune buggy, foiling evil schemes by grown-ups.

See also BROWN, ENCYCLOPEDIA; HARDY BOYS; NANCY DREW

CNN

A pioneer in defining the nothing-but-one-thing-24-hours-a-day philosophy of cable television. Nobody knew that we needed to see the world's events all day long until Cable News Network showed how it could be done on

June 1, 1980. Meanwhile, MTV and Nickelodeon demonstrated that the world could support 24 hours of cheesy videos and goofy kid shows, too. Nonstop cablecasting of most other human activities soon followed.

See also CABLE; HBO; MTV; TURNER, TED; YUPPIE PUPPIES

COCA-COLA CLOTHES

For a few months there in 1987, you just weren't cool if you didn't own a sweatshirt or rugby shirt emblazoned with the Great American Beverage's logo. The fad died quickly, though, and Pepsi's own efforts at fashion never really got off the ground.

See also LIKE COLA; NEW COKE; TAB

COCAINE

A drug relatively unknown before the '80s, it took hold and changed the underworld forever. The use and traffic of cocaine and crack transcended all social boundaries and tarnished/enhanced the images of so many social classes: rich white kids, poor black kids, South Americans, stockbrokers, rock stars, whatever. A real success story of the decade.

See also BRIGHT LIGHTS, BIG CITY; COLORS; ESCOBAR, PABLO; LESS THAN ZERO; MIAMI VICE; NEW COKE; NORIEGA, MANUEL

COCKTAIL

In our humble opinion, this may be the ultimate 1980s movie.

BONUS PLOT SYNOPSIS: Tom Cruise is a bartender of working-class Irish stock who becomes celebrated at a ludicrously hip New York hot spot, which features about 16 levels but only one bar (that would be the 1980s emphasis on glam over substance) for his ability to twirl bottles while making drinks and for his smart-ass grin (again, glam over substance). Our hero dreams of one day owning his own bar (pull-yourself-up-by-the-bootstraps capitalism, a popular myth of the '80s). His mentor, fellow slinger Bryan Brown, tells him that marrying a rich girl is the only way this will happen (devaluation of the marital bond). The boys go to Jamaica, where our hero falls in love with Elisabeth Shue as Brown looks on disdainfully. Our hero then, remembering Brown's advice, disses Shue and screws a wealthy woman who tries to turn him into a corporate type (powerful women are scary and greed is good—two very popular '80s myths). Our hero chafes under her, and at the same time finds out that Shue is fabulously rich but didn't tell him because she wanted him to love her for who she was, not what she was (element of Greek tragedy serving as convenient plot point, which is not unique to the '80s but certainly got a bigger workout then than in decades past). Brown takes up with another rich woman and appears content but later kills himself (in 1980s filmmaking, suicide = having a soul). Our hero fights with Shue's dad, a Park Avenue snob with disdain for the working class (see Leona Helmsley, Donald Trump *et al.*). Our hero gets a loan from his uncle to open his own bar, Cocktails and Dreams, proving his worth to Shue and winning her back

Mr. Coleman hobnobs with Benji backstage at the Emmys.

(tragic element discarded for "up" ending, another common filmmaking device that enjoyed a peak in the '80s). The end.

See also BACK TO THE FUTURE; BRIGHT LIGHTS, BIG CITY; CALL TO GLORY; CRUISE, TOM; GREED; *F/X*; TOP GUN

COLECOVISION

In the early world of video games, this system kicked butt. Great graphics, cool joysticks, and a bunch of games straight from the arcade, like Donkey Kong. The popularity of this and the upgraded Atari 5200 fizzled, though, as the first home computers popped up with tape drives and better graphics. One of these was the Coleco Adam, which could play Colecovision games.

See also ATARI; COMMODORE 64; INTELLIVISION

COLEMAN, DABNEY

This guy always seemed to play the throwaway characters in '80s movies (like *Hot to Trot* and *Dragnet*) and do it better than most. He did offbeat sitcoms called *Buffalo Bill* and *The Slap Maxwell Story*, but neither was conventional enough to succeed.

See also CLOAK AND DAGGER; *9 TO 5*

COLEMAN, GARY

Childhood sensation star of *Diff'rent Strokes*. What he lacked in stature he made up for in spunk, à la his famous phrase "Whatchootalkinbout?" He also managed to stay out of jail, unlike some of his fellow cast members. And just for the record, we think

he would have kicked Webster's ass.

See also CHILD STARS GONE BAD; *DIFF'RENT STROKES*; LEWIS, EMMANUEL; "WHATCHOOTALKINBOUT?"

COLLARS TURNED UP

The most obvious sign that the Prep Look had invaded a guy's fashion consciousness. No pastel Izod shirt would look quite right without the collar flipped up. Wearing a jeans jacket collar up, however, signaled somebody torn between several images, perhaps prep and the heavy-metal "stoner" look.

See also IZOD; JEAN JACKETS; PREPPIES

COLLINS, JOAN

The bitch-queen of the 1980s, her too-dark black hair and conniving ways on *Dynasty* made her more fun than anyone over at the South Fork Ranch. She did battle, of course, with Linda Evans, who was blond and good, and we just couldn't get enough of her.

See also DYNASTY; EVANS, LINDA

COLORED HAIR SPRAY

A minor rage in mid-'80s junior high schools, especially if you were a girl. This spray of colorful glittery gunk was the natural collision of several fashion trends: 1) The proliferation of hair-molding products, like gel and hair spray (which often came in foot-tall cans) and mousse (which also came in different colors), and 2) the brief popularity of glitter on T-shirts and on your face.

See also JELLIES; LEG WARMERS; PUNK; SPLATTER PAINT; SWATCH

COLORIZATION

A technique that was supposed to create "color" versions of old black-and-white movies. But, in the end, it just looked like Jimmy Stewart and that little girl from *Miracle on 34th Street* and everybody else had very rosy cheeks and wore pastel shirts. Ted Turner must have sniffed some strange chemicals and decided in the early '80s that colorization was the Next Big Thing and started airing new versions of the classics (*Casablanca*, *The Maltese Falcon*, etc.) on WTBS. A public outcry followed, "colorized" became a bad word and the madness ended.

See also TURNER, TED; WTBS

COLOR PURPLE, THE

Tough, emotional movie about black women growing up in the early 20th-century South, based on the book by Alice Walker. Oprah Winfrey, Whoopi Goldberg, and Danny Glover starred, and Steven Spielberg directed, although this was such a weird movie for him: None of the characters came from outer space and a bunch of kids didn't outsmart dangerous bad guys.

See also ROOTS; SPIELBERG, STEVEN

COLORS

The first major film to feature modern street gangs. *West Side Story* and *Grease* don't count because they deal with a different era; they were goofy musicals and nobody ever got shot in the theaters on opening night. Despite the violence and open talk about Bloods and Crips surrounding *Colors*, it was mostly about two white cops (Robert Duvall and Sean Penn). This was in 1988, and we didn't get a good cinematic look at the inner city until 1991 with *Straight out of Brooklyn* and *Boyz N the Hood*. The *Colors* soundtrack had some good stuff, though, including the title song by Ice-T, who is, as you know, a nightmare walking, psychopath talking.

See also BLUE VELVET; PENN, SEAN; RAP; RUBIN, RICK

COMMODORE 64

The most popular and versatile of the first home computers, this beige monster could handle actual floppy disks (though many used tape drives) and, of course, played all kinds of games. It put to shame its cousin, the Vic 20 (for which William Shatner did TV ads), and was made obsolete by the visual genius of the Amiga (for which Tip O'Neil did an ad). But to this day, some fanatics still use and worship the C-64.

See also APPLE IIE; ATARI; BACKLESS CHAIRS; O'NEIL, TIP; STAR TREK

COMPACT DISCS

Amazing new technology unleashed in the late '70s that made sure it sounded like Rick Springfield and Starship were in the same room with us. These were radical and expensive in the early '80s and became commonplace and expensive a few short years later.

See also CD LONGBOXES; MINIDISCS

Another big moment in our lifetimes

On September 13, 1982, a *People* magazine story on Valley girls describes San Fernando Valley culture as "only slightly less foreign than the culture of Bosnia-Herzegovina."

The right man for the right role at the right time: Arnold Schwarzenegger as Conan the Barbarian.

CONAN THE BARBARIAN

Our first real exposure to Austrian überhuman Arnold Schwarzenegger, because nobody saw *The Villain* or *Hercules in New York*. Surprisingly (or not), James Earl Jones also starred, and Oliver Stone had a writing credit on this 1981 film.

See also FALCO; LUNDGREN, DOLPH; SCHWARZENEGGER, ARNOLD; STONE, OLIVER; ÜBER-

CONDOMS

Though "rubbers" had been around a long time, the 1980s was the decade that they became a part of everyday life—talking about them, or buying them, was no longer such a big source of embarrassment or laughter (as long as you were older than 15). Thanks to the spread of AIDS and a huge jump in teen pregnancies, condoms (especially brand leader Trojan) became just something else you bought at the drugstore to protect your health.

See also AIDS

CONNECT FOUR

An age-old game sold to us by a brother and sister trying to outwit each other in a TV commercial. The sister finally wins, lining up the fourth plastic circle in a vertical plane. Her brother's immortal retort as he sends the chips tumbling on the table: "Pretty *sneaky*, sis."

See also ELECTRONIC BATTLESHIP; HUNGRY, HUNGRY HIPPOS; TRIVIAL PURSUIT

CONTRAS

Anti-communism rebels causing some sort of trouble in Central America. Reagan loved 'em, but they got him and Oliver North and Admiral John Poindexter into a little trouble. Surprisingly few movies were made about the struggle or even the Iran-Contra Affair, and the arcade game called Contra was about drooling aliens invading Earth.

See also IRAN-CONTRA THING; NORTH, OLIVER; REAGAN, RONALD

COOKIE CRISP

Cereal whose ads, featuring a cartoon convict angling to get the little cookies and the cop who always caught him, were better than the cereal itself. The Saturday morning spots again brought up the age-old mystery of why kids and cartoon characters are always keeping cereal away from each other: The Trix rabbit never gets

Trix. Lucky the leprechaun plays hard to get with the Lucky Charms. Barney's always itching for Fred's Fruity Pebbles. The cookie thief gets caught every time. What's that about, anyway?

See also CAP'N CRUNCH; CINNAMON TOAST CRUNCH; SMURFBERRY CRUNCH; WAFFLE-OS

COOTIES

What you caught if you had too much contact with the opposite sex when you were little. Also a Playskool item with which you could build segmented bug-like creatures with lots of legs, antennae, and happy faces.

See also GLO-WORM; INCHWORM; LEGO; PAPER FOOTBALL

COREYS

Haim and Feldman, that is. Some studio exec probably thought it would be a good idea to try to make these guys into a teenage Jerry Lewis and Dean Martin. But then they made films like *License to Drive* and *Dream a Little Dream*. Oy.

See also STAND BY ME

COSBY SHOW, THE

This was NBC's black nuclear family, the Huxtables of New York City, who ruled prime-time television for half a decade. We watched the doctor-lawyer parents (Phylicia Rashad, Bill Cosby) raise the dim Theo (Malcolm-Jamal Warner), the even-dimmer Denise (Lisa Bonet), the always-at-college Sondra (Sabrina Le Beauf), the Jan Brady–like Vanessa (Tempestt Bledsoe), and the cutesy Rudy (Keshia Knight Pulliam).

The extra characters were great, too, like Cockroach (the Dumb Guy), Kenny (Rudy's "boyfriend," whom she called "Bud"), Elvin (Sondra's husband), and Olivia (Denise's kid, who joined the cast when Rudy grew out of the cute stage). Of course, there was the spin-off, *A Different World*, about Denise at the fictional, all-black Hillman College. And, of course, Bill Cosby always wore cool sweaters.

See also ANGEL HEART; DUMB GUY; MCFERRIN, BOBBY; NEW COKE; THURSDAY NIGHT LINEUP; WILLIAMS, JOHN

COSMOS

Our first lesson in astronomy and special relativity and all the strangeness of science. Billions and billions of years ago . . . or, rather, in the late '70s, a man named Carl Sagan introduced our generation to these things with the much-watched PBS series *Cosmos*. For some, it was an eye-opening glimpse at the surface of Mars and really huge numbers like googolplex. For others, Sagan was just another droning science teacher who eventually led to their major in sociology or philosophy.

See also CHAOS; HAWKING, STEPHEN

COSTELLO, ELVIS

Rarely appreciated postpunk singer and leader of the Attractions, who deserved many more hits than "Every Day I Write the Book." Because Costello, né Declan MacManus, dabbled in so many styles of music, from New Wave to country, programmers could not put a finger on him, and he toiled in unjust semi-obscurity for many years, his albums turning up in the bargain bins of record stores.

See also AMERICATHON; JACKSON, JOE; NEW WAVE; PRESLEY, ELVIS

COSTNER, KEVIN

Never has someone gone on to be so famous after his first big role ended up entirely on the cutting-room floor. We are referring to that Boomer angstfest called *The Big Chill*, in which he played the dead guy but was not seen in the final cut of the film. Somehow, though, we all came to know this after he did *Bull Durham* and went on to become just about the biggest movie star in Hollywood after *The Untouchables*.

See also BIG CHILL, THE; SARANDON, SUSAN

COUGAR, JOHN

See COUGAR MELLENCAMP, JOHN

COUGAR MELLENCAMP, JOHN

See MELLENCAMP, JOHN

COX, COURTENEY

Waif (now on *Friends*) whom many remember first seeing in 1987 as the feathered-haired Lauren Miller, girlfriend to Alex P. Keaton on *Family Ties*. Others recall her as the girl from Springsteen's "Dancing in the Dark" video. And those who really paid attention watched her as a telekinetic wonderchild in *Misfits of Science* and then as an average-teen-caught-up-in-some-intergalactic-mess-involving-action-figures in the *Masters of the Universe* movie.

See also BILLY VERA AND THE BEATERS;

FAMILY TIES; FOX, MICHAEL J.; LUNDGREN, DOLPH; MASTERS OF THE UNIVERSE; MISFITS OF SCIENCE

CRAZY LIKE A FOX

Stupid detective-comedy show set in San Francisco, starring Jack Warden as an old-sage investigator and some tool as his straitlaced grandson. Somehow, this show was No. 10 in the Nielsens in 1985, but it died a quick death shortly after that.

See also CAGNEY & LACEY; EQUALIZER; MOONLIGHTING; REMINGTON STEELE; SIMON & SIMON

CRIME FIGHTING

OK. Pretend you're an '80s TV character looking for a plotline. You've got a spare billion dollars hanging around. What do you do with it? You use it to set up a secret crime-fighting operation, that's what. And what if you're specially trained in military combat but have to remain in hiding because you're "legally dead"? Do some freelance crime fighting. Need money? Fight crime. Got a special mutant power? How about a spiffy, hyped-up piece of technology? Use it to fight crime. Can you time travel? Use that gift, young idealistic one, to *fight crime*. So many people combated evil and solved mysteries in the decade, that there's nothing left for '90s characters to do.

See also A-TEAM, THE; AIRWOLF; CAGNEY AND LACEY; CAPTAIN CAVEMAN; CLUE CLUB; CRIME STORY; ENOS; EQUALIZER, THE; FALL GUY, THE; GREATEST AMERICAN HERO, THE; INSIDERS, THE; INSPECTOR GADGET; KNIGHT RIDER; MACGYVER; MAGNUM, P.I.; MANIMAL; MATT HOUSTON; MIAMI VICE; MISFITS OF SCIENCE; MOONLIGHTING; MR. T AND THE T-FORCE; REMINGTON STEELE; RIPTIDE; SCOOBY DOO; SHIRT TALES; SIMON & SIMON; SLEDGE HAMMER!; WHIZ KIDS, THE; WONDER WOMAN

CRIME STORY

This very violent, very good series from '80s superproducer Michael Mann was on after *Miami Vice* on Friday nights. Despite its impressive lead-in and a good cast that featured Dennis Farina (himself a former cop), it only lasted two seasons—one set in Chicago and one in Las Vegas.

See also MANHUNTER; MIAMI VICE

CROAKIES

Strips of foam rubber that fit onto the ends of sunglasses, allowing them to hang around your neck. Luckily, these came in neon colors.

See also JELLIES; NEON CLOTHES; VUARNET

CROWE, CAMERON

Screenwriter/director with perhaps the best eye for Baby Buster middle-class life. His movies are all classics (*Fast Times at Ridgemont High*, *say anything . . .*) and aren't just about Young People, but about life and humor and music from a young point of view. The films have a certain inside-edge feeling that John Hughes missed.

See also BOOM BOX; CARROT TRICK; FAST TIMES AT RIDGEMONT HIGH; HUGHES, JOHN

CRUISE, TOM

The ideal male. The perfect man. The überguy, if you will. He spent the '80s specializing in being the Best Damn *(fill in the blank)* in the World. Just have a look: *Top Gun* (Best Damn Fighter Pilot in the World), *Cocktail* (Best Damn Bartender in the World), *Days of Thunder* (Best Damn Injured NASCAR Driver in the World), *Rainman* (Best Damn Brother of an Autistic Guy in the World), *The Color of Money* (Best Damn Pool Player in the World), etc. Other career high points included *Risky Business* (One of the Better Damn Pimps in the World) and *The Outsiders*, while low points were Ridley Scott's *Legend* (Best Damn Questing Hero in an Alternate Dimension) and *Losin' It* (Best Damn Guy Having Sex with Shelley Long in the World).

See also COCKTAIL; GOOSE; RISKY BUSINESS DANCE; TOP GUN

CRUSH

Fruit-flavored soft drinks that were huge in the late '70s and early '80s. They were wildly successful when there was just orange and grape

The Best Damn On-Screen Lover of Kelly McGillis in the World.

Crush (and had a pretty good ad campaign—"Hold my Crush, but don't drink it"), but kind of fell apart when red Crush was introduced.

See also JOLT COLA; NEW COKE; TAB

C-3POS

Sugary cereal named for the protocol droid proficient in six million forms of communication (including, of course, Bocce, Ewokese, and the binary language of moisture vaporators). The cereal bits were shaped like little infinity symbols (∞) and tasted like Cap'n Crunch.

See also CAP'N CRUNCH; STAR WARS; WAFFLE-OS

CULTURE CLUB

Just about one of the biggest bands going in 1983–'84, these guys all dressed up like girls and gave us "I'll Tumble 4 Ya," "Miss Me Blind," and "Do You Really Want to Hurt Me."

See also DURAN DURAN; GEORGE, BOY; I WOULD DIE 4 U SIGN LANGUAGE

CUTTING CREW

Flash-in-the-pan group that recorded one annoying hit in 1987, "I Just Died in Your Arms." Dutifully returned to the state-fair circuit after their 15 minutes expired.

See also BALTIMORA

CYBER-

A prefix, associated with intelligent computers and the Future, that began a popularity surge in the '80s. It's ripped from the word "cybernetics," basically the study of brains and computers. *Cyber-* can be applied to almost any word to give it a futuristic, technological edge: Cybertron would be an android bad guy, cybernerds are just that, and a Cyberman would be a portable robot made by Sony.

See also -MAN; TECHNO-

CYBERPUNK

A new subgenre of science fiction born in the '80s and bent on painting the Future as a dark, dreary, and downright scary place. It explores the dirty underside of information technology somewhere around or after the year 2000, and it tends to be much more realistic and immediate than space sci-fi or D&D fantasy stuff. Authors William Gibson and Bruce Sterling are credited with inventing the whole thing, and director Ridley Scott's *Blade Runner* is considered the genre's seminal film.

See also AKIRA; BLADE RUNNER; HEADROOM, MAX; NEUROMANCER

CYBERSPACE

A term coined by sci-fi god William Gibson in the mid-'80s to describe, essentially, the "place" where telephone conversations happen. It follows that phones hooked up to computers would flesh out that place, making it resemble physical reality. Many stories—both real and sci-fi—started to use this pseudolocale as their setting.

See also CYBERPUNK; NEUROMANCER; WARGAMES

DALLAS

When our parents would let us, we got to stay up on Friday nights to watch the saga of the Ewings—Sue Ellen (Linda Gray), Bobby (Patrick Duffy), and that nasty J.R. (Larry Hagman). The Nov. 21, 1980, episode, where we found out who shot J.R., is the No. 2–rated show ever, behind the finale of *M*A*S*H*.

See also DYNASTY; LAST EPISODE OF *M*A*S*H*; TEXAS

DALLAS COWBOY CHEERLEADERS

These high-kicking, low-cut, All-American girls who made up the sideline squad for "America's Team" turned cheerleading into, uh . . . well, they were on camera a lot. And they set the women's movement back about 10 years. They had not one but two TV movies made about them and did cameos on *The Love Boat*. And even Steeler fans could enjoy the aesthetic quality they brought to the game.

BONUS FACT: Jane *"Dr. Quinn"* Seymour starred in the first TV movie.

See also DALLAS; TEXAS

DANCE FEVER

The fact that the contestants on this disco-dancing competition show, hosted by Danny "The music is taped, but the audience is LIIIVE!" Terrio, took themselves seriously only made it that much funnier.

See also PUTTIN' ON THE HITS; SOLID GOLD

DANTE, JOE

His name rarely comes up when people mention good directors, but maybe it should. His specialty for a while was combining comedy and horror. Career high points include both *Gremlins* movies, *The Howling*, and one segment of *Twilight Zone, The Movie*.

See also AMAZON WOMEN ON THE MOON; GREMLINS; LANDIS, JOHN

D'ARBY, TERENCE TRENT

No one was sure what to make of this guy when he hit the scene in 1988. He was basically a smooth-voiced soul singer who liked to rock out. Suffered some by comparing himself to the Beatles and then being confused with Milli Vanilli (they had the same hairstyle).

See also MILLI VANILLI

Another classic '80s outfit

You're on your way to the mall in 1983. You're all set in a pink Izod shirt underneath an argyle sweater vest and shorts the color of some cross pattern in the argyle. You're wearing bobby socks and saddle shoes. Your favorite song, which sort of shows your dark side, is "Blasphemous Rumors." You bought all this in the boutique in the mall. There used to be boutiques in malls.

DARK CRYSTAL

Along with *The Neverending Story* and *Labyrinth*, this signaled the resurgence of fantasy adventures in the early '80s. They all depended heavily on puppets, and Muppetmaster Jim Henson had a hand in the creatures of *Dark Crystal* (which featured not a single human) and *Labyrinth* (which featured David Bowie, who is often mistaken for a human).

See also FRAGGLE ROCK; HENSON, JIM; MUPPET SHOW, THE

DARK KNIGHT RETURNS, THE

A bleak and futuristic comic book series about an elderly Batman coming out of retirement. He battles the Joker, takes on a female Robin, and skirmishes with a withered Superman. The four books by artist Frank Miller renewed the Batman mystique in 1986 with a funny, dark strangeness that fueled the films three years later. The Dark Knight series also gets extra pop culture points for featuring illustrated cameos by David Letterman and Dr. Ruth Westheimer.

See also BATMANIA; CYBERPUNK; LETTERMAN, DAVE; SUPERMAN: THE MOVIE; WESTHEIMER, DR. RUTH

DARK STAR

Weird cult movie about how boring life can be on a spaceship, made in 1974 and seen by many of us either on video or at midnight shows. Also John "*Halloween*" Carpenter's first movie.

See also BAMBI VS. GODZILLA; HARDWARE WARS

DAT

Another revolutionary technological breakthrough that we kept hearing about but never saw. Digital Audio Tape hardly made it out of the lab because the players cost about $1,100 and the recording industry blocked manufacturers from making DAT machines that could record. A CD copied onto a DAT sounds just exactly like a CD, you see, so the honchos thought we'd all just copy our friends' collections instead of buying our own. But we did that with crappy tapes anyway, so what's the big deal?

See also BETAMAX; HDTV; MINIDISCS

DAVID AND DAVID

Pop-rock duo whose minor hit, "Welcome to the Boomtown," was probably ahead of its time. The song was about excess and shattered lives, and in 1986 we just weren't interested. One of the Davids (Baerwald) has enjoyed a moderately successful solo career since then.

See also BALTIMORA; BRICKELL, EDIE

DAVIS, GEENA

How this beautiful Barbie doll of a woman went basically unnoticed until her role as the slightly geeky, somewhat mousy-looking Larry in *Fletch* is a mystery to us, as is the fact that she went out with Jeff Goldblum.

See also BARBIE; *FLETCH*

DAY AFTER, THE

In 1983, at the height of the nuclear war of nerves, this movie about a Soviet first strike scared the crap out of those of us who were allowed to stay up for the whole thing or lucky enough to see it in school. Often confused with *Threads*, a more gruesome British movie with a similar plot.

See also NIGHT OF THE COMET; WARGAMES

DAYS AND NIGHTS OF MOLLY DODD, THE

A boring TV show about the everyday dramas of Molly Dodd (Blair Brown), a single thirtysomething woman who worries a lot. While the show was sitcom-sized (30 minutes), it looked more like a drama. There was no laugh track or "live studio audience," and the directors sometimes went for that cozy, homemade look, using only one camera, which would zip around the set and make us at home feel nauseous. This moved to the Lifetime cable network (nothin' but stuff for women, 24 hours a day) after being dumped by NBC in 1988.

See also CNN; THIRTYSOMETHING

DEAD

Take a proper noun, like Kennedys, Milkmen, or Pets. Put the word "dead" in front of it, and what do you get? Presto! Instant '80s punk band!

See also PUNK ROCK; TRULY TASTELESS JOKES

DEAD OR ALIVE

Freakish limey dance band that straggled in on the end of the second British Invasion of the mid-'80s. They had two minor hits: "You Spin Me Round (Like a Record)" and "Brand New Lover." No one has ever seen the lead singer and Dr. of Dr. and the Medics in the same room, which suggests that they are, in fact, the same person.

See also DR. AND THE MEDICS; SYNTH-POP

DEBARGE, EL

Motown recording artist, pseudopop ministar, fleeting film star, and leader of Debarge, the supposed heir to the Jacksons. He starred in the martial-arts musical/thriller *The Last Dragon*, and the last we heard from him was "Who's Johnny?" from the *Short Circuit* soundtrack.

See also JACKSONS; MENUDO; SHORT CIRCUIT

DEEZEN, EDDIE

You've seen him, but you probably don't know it. If there was a low-budget movie that called for a squeaky-voiced *über*nerd, he was probably it (although, strangely enough, he wasn't in *Revenge of the Nerds*). He is best known as Eugene in *Grease*, and for localized commercial spots and films like *Surf 2*, *Polish Vampire in Burbank*, and *Teenage Exorcists*.

See also NERD; THAT "HEY VERN" GUY; ÜBER-

DEFENDER

Early video game that is significant for two innovations: It had a little radar-screen thing in the corner, so you could see the enemy before it got on the regular screen, and you could go both east and west on the screen, something previously unseen in flying-ship games.

See also ATARI; GALAGA; SPACE INVADERS

DEF LEPPARD

This band's angular logo was doodled on many a school notebook in the '80s, often next to the winged "VH" of Van Halen and distorted "TS" of Twisted Sister. Most people heard about this melodic metal band after their third album, *Pyromania*, but the next mental disorder, *Hysteria*, was huge. Also, one of the guitarists died and the drummer lost his arm.

BONUS GRAMMAR POINT: The band name is a fun homonym.

See also HEAVY METAL BOOM; TWISTED SISTER; VAN HALEN

DELIRIOUS

Eddie Murphy stand-up concert that, along with his *Raw*, became part of many guys' repertoire of instantly quotable material. Other films in the canon include *Fletch, Fast Times at Ridgemont High,* and *Top Gun.*

See also CADDYSHACK; FAST TIMES AT RIDGEMONT HIGH; FLETCH; TOP GUN

DeLOREAN

Part Edsel, part Yugo, and part Stealth bomber, this car-of-the-future-now looked like it flied and would never stain. But it might as well have been designed exclusively for *Back to the Future*, which is the only place we ever saw one.

John DeLorean, the man behind these stainless-steel cars with doors that look like wings, was brought up on charges that he smuggled cocaine in league with some South American heavies. How the two are connected, we're not sure, but, you know, cool car.

See also AUTOMAN; BACK TO THE FUTURE; KNIGHT RIDER; SUZUKI SAMURAI; YUGO

DEPECHE MODE

Brooding British New Wave band that had an underground following in the early '80s and helped start the whole synthesizer-only music craze. While "People Are People" was probably their most popular song, the atmospheric (but obscure) "Somebody" was great for slow dancing and making out. One member of the band (Vince Clarke) left to form Yaz and then Erasure.

BONUS FACT: The name Depeche Mode is French for something.

See also ERASURE; NEW WAVE; SYNTH-POP

DIE HARD

When we first heard about this movie in the early summer of 1988, we said, "Bruce Willis is going to star in an action movie? That same weisenheimer from *Moonlighting*? Nope, can't work." But lured by a pretty good trailer and the novelty of it all, we went and saw it anyway. What we saw was the blueprint for all action movies since.

See also MOONLIGHTING; RAIDERS OF THE LOST ARK

DIE YUPPIE SCUM

Popular bumper sticker and T-shirt slogan seen in the late 1980s, most often on the back of a beat-up Datsun 510 or Chevrolet Chevette, right between the "War is Costly, Peace is Priceless" and "Kill Your Television" stickers.

See also MEAN PEOPLE SUCK; SHIT HAPPENS; YUPPIES

DIFF'RENT STROKES

Long-running NBC sitcom about Phillip Drummond (Conrad Bain), a wealthy white man from Park Avenue, who adopts Arnold and Willis Jackson (Gary Coleman and Todd Bridges), two black kids from Harlem and the children of a former servant. This went downhill fast after Mr. Drummond married Dixie Carter, and her annoying son, Sam (Danny Cooksey), moved in. Also notable for the run-ins Bridges and Dana Plato, who played Kimberly, had with the law after the show went off the air.

See also CHILD STARS GONE BAD; COLEMAN, GARY; FACTS OF LIFE; WEBSTER; "WHATCHOOTALKINBOUT?"

DIG DUG

Atari did this arcade game, where you were the title character, digging around underground and alternately dropping rocks on the bad guys or pumping them full of air until they

blew up.

See also ATARI; MR. DO

DIRTY DANCING

This movie, sappy as it was, captured the collective heart of teenage America in 1987, continuing a long line of hits with hot young stars and smash soundtracks. Other films of this type included *Footloose*, *Vision Quest*, *Top Gun*, *The Breakfast Club*, *say anything . . .* , *Ghost*, and *Pretty Woman*.

See also FLASHDANCE; FOOTLOOSE; LAMBADA!; LOGGINS, KENNY; TOP GUN

DISCO

A musical movement of the mid- and late-1970s featuring watered-down funk beats, lyrics about dancin' all night and the resulting love hangover, lighted floors, gold medallions, and miles and miles of white polyester. The soundtrack to *Saturday Night Fever*, which featured the Bee Gees and others of their ilk, was for a while the best-selling album of all time. Dead by 1981, until resurrected in the '90s.

See also ABBA; DANCE FEVER; SATURDAY NIGHT FEVER; SOLID GOLD

DISINTEGRATION

This album did for The Cure what *Green* did for R.E.M.

See also R.E.M.

DISK CAMERAS

Kodak introduced these slim, easy-to-carry little cameras in the mid-1980s.

Movie lines we said a lot

"So . . . have you ever seen a grown man naked? . . . Do you like to hang around the gymnasium? . . . Do you like movies about gladiators? . . . Have you ever been in a Turkish prison?"

—A complete non sequitur from *Airplane!* pilot Clarence Oever (Peter Graves), who asks these questions of a young boy who's come to see the cockpit. Most often used to make others uncomfortable. Or when we're drunk.

The film was a 15-frame wheel that sort of looked like a Viewmaster disk, and it was easier to load than a regular roll. The cameras were cheap, sort of fun, and eventually came in several colors. The only problem was that they didn't take very good pictures, and so the whole idea died a few years later.

See also BETAMAX; HDTV; POLAROID

D.J. JAZZY JEFF AND THE FRESH PRINCE

Before making it big in sitcoms, they were the kings of easy-to-understand storytelling rap that helped the genre become hugely popular. Who didn't know at least some of the words to "Parents Just Don't Understand"? Groups like Public Enemy and NWA would later make the group's almost suburban tales seem light-and-easy by comparison.

See also PUBLIC ENEMY; RAP; YOUNG MC

DOBBS, J.R. "BOB"

Central figure in the postmodern "religion" the Church of the SubGenius. Dobbs is a mythical god creature who manifests himself as a '50s-esque father figure with Ward Cleaver hair, a Clorox smile, and a pipe. He advocates the philosophy of "having slack," which probably has something to do with drugs.

See also GOD; SUBGENIUS, CHURCH OF THE

DOLBY

First of many sound processes designed for stereo equipment to make our music clearer, sharper, and more expensive to listen to.

See also COMPACT DISCS; *THX 1138*

DOMO ARIGATO

What you were expected to say to Mr. Roboto.

See also CARPE DIEM; DEPECHE MODE; QUEEN

DONALDSON, SAM

ABC news White House correspondent who became famous in the 1980s for his–how to put this–aggressive style of questioning and beady little eyes. Subject of many a fine parody, especially by SNL's Kevin Nealon.

See also KOPPEL, TED; *SATURDAY NIGHT LIVE*

DONKEY KONG

The game that made Nintendo. This was a variation on King Kong stories, with a suitably mean ape, and graphics that were pretty good for the time (1981). That little guy who looked suspiciously like Mario was simply called "Jumpman" in the original game. The second incarnation, Donkey Kong Jr., followed the much more lovable son of the original ape on his quest for revenge and fruit. Then came Donkey Kong III, which no one really played. Mario and his brother Luigi then took over the franchise with Mario Bros., Super Mario Bros., Super MarioLand, and on and on.

See also ATARI

DORITOS

If the question is "What is the preeminent corn-based snack food of our era?" then the answer can be only one thing: definitely Doritos.

See also RANCH

DOUBLE TROUBLE

Short-lived 1984 NBC sitcom with the Sagal twins (from Doublemint gum commercial fame) as Kate and Allison, who lived with their savvy aunt and toyed with men by pretending to be each other.

See also KATE & ALLIE

DOWN AND OUT IN BEVERLY HILLS

Notable because it was, in 1986, the first R-rated film put out by Disney. It technically came from the new Touchstone Pictures studio, so Bette Midler's orgasm while being massaged by a vagrant (Nick Nolte) had no real connection to *Steamboat Willy*.

See also BLACK CAULDRON, THE; MIKE THE DOG; PG-13

DRAGON'S LAIR

The first "laser" video arcade game. It told of Dirk the fearless knight's quest to save a princess, and it looked like a cartoon that you could control. The lines to play this were ridiculously long, *and* the machine took like three tokens.

See also DUNGEONS & DRAGONS; GAUNTLET; M.A.C.H. 3

DR. AND THE MEDICS

Frightening-looking English band that got extensive MTV play in the mid-'80s with its rather faithful cover of Norman Greenbaum's "Spirit in the Sky."

See also BALTIMORA; *DEAD OR ALIVE*; TIMELORDS, THE

DREAM ACADEMY

Ethereal, dark English pop band whose song "Life in a Northern Town" was a favorite among moody types for a few months in 1988. We ask: Why is it that almost all these bands are English?

See also BALTIMORA

DREAMSCAPE

Silly movie about mind control or something. Significant because it was one of the first-ever PG-13 films.

See also PG-13; *RED DAWN*

DREW, NANCY

The girl version of The Hardy Boys. Nancy and she-buddy George fought evil and sleuthed in the books by Carolyn Keene, an author who existed in the same fictional universe as Franklin W. Dixon. The Nancy Drew character had her own show on ABC (alternating weeks with *The Hardy Boys Mysteries*) in 1977, but Nancy later joined Joe and Frank when the shows combined.

See also BABYSITTER'S CLUB, THE; BROWN, ENCYCLOPEDIA; *CLUE CLUB*; HARDY BOYS

DUDE

While this word has been around for, we suspect, centuries, its use as a pronoun became a phenomenon only in the 1980s. Anyone who uses the word in public is either of our generation, making fun of our generation, or talking to one of us. We're hopelessly stuck with it.

See also BACKWARD BASEBALL HATS

DUDES

Actually the name of a movie! It's a fish-out-of-water road tale about a pack of New York punk-scene burnouts who brave the Great American West on their way to Los Angeles. A few of the good-natured music lovers get killed during a *Deliverance*-esque run-in with an outlaw biker gang . . . and there's a-gonna be trouble. Starred Jon "Remember? Duckie, from *Pretty in Pink*?" Cryer.

See also HUGHES, JOHN; PUNK ROCK

DUH

All-encompassing negation/put-down that gained wide popularity and acceptance during the Valley Girl era, circa 1982–83. Used most commonly in response to an obvious question:

"*So are you going to the party tonight?*"

"*Duh!*"

Variations include the redundant "No duh," the alternate pronunciation "Doyee" (commonly heard among boys age 8 to 11), the ultra-sarcastic, "Duu-uhh" (sometimes preceded by a

sigh or click of the tongue), and the lesser known, somewhat nonsensical "Duh-hickey."

See also VALLEY GIRL DICTIONARY

DUKAKIS, MICHAEL

The guy who, during perhaps the only interesting presidential election of our lifetimes, eventually won the right to lose to George Bush. Dukakis' lasting image will remain that of him wearing a helmet, riding in a giant tank, and waving.

See also HART, GARY; HORTON, WILLIE

DUKES OF HAZZARD, THE

CBS sitcom of the late 1970s and early '80s capitalizing on the first wave of enchantment with all things Country. Featured a cast made up of almost all dumb guys, including John Schneider as Bo, Tom Wopat as Luke, James Best as Sheriff Roscoe P. Coltrane, Sonny Shroyer as Deputy Enos, and the late Sorrell Booke as Jefferson Davis "Boss" Hogg. Catherine Bach played the always underdressed Daisy (although we heard a body double performed her butt shots), and Denver Pyle headed the Duke clan as backwoods sage/moonshiner Uncle Jesse. Bo and Luke drove a 1969 Dodge Charger called the General Lee. Waylon Jennings did the theme song and scene-by-scene narration.

See also CB RADIOS; ENOS; MOUNTAIN DEW; SMOKEY AND THE BANDIT

DUMB GUY

A standard character in almost any sitcom. You can spot this creature by its natural habits: The Dumb Guy usually lives next door to the main characters. He's got a one-word name. He never knocks before entering a room, especially if he's about to interrupt a tense situation. He's goofy-looking, dim, lovable, and often hopelessly in love with the most attractive female on the show.

The archetype is Norton on *The Honeymooners* (the *alpha* Dumb Guy) and was taken to a higher level of stupidity with Maynard G. Krebs on *Dobie Gillis*. From there, the '70s and '80s created an army of Dumb Guys: Lenny and Squiggy (*Larverne and Shirley*), Skippy (*Family Ties*), Latka (*Taxi*), Furly (*Three's Company*), Urkel (*Family Matters*), Larry-Darryl-&-Darryl (*Newhart*), Bull (*Night Court*), Cockroach (*The Cosby Show*), Eli (*It's Your Move*), Monroe (*Too Close for Comfort*), Rerun (*What's Happening!!*), Boner (*Growing Pains*), and Screech (*Saved by the Bell*).

See also Dukes of Hazard, The; Family Ties; Gilligan's Planet; Growing Pains; Three's Company; Thursday Night Lineup

DUNE

David Lynch's 1984 interpretation of Frank Herbert's classic sci-fi book was too weird for those who hadn't already read it, and too short for those who had. Kyle MacLachlan, Sting, and some worms starred. Lynch was so embarrassed with the TV version (the producers added some 50 minutes) that the credits said that a guy named "Alan Smithee" directed it.

See also Blue Velvet; Eraserhead

Another big moment in our lifetimes

In January 1980, *Seventeen* magazine makes the following predictions about life in the year 2000: We will have phones that we can carry with us wherever we go. There will be a cure for cancer. Lots of people will work out of their homes, connected to their bosses and coworkers through computers in the home. Doctors will perfect surgery to correct nearsightedness or farsightedness. People will be able to travel to spots in space just as they would fly across the country. Many of us will have household help in the form of robots. We will be able to shop without leaving the living room. There will be vast underwater agriculture projects. The superpowers of the world will settle their differences peacefully, and the threat of war will disappear from the globe.

Under David Lynch's guidance, Dune was only slightly more explicable than Blue Velvet. And almost as cool.

DUNGEONS & DRAGONS

The archetypal role-playing game.
Preadolescents and hermit-like college students would (and still) play it
for hours and even days, submerging
themselves in alter egos (elves and
mages and dwarves), casting spells,
and fighting ogres, dragons, and a
giant eyeball called the Beholder. We
heard horror stories about teenage
boys taking it too seriously and sacri-
ficing themselves to demons, and then
eventually D&D became a cartoon
series.

See also CHOOSE YOUR OWN ADVENTURE;
JUDAS PRIEST; *MAZES AND MONSTERS*

DURAN DURAN

Hunky British band that became
supernaturally popular with some
very bizarre songs and cool videos
(What were "The Reflex" or "Union
of the Snake" about, anyway?).
Beatles comparisons abounded as
stadiums full of females screamed
for Simon, John, Roger, Andy, and
Nick. Also, the band's name, as
was commonly known, came from a
Jane Fonda sci-fi film called
Barbarella.

See also ARCADIA; FONDA, JANE; NEW
WAVE; POWER STATION

DYNAMITE MAGAZINE

Hard-hitting teen rag that tackled
such meaty topics as "Bee Gees vs.
Beatles: Who's Cooler?" If you turned
it upside down and backward, you
could read some zany thing called
Bananas magazine.

See also DISCO; TROLL/SCHOLASTIC PRESS

DYNASTY

ABC's rich-family-in-turmoil answer
to *Dallas*. The show chronicled the
life and times of the Carrington family, with John Forsythe as patriarch
Blake Carrington, Linda Evans as his
statuesque wife, and Joan Collins as
her bitch of a sister. Also included one
of the first gay characters in the
world of network Prime Time, Blake's
son, Stephen (played by Al Corley and
then—after a fiery accident, death,
realization-that-the-death-wasn't-
actually-that-fatal, and some plastic
surgery—by Jack Coleman). A spin-
off, *The Colbys*, was far worse.

See also COLLINS, JOAN; *DALLAS*; SPELLING,
AARON

E

EASTERN AIRLINES

These guys went spectacularly bankrupt in the mid-'80s, causing much hand-wringing among people who cared about this sort of thing. Another news event we didn't quite understand.

See also BRANIFF AIRLINES; IRAN-CONTRA THING; IRANIAN HOSTAGE CRISIS; OCTOBER 19, 1987

EDDIE AND THE CRUISERS

An '83 movie about a band that became huge long after the lead singer died. In the sequel (*Eddie and the Cruisers II: Eddie Lives!*), of course, we find that Eddie's actually alive and working on a comeback. John Cafferty and the Beaver Brown Band did a very Springsteen-esque soundtrack.

See also BORN IN THE USA; JOHN CAFFERTY AND THE BEAVER BROWN BAND

EDWARDS, ANTHONY

The quintessential loser-who-thinks-he's-cool '80s actor. In *Gotcha* he thought he was cool playing paint-gun assassin on campus, but was proven wrong by French thugs and *une femme belle*. In *Revenge of the Nerds* he thought he was a loser but, through hard work and smarts, realized that anybody can be cool. And in *Top Gun* he played Maverick's (Tom Cruise) navigator Goose, who got smoked.

BONUS FACT: He and two other *Top Gun* veterans (Michael Ironside and Rick Rossovich) starred in the first season of NBC's *ER*.

See also GOOSE; *REVENGE OF THE NERDS*; *TOP GUN*

EIGHT IS ENOUGH

One-hour show that tried to be something of a semi-serious *Brady Bunch*, with Dick Van Patten as the harried patriarch and Willie Aames and Adam Rich as the most visible children.

See also ALF; CHARLES IN CHARGE; COSBY SHOW, THE; FAMILY TIES; GROWING PAINS

867-5309

Jenny's number.

See also TOMMY TUTONE

ELECTRIC BOOGALOO

The greatest ever subtitle for a sequel, as in *Breakin' 2: Electric Boogaloo*.

See also BREAKDANCING

ELECTRIC COMPANY

For graduates of *Sesame Street*, this PBS show dealt with words and sentences and simple arithmetic, instead of just letters and numbers. Oh, and: "HEEYY you GUUUUYYYYS!!!"

See also SESAME STREET

ELECTRIC DREAMS

A 1984 movie that preyed on people's fear of the coming Information Age— a full decade before anybody used silly phrases like "Information Age." It examined the worst-case scenario for the new all-powerful personal computer: the machine becomes "self-aware," names itself Edgar, locks its owner (Lenny Von Dohlen) out of the apartment, and tries to steal his cellist girlfriend (Virginia Madsen) by playing duets with her. The soundtrack, strangely enough, included new songs from Culture Club and ELO's Jeff Lynne.

See also ATARI; COMMODORE 64; GEORGE, BOY; HEADROOM, MAX; ORWELL, GEORGE

ELECTRONIC BATTLESHIP

As Atari and Commodore threatened to put game machines and personal computers in every American household, the makers of some traditional board games got nervous. They panicked. They created so-called "electronic" versions of their classics (like Battleship and Stratego), hoping to compete with Pac-man and Summer Games. But the "new" Battleship had only one improvement over the original: unrealistic explosion noises when you sunk a ship.

See also ATARI; COMMODORE 64; PICTIONARY; STOP! THIEF; TRIVIAL PURSUIT

ELMO AND PATSY

Perpetrators of that most foul of Christmas ditties, "Grandma Got Run Over by a Reindeer."

See also "JINGLE BELLS" (ALTERNATIVE VERSION); "JINGLE BELLS" (ALTERNATIVE VERSION NO. 2)

ELVIS HAS LEFT THE BUILDING

Although very few of us ever attended an Elvis concert, this phrase, originally announced to try to make screaming fans leave after a show, has infested itself in our lingo as a common non sequitur. In times of either mass confusion or eerie silence, you can usually expect one smart-ass to say, "Elvis has left the building!"

See also POP-TOP COLLECTING; "MONY MONY" CHANT; MYTHS; PRESLEY, ELVIS

EMMANUELLE

Queen of soft-core pornography, usually found on Cinemax late at night. Since her sexual adventures began in 1974, she has been played by at least six different actresses, has gotten at least one cosmetic facial overhaul, and has screwed in 3-D.

See also 3-D MOVIES; WEBSTER

ENOS

Dukes of Hazzard spin-off, where Deputy Enos heads off to the Big City (read: Los Angeles) to fight crime.

See also ART OF BEING NICK, THE; DUKES OF HAZZARD, THE; FLO

ENUFF Z'NUFF

These guys looked just like Poison, but the drummer had a peace sign on his bass drum and they sang about peace and love, under the guise of another big-haired metal band. Neither metalheads nor hippie-types liked it, but that didn't stop *Rolling Stone* from naming these guys the "Hot Band" in 1989.

See also HEAVY METAL BOOM; MOUSSE; POISON

EPCOT

A giant mall in Orlando whose name stands for Experimental Prototype Community of Tomorrow. Walt Disney World opened this in 1982 in an effort to get every American family with a station wagon to drive to Florida for a few days. A very large percentage of us have gone there, taken the slow roller-coaster thing inside the giant silver ball, seen the fake robotic presidents, and toured all the little Disneyfied versions of foreign countries. Whether this brings us closer together as a nation has yet to be determined.

See also CAPTAIN EO; MALLS; MINIVANS; SALT II

EQUALIZER, THE

Short-lived, '80s drama about a middle-aged Englishman who did contract hits on bad guys for downtrodden people. People always contacted The Equalizer (Robert McCall) by phone, and he would listen to their pleas on his remote-control answering machine.

See also A-TEAM, THE; ANSWERING MACHINES; FALL GUY, THE; RIPTIDE; SIMON & SIMON

ERA

Short for the Equal Rights Amendment, which almost became part of the Constitution before petering out, three states short of ratification, in 1980. It was the first, and pretty much the only, significant effort to amend the Constitution in our lifetimes. The *Weekly Reader* ran periodic updates on its progress.

See also BORK, ROBERT; WEEKLY READER

ERASABLE-INK PENS

All the rage at just the time when it was becoming proper for us to use pens for our schoolwork instead of pencils. Basically, the eraser was actually a hard little piece of rubber that "erased" the part of the paper where you made a mistake, and often tore it. The ink smudged easily, too, leaving a lot of left-handed kids with blue or black palms.

See also MECHANICAL PENCILS; STA-SHARP PENCILS; TRAPPER KEEPER

ERASERHEAD

Another very peculiar film from David "I make very peculiar films" Lynch. This, his first, tells of a man whose hair sticks up about two feet in the air and who must deal with a screaming baby and some loud pipes. Or something like that. It's hard to tell. Lynch freaks are pretty much the only people to have ever seen it (because it's so unwatchably bad), but the

Eraserhead hairstyle is universally recognized.

See also **BLUE VELVET; DUNE**

ERASURE

British synth-pop band that evolved from the British synth-pop band Yaz, which itself came out of Depeche Mode. They had hits with veiled gay rights messages, such as "Respect."

See also **DEPECHE MODE; SYNTH-POP**

ESCAPE CLUB

Minor blip on the pop landscape in 1988. Responsible for the song "Wild Wild West," which talked about heading for the '90s. It wasn't a cover of the Kool Moe Dee rap of the same name, nor was it so cool.

See also **INFORMATION SOCIETY; TIMBUK 3**

ESCOBAR, PABLO

A drug lord as synonymous with the word "Colombia" as Juan Valdez and his mule. When the United States started policing the global cocaine market, Pablo and his South American cartel topped the Bad Guy list.

See also **COCAINE; MIAMI VICE; NORIEGA, MANUEL**

ESPN

In the early days of cable, when you still heard that "doot-doot-doot" telephone-dialing noise when shows went to commercial, the Entertainment and Sports Network was launched. It was all sports, all the time (although, on weekday mornings,

We're sorry, but we have to do this: E.T., *phone home.*

the network ran a business affairs show for some reason), and it was a rather low-budget operation at first, when people scoffed at the notion that anyone would want to watch sports twenty-four hours a day.

See also **CABLE; MTV**

E.T.

Or, officially, *E.T.—The Extraterrestrial*, the movie about a boy and his alien. This was, in 1982, the biggest movie ever. It hit us right where it counts, tapping into our imaginations (about the possibility of life in outer space) and reality (about life in the working-parent suburban home). Spielberg's house in the Valley was familiar and real to a lot of us. The movie also paraded brand names we knew about, such as Reese's Pieces and Speak 'n' Spell—another touch of realism (not to mention crafty product placement). It also made truckloads of money and introduced us to Drew Barrymore.

See also BARRYMORE, DREW; MALLS; *NIGHT OF THE COMET*; REESE'S PIECES; SPIELBERG, STEVEN; VALLEY GIRLS

ETCH-A-SKETCH

No one knows for sure what made this little gadget from Ohio Art work, just that it seemed to be full of sand. We could never make the cool drawings like on the commercial. About all we could come up with was a square.

See also MAGIC SAND; RUBIK'S CUBE

EURYTHMICS

In 1984, androgyne Annie Lennox and her weird partner, Dave Stewart, told us about sweet dreams and the coming rain and stuff, crossing that dance-music line and becoming bona fide popsters. Cool videos, too.

See also HART, COREY

EVANS, LINDA

Stately queen of the manor, so to speak, on *Dynasty*. But she was always put upon by the conniving people around her, especially that bitch Joan Collins.

See also COLLINS, JOAN; *DYNASTY*

EVIL DEAD

Almost universally recognized as not as good as *Evil Dead 2*.

See also EVIL DEAD 2

EVIL DEAD 2

Perhaps the greatest cult film of our time. Director Sam Raimi beautifully parodies cheesy gore films with what can only be described as a cheesy gore film. The effects are bad, the acting is worse, and some of the lines evoke groans from all but the most pun-resistant among us. Bruce Campbell, possessor of the world's most perfect jaw, stars as the invincible Ash, who slices off his own hand (possessed by the Evil Dead, you see) and his girlfriend's head (also possessed) in a frantic attempt to save the world from a menace from another dimension.

See also EVIL DEAD

EVIL EMPIRE

That would be the Soviet Union.

See also AFGHANISTAN; *AMERIKA*; ANDROPOV, YURI; BARYSHNIKOV, MIKHAIL; BREZHNEV, LEONID; CHERNENKO, KONSTANTIN; CHERNOBYL; *DAY AFTER, THE*; GLASNOST; GORBACHEV, MIKHAIL S.; GREAT SATAN; *INVASION USA*; KINSKI, NASTASSJA; KOREAN AIRLINES flight 007; McDONALD'S IN MOSCOW; RAMBO; *RED DAWN*; *RED HEAT*; RUBIK'S CUBE; *RUSSKIES*; RUST, MATHIAS; SALT II; SMIRNOFF, YAKOV; *WARGAMES*; *WHITE NIGHTS*

EXPLORERS

Three kids—a nerd (Ethan Hawke), a dreamer (River Phoenix), and a likable misfit (Jason Presson)—build a spaceship out of an old Tilt-a-Whirl and some things you find around the house. And here's the catch: It works. This was kid empowerment through smarts and imagination at its best, plus it paired two of our generation's sexiest screen stars before they even sprouted pubes. If only Brad Pitt could have been in this.

See also DANTE, JOE; *NIGHT OF THE COMET*; *STAND BY ME*

EXXON *VALDEZ*

Capt. Joseph Hazelwood had a few too many (if you know what we mean), and the result was just about the biggest environmental disaster ever to happen in the United States. Taught many of us to hate big oil com-panies the way lines for gas taught our parents to hate big oil companies 15 years earlier.

See also ALASKA PIPELINE; MADD

EZ BAKE OVEN

An actual tiny oven that cooked actual food. Supposedly a girl toy, but a few boys used these to make little brownies and stuff.

See also ROB BASE; D.J. E-Z ROCK; SNOOPY SNO-CONE MAKER; STRAWBERRY SHORTCAKE

F

FABULOUS THUNDERBIRDS, THE

For most of the 1970s and early '80s, they were a moderately well-known blues-rock band from Texas. But thanks to the magic of MTV, some scantily clad women, and the terrible dearth of good pop songs in 1985, they had two hits that year, "Tuff Enuff" and "Wrap It Up."

See also ENUFF Z'NUFF

FACTS OF LIFE

A spin-off of *Diff'rent Strokes* that started out when Mrs. Garrett (Charlotte Rae) took a job at Kimberly's boarding school. The very large original cast featured Molly Ringwald, but later focused on four girls—the princess Blair (Lisa Whelchel), the neurotic Tootie (Kim Fields), the overweight Natalie (Mindy Cohen), and the streetwise Jo (Nancy McKeon). Somehow they all ended up working for Mrs. Garrett in a knick-knack shop in town and lived above it.

See also DIFF'RENT STROKES; RINGWALD, MOLLY

FALCO

OK, let's see. He was this Austrian guy who dressed up like Mozart and sang a campy synth-drenched song called "Rock Me Amadeus," the lyrics to which about seven people understood. And, in 1986, it was a No. 1 hit.

See also AMADEUS; CONAN THE BARBARIAN

FALCON AND THE SNOWMAN, THE

Movie about two guys who sell government secrets to the Soviets. Also the film that proved Sean Penn could act if he wanted to.

See also COLORS; FAST TIMES AT RIDGEMONT HIGH; PENN, SEAN

FALKLAND ISLANDS

They were the center of attention for a while there in 1982 and 1983, when Britain and Argentina fought a little war over them. See, Britain had claimed them for a long time, but they were a lot closer to Argentina.

See also GRENADA

FALL GUY, THE

After his bionic career ended, Lee Majors starred in this ABC series about a movie stuntman who drove a badass truck and solved crimes with the help of his two young sidekicks, some guy no one remembers and Heather Thomas.

See also EQUALIZER, THE; SIX MILLION DOLLAR MAN, THE

FAME

An NBC show about the life and times of a diverse group of kids at a performing arts school in New York. The cast included Debbie Allen, Nia Peeples, Janet Jackson, and Lori Singer. It was based on the 1980 film and had a theme song performed by Irene Cara.

See also CARA, IRENE; FLASHDANCE; FOOTLOOSE

FAMILY FEUD

Big game show of the 1970s, first hosted by Richard Dawson, in which five members of one family squared off against five members of another family and answered "most likely to" questions. We dug it because kids were allowed to play and because of Dawson's enthusiastic "Survey SAYS!!" bellowing. Another product of the Mark Goodson game-show machine.

See also GOODSON, MARK; WHAMMY; WHITE, VANNA

FAMILY TIES

The story of the Keatons of Columbus, Ohio, NBC's most complete and complex nuclear family. They were: Michael Gross (Steve, dad, and a PBS station manager), Meredith Baxter-Birney (Elyss, mom, and an architect), Michael J. Fox (Alex P. Keaton,

young Republican), Justine Bateman (Mallory, sort of a ditz), Tina Yothers (Jennifer, the least interesting character), and Brian Bonsall (Andrew, the new younger brother, who went from being an infant one season to being 4 the next). Hangers-on included Marc Price (Skippy, the Dumb Guy), Scott Valentine (Nick, Mallory's boyfriend), and Courteney Cox (Lauren, Alex's girlfriend). Tom Hanks and Crispin Glover also showed up a few times. The show pretty much belonged to Fox, who had one memorable episode all to himself (Alex paced a darkened stage and talked about a friend who had recently died). The made-for-NBC movie *Family Ties Vacation* had the Keatons go to England and cause the kind of royal ruckus only they can. Unfortunately, Skippy stayed home.

See also ART OF BEING NICK, THE; BILLY VERA AND THE BEATERS; COX, COURTENEY; DUMB GUY; FOX, MICHAEL J.; THURSDAY NIGHT LINEUP

FANGFACE

Good-natured, one-fanged werewolf who wore a hat and had his own Saturday morning cartoon for a while.

See also CAPTAIN CAVEMAN

FANTASY ISLAND

Starred Ricardo Montalban as a shadowy figure who let people live out their dreams on his private isle, teaching them the lesson that maybe real life isn't so bad after a week with him and Tattoo (the late Herve Villechaize).

And, we have to say this, "Da plane! Da plane!"

See also GILLIGAN'S PLANET; LOVE BOAT, THE; SPELLING, AARON; STAR TREK

FARM AID

While New Wave and R&B types scrambled to put together tributes for starving Ethiopians right around 1985, Willie Nelson and John Cougar Mellencamp and some other country-rockers put together this big concert for folks who actually grow food.

See also USA FOR AFRICA

FARRAH POSTER, THE

'Nuff said.

See also KINSKI, NASTASSJA

"FAR SIDE, THE"

Esoteric comic world-in-a-box by Gary Larson. Weird, full of talking live-stock, and popular with almost every-body on Earth, even those who didn't *get it.*

See also "BLOOM COUNTY"; "CALVIN AND HOBBES"

FAST TIMES AT RIDGEMONT HIGH

Too cool and too influential to describe in one short entry, so look at all the cross-references.

See also CARROT TRICK; CROWE, CAMERON; GERE, RICHARD; MALLS; PENN, SEAN; SQUARE PEGS; STOLTZ, ERIC; VAN HALEN; VANS (THE VEHICLE); VALLEY GIRL; VALLEY GIRL DICTIONARY; VALLEY GIRLS

FATAL ATTRACTION

The quintessential obsessed-other-woman-stalks-married-man-and-makes-his-life-miserable-by-boiling-his-household-pet movie. For some reason, this Glenn Close/Michael Douglas film was probably the most talked about cultural event of 1987. And the name, suggesting the duality of love or something, has inspired a genre of similar-sounding films: *Basic Instinct, Deadly Desire, Deadly Obsession, Fatal Beauty,* and *Fatal Instinct.* And despite the movie's title, the affair was only fatal to Ms. Close's character and a bunny.

See also FATAL VISION; WALL STREET

FAT ALBERT AND THE COSBY KIDS

Bill Cosby's cartoon-with-a-message was the first to feature an all-black cast of characters, and it was really funny, too. Dumb Donald, Mushmouth, Rudy, Bill, Russell, Weird Harold, and Bucky hung with Fat Albert, and they all went to the clubhouse to watch *The Brown Hornet.* Oh, and "Hey, Hey, Hey."

See also BLUE FALCON AND DYNOMUTT; COSBY SHOW, THE

FATAL VISION

Sort of an *Executioner's Song* for the '80s. The Joe McGinniss book—a true story of a doctor who killed his wife and convinced everybody that a burglar did it and then got caught—was thick and hugely popular. And the miniseries proved that tragedy in

ANOTHER OVERUSED CATCH-PHRASE: "Go ahead. Make my day."

YEAR: 1984

SOURCE: *Sudden Impact*

COMMON USAGE: To sound, in a completely facetious way, bad as shit.

ADVICE FOR THOSE WHO USED IT: It's OK, because Reagan did, too.

America doesn't *have* to turn into a bad Sunday night movie. It can be a quite good Sunday night movie.

See also **FATAL ATTRACTION; MINISERIES**

FAT BOYS

For a while, it seemed like they had cornered the growing market for obese rap stars. But that was before Heavy D and Chunky A, and that was before the Fat Boys tried—and failed—to single-handedly revive the golden era of '60s surf music. Their valiant effort began with a remake of "Wipeout," a tag-team deal with the Beach Boys, who hadn't yet achieved their only No. 1 hit of the decade ("Kokomo" from the *Cocktail* soundtrack). Then they covered the immortal "Twist" with history's most persistent one-hit wonder, Chubby Checker. And, of course, the Fat Boys' movie (because everybody got a movie), *Disorderlies*, bombed like a Jerry Lewis routine at the Apollo.

See also **CHUNKY A; COCKTAIL; RAP**

FAT SHOELACES

A fashion trend that moved from the world of breakdancing and onto the feet of America's youth in the form of inch-thick shoelaces. You didn't lace them crisscross, but in parallel, horizontal rows. And the traditional style (as popularized by Run-D.M.C.) involved white laces on black high tops, but neon and fluorescent colors soon entered the scene.

See also **BREAKDANCING; JELLIES; KANGAROOS; NEON CLOTHES; RUN-D.M.C.; VANS (THE SHOES)**

FEDERAL EXPRESS

A concept that became a reality right about when we started licking our own stamps. We can hardly remember a world where you couldn't send whatever you happened to be holding to any place on the planet by this time tomorrow.

See also **GUY WHO TALKS REALLY FAST, THE**

FERRARO, GERALDINE

Doing wonders for the advancement of female creatures everywhere, she was the first-ever chick on a presidential ticket. After she and partner Walter Mondale lost to Reagan in a 1984 landslide, Ferraro picked herself up and did the next best thing to being vice president: She taped a TV spot for Diet Pepsi.

See also **MONDALE, WALTER; REAGAN, RONALD**

FIBER OPTICS

Many of us first encountered this Substance of the Future on toy flashlights that had big bundles of fiber optics coming out from the lenses. When you turned on the flashlight, only the tips of the fibers would light up. Pretty cool.

See also **FLUORESCENT ODDITIES; SDI; WACKY WALL WALKERS**

FIDO DIDO

Simple cartoon doodle with a long face and squiggly hair who spontaneously appeared in late '80s cultural outlets like T-shirt designs, books, and Sprite commercials.

See also "Far Side, The"; "Garfield"; Haring, Keith

FIELD, SALLY

We like her. We really like her.

See also Gere, Richard; Reynolds, Burt

FIREFOX

A 1982 Clint Eastwood film about a U.S. spy/pilot/badass who steals a Stealth-like superplane from the Russians. As if they could build something like that. Ha!

See also Amerika; Carmel, Calif.; Red Dawn; Red Heat; Stealth

501 BLUES

A lifestyle developed through advertisements for Levi's 501 jeans. The idea strayed, however, to perfume, beer, and other jeans ads. Those who live the "501 Blues way" inhabit bare studio apartments located in deserted metropolitan arts districts. Guys wear only Levi's and T-shirts; women wear only Levi's and tank tops. They lounge in their white-walled angst boxes, staring at the ceiling fans. They find romance on fire escapes and sing doo-wop on street corners. They walk through alleys in slow motion, carrying heavy musical instruments. Nothing bothers them. Often, usually at the end of an ad, they throw their heads back in spontaneous silent laughter. And they speak only in voice-overs, providing commentary on their lives with snippets of dialogue or philosophy.

See also Acid Wash; Beerland

FIXX, JIM

This prophet of the '70s jogging craze and author of several books on getting in shape by running dropped dead from a heart attack while out on a run in 1988. He also wrote a quiz book for smart people called *Games for the Superintelligent.*

See also Chariots of Fire; Geek Era

FLASHDANCE

The first '80s movie that featured several elements that appealed to Teen America all in one package. You had the dreamy story line (welder/stripper from Pittsburgh yearns to be a prima ballerina), the huge-selling pop-music soundtrack (featuring the title song by Irene Cara), the fast, MTV-style editing (this was one of the first films to use the music-video style), and, of course, the fashion statement (ripped sweatshirts and leg warmers).

See also Baryshnikov, Mikhail; Beals, Jennifer; Cara, Irene; Dirty Dancing; Fame; Footloose; Leg warmers; MTV; Ripped sweatshirts

FLASH GORDON

Cheesy space epic that adhered to the fundamental principle that if you can't make stuff look real, make it look very, very fake. The effects were bad, but in 1980, that was sort of cool.

Two other things to remember: 1. The soundtrack by Queen ("Flash!! Aahh-aahhh!"), and 2. Max von Sydow as a perfect Ming the Merciless.

See also Banzai, Buckaroo; Evil Dead 2; Queen; Star Wars

FLETCH

Perhaps the most quoted movie in conversations among today's twentysomething men. Based on a series of Gregory McDonald mystery novels, the film starred Chevy Chase as smart-ass newspaper reporter Irwin Maurice Fletcher, and also Tim Matheson, Kareem Abdul-Jabbar, Geena Davis (as Larry), and George ("Norm!") Wendt. Favorite lines include (out of context, as they are usually quoted): "Not as far as you know." "Saw my pimp today." "Look! Defenseless babies!" "Could you just bring me a glass of hot fat? Oh, and bring me the head of Alfredo Garcia while you're out there." "Did you decorate the place yourself, or did Mrs. Chief of Police help out?"

See also CADDYSHACK; DAVIS, GEENA; MATHESON, TIM

FLINTSTONES CHEWABLE VITAMINS

So much fun to eat, we hardly knew they were good for us.

See also ST. JOSEPH BABY ASPIRIN

FLO

Fleeting 1980 spin-off of *Alice*, starring Polly Holliday (also the old lady in *Gremlins*) as spunky waitress Florence Jean "Kiss My Grits" Castleberry, or Flo. If this had been a hit, it would have made living in a trailer park *the* thing to do.

See also ART OF BEING NICK, THE; ENOS; GREMLINS

FLOCK OF SEAGULLS, A

New Wave band with lots of hair, which disappeared shortly after the band members did when DJs stopped playing their song "I Ran" in the early '80s.

See also BALTIMORA; NEW WAVE

FLUORESCENT ODDITIES

For a while there, it was cool for toys to glow in the dark. Or at least to have accessories (swords, eyeballs, decals, heads) that did. Among the rash of mysteriously illuminated objects we saw: Frisbees, necklaces, bracelets, and yo-yos. Not to mention Glo-Worms and Yo-Balls (both of which sound like venereal diseases) and Wacky Wall Walkers and plastic, fluid-filled sticks that shined when cracked. You had to be careful not to drink the stuff that oozed out after one glow too many, though.

See also GLO-WORM; WACKY WALL WALKERS; YO-BALL

FONDA, JANE

Possessor of the world's most famous leotards (the red and black ones) and a major instigator of the '80s biggest exercise craze: aerobics. Other generations know her as an actress as well, but our experience with Fonda involves her wearing something striped and tight and posing on the cover of videocassette boxes for "Jane Fonda's Workout."

See also AEROBICS; CNN; DURAN DURAN; L.A. GEAR; REEBOK; TURNER, TED

FONZIE CARTOON

Saturday morning series in which Arthur Fonzarelli gives up on getting lots of babes and just being the coolest guy in Milwaukee . . . and travels through time with a bunch of little kids in a flying saucer. *You* figure it out.

See also ALF CARTOON; GILLIGAN'S PLANET; MR. T AND THE T FORCE; PUNKY BREWSTER

FOOD FIGHT

For our money, one of the most underrated video games ever. The object was simple: Obliterate a bunch of crazed chefs with various foodstuffs placed around the board. The watermelon screen, with its limitless supply, was especially fun. If you did something really cool, the game gave you an instant replay.

See also ATARI; BURGER TIME

FOOTLOOSE

Imagine a small Colorado town so backward as to think dancing and rock 'n' roll are evil. Now, imagine Kevin Bacon swooping onto the scene and stirring up some rip-roaring, '80s-style trouble. Now imagine this being just about the biggest movie of 1984. Amazing, isn't it? The soundtrack featured, among others, Kenny Loggins, Deniece Williams, Shalamar, and Sammy Hagar.

See also LOGGINS, KENNY; VAN HALEN

FORD, HARRISON

Star of two of the biggest and coolest movies of our lifetime (and we think

you know which ones). Probably the only guy we were capable of believing in the role of Indiana Jones, because, aside from the incredible stunts and action that 1930s archaeology provided, he was a pretty normal guy.

BONUS FACT: The role of Indiana Jones was originally offered to Tom Selleck.

See also CLANCY, TOM; MAGNUM P.I.; MILLENNIUM FALCON; RAIDERS OF THE LOST ARK; STAR WARS

FORD, LITA

Armed with some tight black leather pants, she tried to make heavy metal sexy by singing "Kiss Me Deadly" and then dueting with Ozzy Osbourne on "Close My Eyes Forever."

See also BENETAR, PAT; FOX, SAMANTHA; JETT, JOAN; OSBOURNE, OZZY

FOREVER

The most sexually advanced of Judy Blume's puberty books (including *Are You There God? It's Me, Margaret* and *Then Again, Maybe I Won't*). This was among our early exposures to the concept of blow jobs.

See also CARROT TRICK

FOR SURE

Yet another way to say "Yeah." Like many clearly '80s phrases, this came from the Valley Girl lexicon. Also pronounced "Fer sher."

See also GAG ME WITH A SPOON; GNARLY; GRODY; LIKE; VALLEY GIRLS; WAS ALL

42

The answer to the ultimate question of life, the universe, and everything.

See also HITCHHIKER'S GUIDE TO THE GALAXY, THE

FOSTER, JODIE

A rare child actress who grew up and became a successful adult actress without picking up a rap sheet along the way. John Hinckley was a fan.

See also BARRYMORE, DREW; CHILD STARS GONE BAD; DIFF'RENT STROKES; HINCKLEY, JOHN; MCNICHOL, KRISTY; O'NEAL, TATUM

FOX

The fourth network, the one that challenged the conventions of the Big Three, brought a cable mentality to over-the-air broadcasting and forever lowered the common denominator in television programming. Still, its gradual buildup from one or two shows to a full-fledged lineup changed the face of television.

See also CABLE; IN LIVING COLOR; 21 JUMP STREET; ULLMAN, TRACEY

FOX, MICHAEL J.

The quintessential actor of the 1980s. If he was a few feet taller, he'd be perfect to play President Ronald Reagan in 40 years. As *Family Ties* son Alex P. Keaton, he took part in the greatest TV lineup ever. As Marty McFly in *Back to the Future*, he became a character in the divine shadow of Spielberg.

See also BACK TO THE FUTURE; BRIGHT LIGHTS, BIG CITY; FAMILY TIES; THURSDAY NIGHT LINEUP

FOX, SAMANTHA

Unlike Traci Lords, who moved into mainstream acting, this ex-porn star turned to the music world, where she crooned the (regrettably) unforgettable "Naughty Girls Need Love Too." The song was a hit for about three hours in 1988.

See also BALTIMORA

FRAGGLE ROCK

Muppet sitcom on HBO about a society of little creatures (Fraggles) who live underground and sometimes hang out with the bigger creatures who live above ground. Usually, they would all sing.

See also DARK CRYSTAL, THE; LITTLES, THE; MUPPET SHOW; SMURFS; SNORKS

FRANKIE GOES TO HOLLYWOOD

Trifling British synth-pop band popular for about three Tuesdays in the mid-'80s because of songs such as "Relax" and "Two Tribes," and for all those T-shirts that said things like "Frankie say relax." The shirts were of course parodied, and you'd find clothes that said, "Who gives a shit what Frankie say."

See also DURAN DURAN; PET SHOP BOYS; WHAM!

FREAKY FRIDAY

First (in our lifetime, anyway) movie in which a kid (Jodie Foster) and a parent (Barbara Harris as Jodie's mom) magically switch personalities, creating a whole bunch of wacky situations that were Disney fun for the whole family.

See also FOSTER, JODIE; SWITCHAROOMANIA

FREE JAMES BROWN

This was the cry that went up across the nation when the Godfather of Soul was imprisoned in the late 1980s for assault and battery.

See also MANDELA, NELSON; VISUALIZE WORLD PEACE

FRIDAY NIGHT VIDEOS

Weak NBC attempt to catch a little of that MTV market. When the show began in 1983, it had no veejays, just a narrator and a steady stream of videos. A couple of years later, prime-timers like Lisa Bonet and Tony Danza sat in a small room and tried to be funny between videos.

See also COSBY SHOW, THE; MTV; NIGHT TRAX; WHO'S THE BOSS

FRIDAY THE 13TH

The quintessential undead/slasher film serial, running from 1980–93 and featuring prominently the "have sex, get hacked to death with a lawn-mower blade by a raving lunatic zombie" story line. Some have theorized that the filmmakers were trying to send a message about the danger of promiscuity. Jason Voorhees, the man in the hockey mask, and his mom, who did the honors in the first install-ment, killed 116 people in the first eight films. The victims included Kevin Bacon, Corey Feldman, and Crispin Glover. There was also a TV

series on Fox, which had little to do with the Voorhees family saga.

See also COREYS; NIGHTMARE ON ELM STREET, A; 3-D MOVIES

FRIDGE, THE

Also known as William Perry, the lov-able, grossly overweight defensive tackle/running back o n the 1985 Super Bowl champion Chicago Bears. The Fridge became a celebrity only because of his enormous girth, and gave a nation of couch potatoes some-one to look up to.

See also SUPER BOWL SHUFFLE

FRIENDSHIP PINS

Small safety pins with a few brightly colored beads attached. They were great around fifth grade, because everyone could see how popular you were just by looking at the collar of your jean jacket or at your shoelaces, the two common places to attach them.

See also JEAN JACKETS

FROGGER

Your mission, in this game that was big in about 1981, was to guide six frogs across a busy highway, then across some floating logs, into their safe havens at the top of the screen, without getting squashed.

See also ATARI; SATURDAY SUPERCADE

FRUIT FLIES

No creature could wreak more havoc in its 18-day lifetime than these little bugs could. California had a major

Most Significant Scientific Advances of the '80s

Velcro

Big Gulps

Answering machines

Jolt Cola

Magic Shell

Space shuttles

Post-It notes

Computer mouses

Liposuction

Compact discs

Stonewashed jeans

Fax machines

Stealth airplanes

Cold fusion . . . oh, wait, cancel that . . .

Cool Ranch Doritos

infestation problem, but to listen to the news in the early '80s, you'd think one fly was capable of destroying an entire orange grove all by itself.

See also KILLER BEES

FRUIT PIE MAGICIAN

Hostess snack cake poster boy.

See also TWINKIE THE KID

FRUIT ROLL-UPS

They were thin, they were sticky, they could be bent into gross shapes, and they had real fruit in them, so your parents couldn't really complain when you stretched a piece out or ate a hole in a square and stuck your tongue through it.

See also FUN DIP

FUCK

A word that started to come out of the closet in the '80s. Still considered the worst of the basic cuss words, it's also the most versatile. "Fuck" can be used as any part of speech. And, as all stand-up comics and screenwriters know, it can make someone appear funny when used often enough. You won't hear it in PG movies, but maybe in later PG-13 releases.

See also DELIRIOUS; MOTHERFUCKER; PG-13; SHAZBOT!; STAND-UP BOOM

FUCK TAB

First came the early-'80s innovation where aluminum pop-tops stayed on the soda can when you opened them. This eliminated those annoying, dangerous slips of metal that you had to throw away every time you wanted to enjoy a Sunkist. Then came the fun little game: If you can remove the pop top without breaking the nub underneath, you can give it to someone as sort of a coupon for sex.

See also POP-TOP COLLECTING

FULL METAL JACKET

Surreal Vietnam movie from Stanley Kubrick that came on the heels of *Platoon* and offered both a look at the hell of boot camp (with tyrannical drill sergeant R. Lee Ermey) and the physical and psychological ordeals of combat. Less preachy than its predecessor, with more moments of grim comedy.

See also APOCALYPSE NOW; PLATOON; VIETNAM-MANIA

FUN DIP

Also known as Lik-m-Aid, this post-Little League/youth soccer/YMCA basketball/peewee football treat was basically three packets of Kool-Aid mix that you dipped with a stick made out of sugar. We think it was invented by a dentist.

See also NERDS; PLAQUE; TARTAR

F/X

Had they not made a sequel to this 1986 movie about a special effects guy (Bryan Brown) hired to stage a fake murder of a Mafia guy but who gets double-crossed and must use his skills to survive, it might have become a cult classic of sorts. But instead, it's just another decent movie with a bad sequel.

See also COCKTAIL

G

GACY, JOHN WAYNE

Serial killer who cut up his victims and then put their various parts in trash bins around Chicago and other parts of northern Illinois. Oh, yeah, he also liked to dress up like a clown.

See also BUNDY, TED; WILLIAMS, WAYNE

GADHAFI, MU'AMMAR

See QADDAFI, MU'AMMAR

GAG ME WITH A SPOON

Request made by those perpetrating the Valley Girl persona, meaning that they are displeased with something. For example:

"That like grody, pimply Timmy guy asked me to go minigolf! Like, gag me with a spoon!"

Variations include just "gag me" and exaggerations involving any number of utensils: "gag me with a fork" or "gag me with a pair of Teflon tongs."

See also GO; GRODY; GRODY TO THE MAX; LIKE; VALLEY GIRLS; WAS ALL

GALAGA

This, Galaxian, and Gorf had different names, but damned if we know how these early kill-the-alien video games were different from each other.

See also ATARI; DEFENDER; SPACE INVADERS

GALAXIAN

See GALAGA

GALAXY HIGH

CBS Saturday morning cartoon about a high school floating above the surface of some planet somewhere. It included all the usual high school stereotypes (jocks, nerds, bullies, etc.), some from Earth, some with six arms, and some that looked like chickens.

See also BREAKFAST CLUB, THE; BUELLER, FERRIS; FAST TIMES AT RIDGEMONT HIGH; SCHOOLHOUSE ROCK; SQUARE PEGS

GAME SHOWS

When we stayed home from school, we watched *Press Your Luck, Joker's Wild, Tic Tac Dough, Family Feud, Sale of the Century, The $25,000 Pyramid, Card Sharks, The Price Is Right*, and *Hollywood Squares*. If we were lucky and had the right cable channels, we could see *Jackpot!* (from Canada), *The Gong Show*, and *Let's Make a Deal* (from the '60s and '70s).

See also CABLE; GONG SHOW, THE; $1.98 BEAUTY PAGEANT, THE; WHAMMY; WIN, LOSE OR DRAW

GARBAGE PAIL KIDS

Horrific, hilarious, and popular parodies of the Cabbage Patch phenome-

Another big moment in our lifetimes

July 1979: Skylab falls to earth; Nerf Soccer ball introduced.

The fat cat charms a female feline friend.

non. They started as trading cards of dismembered and disfigured little dolls and, like any great idea taken to its logical extreme, eventually became a movie. We remember something about concerned parents and teachers and lawyers, but that all passed with the fad.

See also CABBAGE PATCH KIDS; SLIME; STRETCH ARMSTRONG

GARFIELD

Cat who, at first, was fat, insolent, lazy, ugly, and loved to eat lasagna and torment dog Odie and human John. Then he started to get a little cuter as he got more popular, and his insolence was a little more good-natured, and a symbiosis developed with Odie. The '80s had that effect on a lot of folks.

The question remains: Why does the gray bar in the background of every strip change from being straight in one panel to angled in the next to being straight again in the last?

See also BILLY AND THE BOINGERS; "CALVIN AND HOBBES"; "FAR SIDE, THE"; SUCTION-CUP GARFIELD

-GATE

Add this to the end of any word to make it sound like a scandal.

See also CYBER-; HYPER-; IRAN-CONTRA THING; MEGA-; ÜBER-

GATES, BILL

The most amazing fact about this Nerd God is that he kept such a low profile during the '80s. All the while he seeded every IBM-compatible computer with his MS-DOS and built the software

empire that has made him, in the '90s, the richest organic being on the planet.

See also GEEK ERA; JOBS, STEVE; MS-DOS

GAUNTLET

Fantasy/adventure arcade game that came along a few years after the huge Pac-man boom of '82. Four people could play at once (usually on one of those flat, tabletop machines), competing to find a magic glove.

See also ATARI; DIG DUG; DUNGEONS & DRAGONS; GALAGA; JOUST; PAC-MAN

GAY

A very tricky word. In elementary and junior high school, it was often accepted as a slang adjective describing something with which you wouldn't want to be associated, something that sucks (i.e., *"I saw the 'Masters of the Universe' movie. It was so gay."*). But it's also a synonym for homosexual, and the coming of Political Correctness made any other use insulting.

HISTORICAL NOTE: For hundreds of years "gay" meant happy and lively, but that usage died out almost completely in the last half of the 20th century.

See also MASTERS OF THE UNIVERSE; RETARDED

GAYLORD, MITCH

Olympic gymnast on the 1984 team, he was as close as the men could get to a Mary Lou Retton. Went on to star in *American Anthem*, a movie about—guess what—gymnastics, with

Janet Jones (that's Mrs. Wayne Gretzky to you and me) and a theme song by John Taylor of Duran Duran.

See also DURAN DURAN; OLYMPICS; POWER STATION; RETTON, MARY LOU

GEEK ERA

A period in the mid-'80s when kids with superior intellect and few social skills were celebrated and romanticized in media outlets. Movies and TV shows took on nerdy high school students as heroes, arming them with computers and bad guys to fight, or just telling their stories. This coincided with the initial explosion of home computers from 1981–83.

BONUS CONSPIRACY THEORY: The whole movement may have been a calculated salvo by Bill Gates in his attempt to take over the world.

See also GATES, BILL; *MANHATTAN PROJECT*; *MISFITS OF SCIENCE*; *REAL GENIUS*; *REVENGE OF THE NERDS*; *WARGAMES*; *WHIZ KIDS*

GEE, YOUR HAIR SMELLS TERRIFIC

A shampoo that didn't lie to you about what it could do for you.

See also COLORED HAIR SPRAY

GEFFEN, DAVID

In 1981, most folks didn't know who he was. In 1988, he was commanding one of the biggest entertainment conglomerates in the free world, thanks largely to the success of his record label. Don'cha just love the '80s?

See also GATES, BILL; *WALL STREET*

GEL

This viscous substance was rarely found in the American household until the early 1980s, when the folks at Crest started making their dental cleaners out of it. Soon, there was a gel revolution under way, and today, rare is the home that does not contain it in some form. It's even in shoes.

See also PLAQUE; PUMP TOOTHPASTE

GENERATION X

First it was a '70s punk band fronted by Billy Idol, then it was a book about people living in Palm Springs, then it was a bunch of people who might buy a book like this.

See also MTV GENERATION; YUPPIE PUPPIES

GEORGE, BOY

This smooth-voiced, cross-dressing frontman for the upbeat English band Culture Club had a lot of us singing, "Karmakarmakarmakarmakarma chameleon" and asking, "Daddy? What's a transvestite?"

See also BAND AID; *ELECTRIC DREAMS*

GEORGIA SATELLITES

Scruffy, hillbilly rockers significant because their one semi-hit, "Keep Your Hands to Yourself," was so cool.

See also R.E.M.

GERE, RICHARD

Though his career began with a movie called *Strike Force*, it didn't really take off until *American Gigolo* and

Movie lines we said a lot

"What did you say your name was?"

"John Coc-teau-sten. It's Scotch-Romanian."

"That's quite a combination."

"So were my parents."

—This exchange between Fletch and Mrs. Stanwyk from *Fletch* is another one that doesn't really mean anything, but it's funny and doesn't need an elaborate "Did you see *Fletch?*" setup to work.

Boy? George?

wasn't legendary until his name was mentioned in *Fast Times*. He made a cottage industry out of playing the potentially dangerous brooding guy and giving long speeches at the Oscars about Tibet. And you all know the rumor.

See also RUMOR ABOUT RICHARD GERE, THE

GHETTO BLASTER

A very large boom box.

See also BOOM BOX

GHOSTBUSTERS

This 1984 film had it all: a great cast (Bill Murray, Dan Aykroyd, Sigourney Weaver, Rick Moranis, Ernie Hudson), insults that we 13-year-olds loved to revel in ("Yes, sir, it's true—this man has no dick."), evil villains in the form of confectionery treats (the Sta-Puft

Marshmallow Man), and slime, slime, slime. But no one who aspired to cool would be caught dead wearing a T-shirt with the 'Busters logo on it.

See also REAL GHOSTBUSTERS, THE; REITMAN, IVAN; SLIME; STA-SHARP PENCILS

GIANT PEANUT WITH A BIG SMILE ON ITS SHELL

Many an editorial cartoonist's rendering of Jimmy Carter while he was in the White House.

See also IRANIAN HOSTAGE CRISIS

GIBSON, DEBBIE

Teenage wunderkind who took the pop charts by storm with her perky song "Only in My Dreams" in 1987 and had a string of similarly bubbly hits ("Shake Your Love") and puppy-love ballads ("Foolish Beat"). Unlike most teen stars, she wrote some of her own songs and had a hand in the production.

See also TIFFANY

G.I. JOE

Some of us first met this fictional grunt in the '70s when he was, basically, a doll for guys. He had changeable fatigues and moving "eagle eyes," a full cache of weaponry, and the dread kung fu grip. The rest of the world got to know G.I. Joe during his more virile mid-'80s comeback as a bunch of tiny action figures, a television series, and a comic book. The plotlines involved a force of hyperMarines fighting the evil members of COBRA. The thing is, none of the characters was named Joe.

BONUS FACT: The show always ended with a little safety tip from Sgt. Slaughter and the sign-off: "And now you know. And knowing is half the battle."

See also ADVENTURE PEOPLE; MASTERS OF THE UNIVERSE

G.I. JOE CEREAL

The box and the ad had Sgt. Slaughter pointing at you and commanding that the food product is "part of this nutritious breakfast."

See also CAP'N CRUNCH; C-3POS; G.I. JOE; MR. T CEREAL; NERDS CEREAL; OJS; SMURFBERRY CRUNCH; WAFFLE-OS

GILLIGAN'S PLANET

Most of the work of this Saturday morning cartoon had been done by sitcom producers a decade before. Except this time, the passengers of the *Minnow* crashed on, get this, a distant and barren *planet!* Throw in a goofy alien and you have, get this, *comedy!*

See also FONZIE CARTOON; PUNKY BREWSTER; SMURFS; *3 ROBOTIC STOOGES, THE*

GIMME A BREAK

NBC sitcom about a heavy, sassy, lovable black woman (Nell Carter) who takes a job as the live-in maid/cook/sage for an aging widower police chief named Carl Kanisky (Dolph Sweet), his three daughters, the chief's father and later, a young boy who was somehow related to the family. Most of your classic sitcom elements are there. Nell sort of wants to leave her dead-end job, but she loves the family too much to go. The chief is nice and crusty. His daughters fit well into the realm of stock characters: The oldest is the sexiest of the three and a touch rebellious; the middle is bright, practical, and not overly attractive; and the youngest is cute but confused. There's even a Dumb Guy in the person of Officer Simpson, who is sort of the chief's assistant. Probably would have been a huge hit if it had aired on Thursday, but as it was, it did OK for a few seasons, until the chief died and the older daughters moved off to other places and new characters, such as a young Joey Lawrence as the aforementioned boy, showed up to fill the void.

See also HOGANS, THE; TARTIKOFF, BRANDON; THURSDAY NIGHT LINEUP

GINGIVITIS

Yet another mouth disease brought out of the closet to sell toothpaste. After everybody got used to gels and cool mint flavoring and pumps and plaque fighters, toothpaste ads started reminding us about this scary gum problem.

See also PLAQUE; PUMP TOOTHPASTE; TARTAR

GIVENS, ROBIN

Would have been just another sitcom actress but for her short-lived, tempestuous marriage to Mike Tyson.

See also HEAD OF THE CLASS; TYSON, MIKE

GLASNOST

Russian word the meaning of which we never knew. News reports always said that it had no English translation, but meant peace or unity or openness or some cozy thing like that. A vital part of the Ronny-Gorby thawing Cold War lexicon.

See also DEPECHE MODE; GORBACHEV, MIKHAIL S.; PERESTROIKA; REAGAN, RONALD; SHAZBOT; SOLIDARITY

GLASS TIGER

Forgettable popsters who held the spotlight for a few minutes in 1986 with their happy ballad "Don't Forget Me (When I'm Gone)," which had Bryan Adams singing backup.

See also BALTIMORA

GLEEK

The bumbling yet lovable pet monkey of Zan and Jana, the Wonder Twins.

He carried Zan in a bucket when he took the form of water and usually provided the episode-ending joke or antic.

See also JUSTICE LEAGUE OF AMERICA; MONKEYMANIA

GLOBETROTTERS

As in, the ones from Harlem. They toured the country with their basketball sideshow, they had their own Saturday morning cartoon and, in a surreal geographic twist, they got stranded on Gilligan's Island in a 1981 TV movie.

See also FONZIE CARTOON; GILLIGAN'S PLANET; 3 ROBOTIC STOOGES, THE

GLOMER

A magical being from another dimension that hung out with Punky Brewster on her Saturday morning cartoon show. Not to be confused with Brandon, Punky's dog on the NBC prime-time sitcom.

See also BREWSTER, PUNKY; SCHMOO; TARTIKOFF, BRANDON

GLO-WORM

The appeal of this toy, a sickly glow-in-the-dark segmented worm wearing a night cap, proved that anything can be marketed as "cute."

See also FLUORESCENT ODDITIES; INCHWORM; STRETCH ARMSTRONG; YO-BALLS

GNARLY

Slang for something particularly unpleasant, according to the Valley Girl dialect. Later usage, such as in Bill&Tedspeak, suggested that something "gnarly" was actually pretty cool.

See also BILL&TEDSPEAK; GRODY; VALLEY GIRLS

GO

Synonym for "say." For example: *She was all, "What happened at the Duran Duran concert?" and I go, "I like ran up to the stage to touch Simon and the security dude was all, 'Hey! Get away from here, punk,' and I go, 'Dick,' and he goes, 'Touch Simon's jacket and die,' and I go, 'Gawd!'"*

See also DURAN DURAN; LIKE; WAS ALL

"GO AHEAD, MAKE MY DAY"

Tied for the "Most Quoted Movie Line" award for the '80s. As delivered by Clint Eastwood in 1983's *Sudden Impact*, it went like this: "Go ahead. (pause) Make my day." Dirty Harry said it only twice, but you wouldn't know it by the aftermath. Variations were featured in several other movies (*Fletch, Hollywood Shuffle, Weird Science*) and included: "Go ahead, make my year," " . . . make my decade," and " . . . make my millennium." The humor either relied on time-frame exaggeration or the actor's delivery, and it never worked. Except, of course, when Reagan said it.

See also CARMEL, CALIF.; *FIREFOX*; *FLETCH*; "I'LL BE BACK"; "MAY THE FORCE BE WITH YOU"; "READ MY LIPS"; REAGAN, RONALD; "WHATCHOOTALKINBOUT?"; "WHERE'S THE BEEF?"; "YOU'RE NO JACK KENNEDY"

GOBOTS

Pitiful entry into the cars-that-turn-into-robots rage started by Transformers. Gobots manifested themselves as toys and an afternoon cartoon, both of which lacked the complexity and competence of the aforementioned Transformers or other Japanese robots. The Gobot story line, for what it's worth, involved a conflict between the Guardian Gobots and Renegade Gobots (lead by Cy-Kill, a motorcycle—get it?) over their home planet, Gobotron.

See also AKIRA; STAR BLAZERS; TRANSFORMERS

GOD

Historically, this all-encompassing deity has been portrayed as an old white guy with a huge wispy beard and flowing robes. We now know that he looks like George Burns.

See also CHRIST, JESUS

GODLEY AND CREAM

New Age types who scored a minor hit in 1985 with their song "Cry." They were more noted for the black-and-white video, which featured the faces of everyday-looking folks all about to burst into tears and melding into one another, even though this was years before anyone uttered the word "morph."

See also MANIMAL

GOETZ, BERNIE

Angry white guy who shot either a bunch of thugs who tried to rob him or some innocent kids who tried to rob him on a New York City subway. Public debate followed about whether he was scum or hero, and many concluded that this was yet another reason not to go to New York City.

See also CENTRAL PARK JOGGER

GO-GOS

Peppy all-female band that defined not only early '80s girl-pop New Wave music but the entire early '80s. The exploits of Belinda Carlisle, Jane Wiedlin & Co. added a splash of pure happiness to MTV, Top-40 radio, and the faces of leg-warmer-and-jellies-clad girls and Jams-wearing skaters all over America. The image that most of us will carry around in our brains like a postcard from the Go-Go era features the band smiling, waving, and water-skiing in the "Vacation" video.

See also CARLISLE, BELINDA; JAMS; JELLIES; NEW WAVE

GOLDMAN, ALBERT

Tell-all biographer who took the King off his throne (except for the one he died on), savaged John Lennon about 8 years after his death, and caused many a stink in the fashion world, not to mention a "Doonesbury" plotline, when he gussied up and published *The Warhol Diaries*. Immortalized in U2's song "God Part II."

See also "ELVIS HAS LEFT THE BUILDING"; KELLY, KITTY; LENNON, JOHN

GONG SHOW, THE

OK, how this worked was regular schmos went on TV and did some act—singing, tap dancing, jokes—

with a hope of winning cash prizes and a near certainty of embarrassment on national TV, especially if they got gonged. Celebrity judges were chosen from the same pool as the crowd on *The Hollywood Squares*. And who can forget Mean Gene the Dancin' Machine, who was a janitor for the show or something and got gonged every time he appeared.

See also HOLLYWOOD SQUARES, THE; $1.98 BEAUTY PAGEANT, THE

GOODSON, MARK

Game-show mogul responsible, with longtime partner Bill Todman, for creating some of the stalwarts of the genre, including *Family Feud*, *The Price Is Right*, and *Joker's Wild*. Though later usurped by Merv Griffin's *Wheel of Fortune–Jeopardy!* juggernaut, Goodman game shows survive to this day.

See also FAMILY FEUD; TIC TAC DOUGH; WHITE, VANNA

GOOD TIMES

Norman Lear's most innovative work (or at least tied with *All in the Family* for the honor) and the first remotely realistic black family on television. Characters were: J.J. (Kid Dyn-O-Mite), Florida (Mom), James (Dad) Evans, Bookman (aka Buffalo Butt), Willona, Thelma, and Michael. Young Janet Jackson was Willona's adopted daughter Penny in later episodes.

See also DIFF'RENT STROKES; FAT ALBERT AND THE COSBY KIDS; ROOTS; WHAT'S HAPPENING!!

The Evans family.

GOOGOL

Anybody who knows what this is probably watched *Cosmos*, the show through which Carl Sagan taught us all kinds of stuff about the universe, including this huge number that looks like:

10,000,000,000,000,000,000,000,000, 000,000,000,000,000,000,000,000, 000,000,000,000,000,000,000,000, 000,000,000,000,000.

See also Cosmos

GOOGOLPLEX

A number too big to fit in this book, which is OK, since this isn't a math book. You'd write it as a "1" followed by a googol of zeros.

See also Googol

GOONIES

While exploiting two of his keenest skills—filming from the kids' point of view and telling a kick-ass adventure story—this 1985 flop still managed to be one of the worst movies with Spielberg's name on it. (He was only an executive producer. Richard *Lethal Weapon* Donner directed.) Corey Feldman and Martha Plimpton starred with a bunch of other kids who look for treasure and outwit pirates and a big dumb guy named Chunk—all by themselves!

See also Night of the Comet; Spielberg, Steven

GOOSE

A stock film character played to greatest prominence by Anthony Edwards in *Top Gun*. The Goose character is the protagonist's partner or sidekick, a nice guy with a family who, from reel one, the audience knows will get wasted at some crucial point in the film. Goose's death will then give the needed motivation our hero needs, after a period of moral crisis in which he feels responsible for the tragedy, to finish his quest. Since *Top Gun*, the Goose character has become a staple of the buddy/action film.

See also EDWARDS, ANTHONY; *TOP GUN*

GORBACHEV, MIKHAIL S.

Along with lovely wife Raisa, the last ruler of the Soviet Union was almost as popular in the United States as Ron and Nancy. He came to power after a rash of stiff general secretaries (Brezhnev, Andropov, and Chernenko) all went the way of Lenin between '82 and '85. By the time his trademarks *glasnost* and *perestroika* became buzzwords, the Cold War was over. His funky head mark thing was cool, too.

See also AFGHANISTAN; REAGAN, RONALD; *WARGAMES*

GORE, TIPPER

In the mid-'80s battle over profanity and free speech, she was the anticulture villain pitted against the patriotic, Constitution-loving crusader, Luther "Luke Skywalker" Campbell from 2 Live Crew. The helmet-haired wife of then-Senator Al Gore pushed to get that Parental Advisory label on CDs and tapes.

See also FUCK; MOTHERFUCKER; PARENTAL ADVISORY LABEL; 2 LIVE CREW

GORF

See GALAGA

GOSSETT, LOUIS, JR.

When Hollywood needed a black actor to play a tough-but-smart or demanding-yet-caring character in the years 1982–87, Gossett was likely the man to do it.

See also IRON EAGLE; OFFICER AND A GENTLEMAN, AN

GOTCHA! GUNS

These low-impact paint pistols came out several years after the movie of the same name and concept, and they didn't have any affiliation with Anthony Edwards. By the time these hit the stores, the whole Laser Tag craze had vanished, so who cared? Plus, the paint was supposed to come out of your clothes but didn't.

See also EDWARDS, ANTHONY; LASER TAG

GOTTI, JOHN

The biggest Mafia boss to get caught in recent history. Not as glamorous as Al Capone, but still a pretty memorable guy. Nicknamed the "Teflon Don" because charges never stuck to him.

See also AL CAPONE'S VAULT

GRANDFATHER CLAUSE

Phrase we became quite familiar with after Reagan forced states to raise their drinking age to 21 in 1986 by threatening to pull federal highway money. But in most states where it was raised, people who were already 18 or 19 were still able to buy beer and wine, so knowing someone who was "grandfathered" was key for many of our first alcohol experiences.

See also BARTLES & JAYMES GUYS; JUST SAY NO; MADD

GRANT, EDDY

Caribbean shaman whose electro-calypso song "Electric Avenue" is essential listening for any chronicler of the one-hit wonders of the early 1980s.

See also BALTIMORA

GRAPE APE

Cool cartoon about a giant purple gorilla who did good deeds with his pal Beagley Beagley and rode around on the top of Beagley's van. Usually on after *Hong Kong Phooey*.

See also HONG KONG PHOOEY; LAFF-A-LYMPICS; VANS (THE VEHICLE)

GREASE 2

This movie had a lively musical sequence about bowling. We repeat: *a musical sequence about bowling*. Embarrassing, both for Michelle Pfeiffer and anybody who watched it.

See also NEWTON-JOHN, OLIVIA

GREAT BRAIN, THE

A series of books by John D. Fitzgerald about a clever kid living in Utah. As do many kid heroes, he spent his free time diligently solving mysteries and outsmarting parents, teachers, bullies, and his little brother, who

actually "wrote" the stories. He also made a big deal that most everyone in town was Mormon, and there was only one other church for all the other denominations and the minister just preached straight from the Bible. Jimmy, the younger Osmond, starred in the 1978 film version.

See also BROWN, ENCYCLOPEDIA; HARDY BOYS; *NIGHT OF THE COMET*

GREATEST AMERICAN HERO, THE

Short-lived series about a klutzy superhero. Starred William Katt, Robert Culp, and Connie Sellecca. Joey Scarbury did the theme song ("Believe it or not, I'm walking on air . . .") and each episode usually featured some groovy '60s tunes.

See also A-TEAM, THE; CANNELL, STEPHEN J.; SUPERMAN: THE MOVIE

GREAT SATAN

That would be the United States of America.

See also EVIL EMPIRE; GOD; KHOMEINI, AYATOLLAH RUHOLLAH

GREAT SPACE COASTER, THE

One of those early morning kids shows that tried to disguise the fact that it was trying to teach you something by showing a cartoon every 15 minutes or so.

See also SESAME STREET

GREAT WHITE

Well, these guys *were* white. And the kids who made their oh-golly-does-

"Autobots, roll out!"

—If we were really
dorky, we might say this
from the back seat of
our friend's car as we all
went searching for a
party. The line was first
brought to life on the
cartoon *Transformers* by
leader Optimus Prime.

He told you not to get them wet.

this-rock "Once Bitten Twice Shy" a hit thought they were pretty great, we guess.

See also Bon Jovi; Living Colour; Poison; Whitesnake

GREED

The unforgivable vice that, according to conventional wisdom, personified the decade between 1981 and 1990. People said that everybody was getting rich and Reagan was running up the deficit and that hawking junk bonds and buy-sell-buying your way into stock market millions was just about the sexiest thing you could do with your life. Sure, a lot of that may have been true, but those who were complaining about it came from the same generational pool as those responsible, those who grew up in a time when the en vogue vice had something to do with free love or something. Perhaps they felt that cap-

italism bashing in some way compensated for all the bad stuff everybody was saying about communism.

See also Boesky, Ivan; *Bonfire of the Vanities;* Evil Empire; Keating, Charles; October 19, 1987; Reagan, Ronald; Tzu, Sun; *Wall Street*

GREEN MACHINE

If tricycles are mopeds and Big Wheels Yamahas, then this contraption would be the chopped Harley of children's riding toys. It was longer and sleeker than a Big Wheel—you had to really reach for the pedals— and it had some sort of steering thing that made you able to execute tight turns, despite the vehicle's length. And it was, naturally, green.

See also Big Wheel; Inchworm

GREMLINS

A 1984 monster movie done with that

classy Spielberg-produced touch. Small-town teens Zach Galligan and Phoebe Cates forget the three rules of maintenance for mogwai, cute little Asian critters that (1) turn nasty when they eat after midnight, (2) multiply when they get wet, and (3) melt in the sunlight. We never understood, though: How do time zone changes affect the "after midnight" rule? Does it matter if you feed them after midnight Pacific Time instead of Central Time? Wouldn't their internal clocks be on Japanese time or something?

BONUS FACT: Howie Mandel was the voice of Gizmo.

See also DANTE, JOE; *NIGHT OF THE COMET;* SPIELBERG, STEVEN

GRENADA

The shortest successful foreign invasion and occupation in U.S. history, engineered by the Gipper himself. Troops parachuted down and rescued some medical students from the seven or eight Cuban nationals who lived on the island. No one told the press about the landing, so it's hard to say what all happened, and to this day, many of us don't know exactly where the island is. The Clint Eastwood Grenada movie, *Heartbreak Ridge*, however, is widely regarded as very cool.

See also DANTE, JOE; EASTWOOD, CLINT; FALKLAND ISLANDS; REAGAN, RONALD

GRIMLEY, ED

Fictional nerd concocted by Martin Short on *Saturday Night Live* in the late '80s, when nerds had already begun their gradual ascension to "cool" status. Ed had a neat crest of solid hair spewing from his forehead and did a little dance that involved his feet being right next to each other and his hands in the air and *he was such a decent guy I must say.* Also, he played the triangle and liked Pat Sajak a little too much. He tried to make it in the outside-SNL world with a Saturday morning cartoon, but, thank God, never made a feature film, so Mr. Grimley will remain a fond memory instead of a failed franchise.

See also GEEK ERA; GEL; NERD; *PAT SAJAK SHOW, THE;* PEE-WEE HERMAN; *SATURDAY NIGHT LIVE*

GRODY

Adjective in Valley Girl slang used to describe anything undesirable. Basically, it means "extremely gross."

See also GAY; GNARLY; GRODY TO THE MAX

GRODY TO THE MAX

Even grosser than grody. Way grosser.

See also GRODY; RAD

GROWING PAINS

This sitcom presented yet another one of those fabled nuclear families, this one (the Seavers of suburban New York) revolving around the psychologist/guru/dad played by Alan Thicke. Teen-throb Kirk Cameron and anorexic-to-be Tracey Gold pretty much dominated the plotlines by screwing up—always in the standard I-borrowed-the-car-without-asking-and-wrecked-it kind of way, never the I-borrowed-the-car-without-asking-and-sold-it-for-crack-and-sex-and-got-syphilis kind of way—and then receiving a dose of Daddy's philosophy.

One minor character, Coach Lubbock (Bill Kirchenbauer), got his own show. But the dumb guy, Boner (Josh Andrew Koenig), deserved it more.

See also ALF; CAMERON, KIRK; COSBY SHOW, THE; DUMB GUY; FAMILY TIES; HOGANS, THE; JUST THE TEN OF US

GUNG HO

Lighthearted morality tale of a movie starring Michael Keaton (who would spend most of the '80s being called "*Mr. Mom*") that pushed the idea that American car makers could get along with the Japanese, even though the foreigners seemed to be taking over everything. But this just didn't make for a funny movie, and, besides, "gung ho" is a Chinese term.

See also AKIRA; BATMANIA; TIANANMEN SQUARE; TRANSFORMERS; TZU, SUN

GUNS N' ROSES

The final, last spectacular gasp of heavy metal in the late 1980s. After much of the genre had become big-haired and bloated (e.g., Warrant, Kingdom Come), along came young Axl, Slash, and the boys with *Appetite for Destruction*, an angry, paranoid, kinetic album that pretty much grabbed you by the balls and wouldn't let go. Even its ballad, "Sweet Child of Mine," had something of an edge to it.

But then, with subsequent efforts *Lies* and *Use Your Illusion I&II*, G n'R fell into the same creative wasteland from which they were supposed to rescue metal. Pounding beats and screechy guitars gave way to pianos and strings, and the band pretty much faded out, swallowed by a sea of flannel and the next big thing in hard rock, grunge.

See also ENUFF Z'NUFF; HEAVY METAL BOOM; VAN HALEN

GUTTENBERG, STEVE

He was the guy next door, your buddy at work, and a middling (at best) actor who had some good early breaks (*Diner* especially) but squandered them on the likes of *Police Academy* and *Short Circuit*.

See also POLICE ACADEMY; SHEEDY, ALLY

GUY WHO TALKS REALLY FAST, THE

He was short, he was balding, and dammit if that little guy couldn't jabber like an uzi. John Moschitta, Jr., who could say like 10 words a second, got into the *Guinness Book of World Records*, became the spokesguy for the emerging Federal Express, had a cameo on the Academy Awards (reading the rules and regulations) and . . . well, that's about his 15 minutes, right?

See also BLU-BLOCKERS GUY, THE; FEDERAL EXPRESS; MICRO MACHINES

H

HACKY SACK

Something that 249,999,999 of us *didn't* think of and become fabulously wealthy from, by taking the interest in soccer, modifying it a little, and packaging it in a quirky but attractive manner.

See also PELÉ; SOCCER

HAHN, JESSICA

This busty secretary took down Rev. Jim Bakker in a motel room and then took down his career, with the help of a criminal fraud conviction. She later hooked up with comedian Sam Kinison (may he rest in peace), starred in his "Wild Thing" video and, last we heard, now frequents Howard Stern's show. The Bakker-Hahn scandal, plus the resignation of Rev. Jimmy Swaggert, should have obliterated mass media evangelism, if not entire religions. But Oral Roberts still got away with saying he needed $5 million or a 900-foot Jesus would "call him home" a few years later.

See also BAKKER, TAMMY FAYE; CHRIST, JESUS; GOD; KINISON, SAM; RICE, DONNA

HAIL TO THE CHIEF

One-season, mid-'80s sitcom notable because it was about Patty Duke

being the President of the United States of America.

See also MR. SMITH; REAGAN, RONALD; SHE'S THE SHERIFF

HALL & OATES

These guys had *so many* hit songs in the '80s, but they sucked. A lot. Big mystery.

See also AIR SUPPLY; RICHIE, LIONEL

HALL, ANTHONY MICHAEL

He started out as the quintessential '80s weenie actor, as sculpted by John Hughes in *Sixteen Candles*, *The Breakfast Club*, and *Weird Science*. For some reason he made a bad career move and beefed up, taking more macho roles like a hot high school quarterback in *Johnny B. Goode*.

See also BREAKFAST CLUB, THE; HUGHES, JOHN

HALL, ARSENIO

After playing sidekick to Eddie Murphy in *Coming to America*, he launched the only successful late-night talk show born in the mid- or late '80s. The syndicated *Arsenio* took on the standard two-guests-and-a-band format and spawned a few pop culture phenoms: 1) That thing where Arsenio

Not real.

made the audience chant "Whoop! Whoop! Whoop!" by pumping his fist, and 2) The "things that make you go 'hmmm,'" which filled his monologues and later became a "song" by C+C Music Factory (featuring Freedom Williams).

See also CHUNKY A; LETTERMAN, DAVE; MURPHY, EDDIE; PAT SAJAK SHOW, THE

HALL, FAWN

Ollie North's secretary, and the woman who made the shredder an essential office machine. Unfairly compared to the other scandalized women of the time.

See also HAHN, JESSICA; IRAN-CONTRA THING; RICE, DONNA

HANDS ACROSS AMERICA

The largest, oddest touchy-feely event in the history of mankind. The idea was to have a line of human beings holding hands from one end of the United States to the other. We're not exactly sure why this would help the hungry and poor, but apparently it did. The whole thing started at the White House, with Ronald Reagan, and stretched to many of our hometowns (there were a bunch of gaps, we heard). So, now let's see a show of hands: Who was one of the 5 million who took part?

See also USA FOR AFRICA

HARDCASTLE & McCORMICK

CBS's effort to capitalize on the culture-clash-and-cool-car buddy formula so successfully used in

Magnum, P.I. As part of his sentence for some crime or other, ex–race car driver "Skid" Mark McCormick (Daniel Hugh-Kelly with a hellacious white-boy 'fro) was forced to live with retired judge Milton "Hard Case" Hardcastle (Brian Keith). Mark drove this bad-ass looking race car, and the pair went around solving crimes and bickering.

See also CANNELL, STEPHEN J.; CRIME FIGHTING; MAGNUM, P.I.

HARDCASTLE, PAUL

Recorded the song "Nineteen," which might have been a nice Vietnam protest tune, but for the fact that it was recorded in 1984 and the only lyric anyone can remember from it is the "N-N-N-N-Nineteen, Nineteen" phrase that runs throughout.

See also LAID BACK; VIETNAM-MANIA

HARDWARE WARS

A film not even well-known enough to be described as "cult." It was a hilarious 15-minute spoof of *Star Wars* that used household appliances as spaceships and put actual cinnamon rolls in the Princess Leia character's hair.

See also BAMBI VS. GODZILLA; DARK STAR; STAR WARS

HARDY BOYS

The boy version of Nancy Drew, and an all-time classic kid empowerment story that began in the early 1900s and peaked about 80 years later. Teenagers Joe and Frank Hardy got into all kinds of trouble, solved mysteries, chased bad guys, hunted ghosts, and did very few things that actual teens do.

The hundreds of books in the series also opened young minds to perhaps their first cynical thoughts about the publishing industry. (*This Franklin W. Dixon guy couldn't be writing all these books, could he? There must be a factory somewhere in Asia.*) Indeed, there was no such guy. The books came from the same writing mill as Nancy Drew and the Bobbsey Twins.

Joe and Frank never hit the Big Time with a full-length motion picture, but *The Hardy Boys Mysteries* (later shortened to *The Hardy Boys*) aired on ABC from 1977–79. Shaun Cassidy and Parker Stevenson played groovy, sexy versions of the brothers quite different from the traditional Boy Scouty sleuths. Nancy Drew hung out on the show, too.

See also BROWN, ENCYCLOPEDIA; CHOOSE YOUR OWN ADVENTURE; DREW, NANCY

HARING, KEITH

Artist best recognized by his minimalist cartoony style and association with AIDS-related causes (he died from "complications" in 1990). His characters, usually drawn in white-on-red or white-on-black, are little more than stick figures who express emotion by exuding little squiggly lines from their heads. His most widely known work appears on the cover for *A Very Special Christmas*.

See also AIDS; FIDO DIDO

HARMONIC CONVERGENCE

Something that was supposed to happen August 16, 1987, when all the constellations were in their right houses or something. We didn't notice much change, except that the phrase "New Age" was bandied about a lot in the days leading up to the non-happening, and more people started wearing crystals.

BONUS FACT: The date of the event was also the 10th anniversary of the death of Elvis Presley.

See also PRESLEY, ELVIS

HARPER VALLEY PTA

A free-thinking mom ruffles a whole bunch of feathers in a small town in this movie, one of the first to be based on a song, which was sung by Jeannie C. Riley. It also became a short-lived TV series.

See also NIGHT THE LIGHTS WENT OUT IN GEORGIA, THE

HART, COREY

Canadian crooner who, we assume, would never surrender his sunglasses at night. What he would do with them during the day is still cause for speculation. Also, some of his songs sounded a lot like the Eurythmics.

See also COREYS, THE; EURYTHMICS

HART, GARY

Former senator from Colorado and presidential candidate who should never have gotten on a boat called the *Monkey Business*.

See also RICE, DONNA

HAVE A NICE DAY

The slogan of the 1970s, illustrated with a yellow smiley face. We always kind of liked the version where the smiley face had a bullet hole between its eyes.

See also WATCHMEN

HAWKING, STEPHEN

Widely regarded as the smartest human being on Earth. It's almost impossible to comprehend what he's talking about, but most everybody knows who he is and what's on his mind (sort of). Confined to a wheelchair and unable to speak without the aid of an electronic voice enhancer because of Lou Gehrig's disease, he wrote the book *A Brief History of Time* about how the universe began and what's up with it now. It's mostly dense, theoretical stuff, but some of the larger points he makes are the kinds of things that make you feel really insignificant as a life form. For all of these reasons, it was one of the best-selling books in the last part of the '80s.

See also CHAOS; COSMOS

HBO

Before this cable channel, few people ever uttered the phrase: "Yeah, I've seen that movie about 50 times." Before Home Box Office, which became popular about the same time as VCRs, it was almost physically impossible to see a movie more than a few times. But after the early '80s, people had the opportunity to encounter *Smokey and the Bandit* every time

they turned on the television, and God knows it was hard to turn away. The new era of history had dawned.

See also CABLE; CNN; MTV; *SMOKEY AND THE BANDIT*

HDTV

A revolutionary new technology called "high-definition television" that we have been hearing about for *decades* but have never seen.

See also BETAMAX; DAT; VCRS

HEAD, MURRAY

His synthed-up "One Night in Bangkok" from the musical *Chess* scored a pop hit in 1985 and got into heavy rotation on the early days of MTV.

See also FALCO

HEAD OF THE CLASS

Howard Hesseman starred in this mid- and late '80s ABC show as the teacher of a gifted class at a New York high school. The class was full of geek stereotypes, including the Math Nerd (Arvid), the Black Girl (Darlene, played by Robin Givens), the Preppy Snob (Alan), the Fat Computer Guy (Dennis), the Poet (Simone), the Basket Case (Maria), the Foreign Student (Joarhalal), the Prodigy (Janice), and the Rebel (Eric).

See also BREAKFAST CLUB, THE; SQUARE PEGS; WKRP IN CINCINNATI

HEADROOM, MAX

A concept way ahead of its time. This fidgety, talking head on a computer screen heralded overwhelming advances in technology and culture like artificial intelligence, worldwide networking, and cyberpunk literature. Max, played by Matt Frewer, is unfortunately best known as a Coca-Cola pitchman. His futuristic ABC series (with Frewer and Amanda Pays) about television reporters in a gritty, dark, and dirty futuristic urban wonderland was one of the most underappreciated shows of the '80s. But it was caught up in the trendy paranoia of Big Brother and was too geeky and weird for most people. A parody of the concept in *Back to the Future II* featured a stuttering, Headroomized Ronald Reagan and Ayatollah Khomeini as waiters in a futuristic, nostalgic "Cafe '80s."

See also BACK TO THE FUTURE; BLADE RUNNER; MTV; NEUROMANCER; ORWELL, GEORGE

HEALEY, JEFF

Blind bluesman noted for playing guitar on his lap, his costarring role in the Patrick Swayze movie *Road House*, and the song "Angel Eyes," a prom-night favorite around 1990.

See also FABULOUS THUNDERBIRDS, THE

HEAR'N AID

The heavy metal version of Band Aid. Their song was called "Stars."

See also BAND AID; USA FOR AFRICA

HEART BEAT

Don Johnson's album.

See also MIAMI VICE; RETURN OF BRUNO, THE; SPRINGFIELD, RICK; WAGNER, JACK

HEATHERS

Perhaps the most popular movie that nobody saw in the theater. This was the first and most significant of the post-Brat Pack films that began portraying our generation as bored slackerpeople (*Pump Up the Volume*, *Bill&Ted*). This was also one of our first good looks at Winona Ryder, Christian Slater, and Shannen Doherty.

See also BEETLEJUICE; BRAT PACK, THE

HEAVY METAL BOOM

It ruled the music world for about five years in the 1980s, and record companies were scrambling to sign just about any group of moussed-up, leather-clad guys who knew three chords. The boom started in earnest with the megasuccess of Van Halen's *1984*, which featured a balance of old-fashioned, sex-drugs-rock 'n' roll songs and a few poppier numbers that Top-40 stations could fit into their formats. From there, a seemingly endless parade of leering guys in loud outfits followed, chief among them were Mötley Crüe, Poison, Warrant, Skid Row, Ratt, and Cinderella. Guns N' Roses came along in 1987 and gave the movement one final kick in the ass, bringing with them an energy reminiscent of punk and the nihilism of speed-metal, which existed on the fringe of mainstream metal. The movement's death knell came late in 1988 with the release of R.E.M.'s *Green*. That was the band's first album for a major label (Warner Bros.) and signaled the coming ascendancy of "alternative" music that would make the term itself an oxymoron.

See also BILLY AND THE BOINGERS; BON JOVI; CINDERELLA; FORD, LITA; GREAT WHITE; GUNS N' ROSES; MÖTLEY CRÜE; OSBOURNE, OZZY; POISON; RAP; RATT; R.E.M.; SCORPIONS, THE; SKID ROW; VAN HALEN; WARRANT; WHITESNAKE

HENSON, JIM

Creator of the furry creatures we call Muppets and Fraggles. Hence, a genius.

See also DARK CRYSTAL; FRAGGLE ROCK; MUPPET SHOW, THE; SESAME STREET

HERB

Star of an ingenious mid-'80s ad campaign by Burger King. The mysterious flame-broiled burger lover never appeared in the first series of ads. These featured friends and relatives talking about how much they all like Herb and wondering (*gosh!*) just where was the guy and why had he never eaten a Whopper? The well-scripted search created a Myth of Herb, an ephemeral cult of personality based on an imaginary nerd/hero. This was, of course, diffused the instant Burger King showed us what Herb looked like.

See also NERD; PELLER, CLARA

HERBIE

The Love Bug to you and me. Not to be confused with the guy who's never had a Whopper.

See also HERB

HILL STREET BLUES

Best cop show ever.

See also BOCHCO, STEVEN; CHiPs; CRIME

STORY; TARTIKOFF, BRANDON; THURSDAY NIGHT LINEUP

HINCKLEY, JOHN

The guy who shot Ronald Reagan in April 1981. He said he was trying to impress Jodie Foster, just as Robert DeNiro's character shot a politician for her affections in *Taxi Driver*. The whole incident created widespread zaniness, including a classic *Saturday Night Live* episode in which Eddie Murphy's Buckwheat gets shot.

See also CHAPMAN, MARK DAVID; FOSTER, JODIE; LENNON, JOHN; REAGAN, RONALD; *SATURDAY NIGHT LIVE*

HINDU LOVE GODS

These were the three instrument-playing members of R.E.M.—Peter Buck, Mike Mills, and Bill Berry—with singer Warren Zevon along for the ride. They put out a self-titled album in 1989, consisting entirely of cover songs. Eight were old blues and folk songs, one was the Georgia Satellites' "Battleship Chains," and one was a wonderful, guitar-and-drum cover of Prince's "Raspberry Beret."

See also GEORGIA SATELLITES; JONES, TOM; PRINCE; R.E.M.

HITCHHIKER'S GUIDE TO THE GALAXY, THE

Farcical sci-fi book that opened a lot of young minds to outer space, philosophy, science, and British humor by making fun of all these things. Author Douglas Adams became a sort of cult leader for smart kids who liked

The Hulkster and Miss Cyndi. Why, we're not sure.

to think about the absurdities of life, many of whom can still quote much of his inaccurately titled Hitchhiker's trilogy—now five books long. (Ex: "Time is an illusion, lunchtime doubly so.") Hard-core fans have the original BBC radio shows on tape and know what "42" means.

See also BLADE RUNNER; 42; *NEUROMANCER;* SNIGLETS

HOBBY, HOLLY

Greeting card character who broke into the "real world" as a fairly cozy toy. She was a country girl with long blond braids and a huge blue bonnet. You could hardly see her features in illustrations, but the Raggedy-Ann type dolls (floppy, soft, and homemade-feeling) had a painted-on face. Unlike most of her contemporaries in the doll

world, she didn't command an army of similar creatures, she didn't star in a TV show, and she didn't combat any form of evil.

See also CARE BEARS; RAINBOW BRITE; STRAWBERRY SHORTCAKE

HOGAN, HULK

Before 1983, he was just some big guy in tights. Then he played the role of Thunderlips in *Rocky III* and proceeded to preside over the huge and weird upward zoom in the popularity of professional wrestling in the 1980s. Along the way, the Hulkster appeared on the cover of *Sports Illustrated*, had his own cartoon, recorded a song with Rick Derringer, and made a few really stupid movies. What a country, huh?

See also ALBANO, CAPT. LOU; LAUPER, CYNDI; SMIRNOFF, YAKOV

HOGAN, PAUL

Nutty Australian from the *Crocodile Dundee* movies of 1986 and '88. He carried a giant knife and was simply a big deal for a while. Um . . . is there anything else to say here? Nope. Guess not.

See also AUSSIEMANIA; JOCKO; *MAD MAX*; MEN AT WORK; MINOGUE, KYLIE; SERIOUS, YAHOO

HOGANS, THE

A show with four names. It was much better when it was (1) *Valerie* and (2) *Valerie's Family*. After Valerie Harper left and Sandy Duncan took over, it was (3) *The Hogan Family* and later, as (4) *The Hogans,* it deteriorated. But it was good to see Jason Bateman again, and the father, Josh Taylor, was later Dylan's dad on *Beverly Hills 90210*.

See also IT'S YOUR MOVE; SILVER SPOONS

HOLLYWOOD SHUFFLE

Brilliant 1986 movie by Robert Townsend that poked a large amount of fun at the movie industry and how it treats black actors and filmmakers. The central story was that of a struggling black actor, played by Townsend, who gets offered a demeaning part. Does he take the break or keep his integrity? Weaved into that, though, were a bunch of hilarious sketches and movie parodies that, had more people seen the movie, would have put it on the level of *Fletch* as quotability goes.

See also AIRPLANE!; FLETCH; I'M GONNA GIT YOU SUCKA!; SUPER BOWL SHUFFLE

HOLLYWOOD SQUARES, THE

Both the title of a game show and an apt description of the B-list celebs who appeared on it.

See also GONG SHOW, THE; WIN, LOSE OR DRAW

HOOKED ON CLASSICS

A bunch of classical music themes set to a cheesy disco pulse and turned into a Top-10 hit in 1982. This spawned a wave of *Hooked on . . .* albums, including jazz and swing versions.

See also DISCO; MECO

HOOSIERS

Story of a small-town high school basketball team with a tough-but-fair coach and their march to the state championship. Better than most basketball movies because the action looked real. Also notable because Dennis Hopper played one of his most normal roles, as a former-star-turned-town-drunk, who coach Gene Hackman then takes on as his assistant.

See also BLUE VELVET; HOPPER, DENNIS

HOOTERS, THE

They came from Philadelphia in 1985, bearing a goofy mouth-keyboard-type of instrument that gave the band its name, and they sang super-peppy songs like "And We Danced" and "Day by Day" (from their album *Nervous Night*). Then, as quickly as they had arrived, they were gone. The video for "And We Danced" should be studied by those who want to know exactly how teenagers dressed in the mid-'80s.

See also JELLIES; OP; SWATCH; VANS (THE SHOES)

HOPPER, DENNIS

Just once we'd like to see Dennis Hopper play somebody who isn't psycho. To his credit, though, he does it well.

See also APOCALYPSE NOW; BLUE VELVET; RIVER'S EDGE

HORTON, WILLIE

A convicted murderer and rapist who, strangely enough, came to embody all things evil and racist in Republican politics. The whole business started when acknowledged sleazebag Horton killed somebody, went to prison, and then got out early on some program that Massachusetts governor Michael Dukakis had set up. Horton then raped and killed somebody else.

This incident was used against Dukakis in his 1988 push to be president. A group supporting George Bush flashed a picture of the killer in a TV ad, and a lot of people said this was racist: *Horton (a black guy) was very scary-looking indeed. Why couldn't these two white guys fight about a scary white person instead of a scary black person?*

And now, any sort of race-baiting political scapegoating (or whatever that stuff is called) usually brings up the name of Willie Horton. (Not to be confused with Horton, the lovable elephant from the Dr. Seuss classic, *Horton Hears a Who*.)

See also DUKAKIS, MICHAEL; SEUSS, DR.

HOSER

A toothless insult made popular by *Strange Brew*, in which Bob and Doug MacKenzie (Rick Moranis and Dave Thomas) call each other Hoser and Hosehead and the like.

See also STRANGE BREW

"HOT FOR TEACHER"/ "JUMP"/"PANAMA"

You could argue that Van Halen's cheesy videos essentially made MTV what it was. "Hot for Teacher" defined the story/flashback video, and the other two took the straight performance video and gave it some style.

See also MTV

HOW

Common Indianspeak for "Hello," at least according to decades of television and movies. Often accompanied by one stiff, raised hand.

See also PHILLIPS, LOU DIAMOND

HOWARD THE DUCK

The most notorious bomb of the '80s. This story of a duck from another planet who came to Cleveland was supposed to be the hugest movie of its time, a ground-breaking epic-with-an-attitude. The idea came from an obscure old comic book, the movie was produced by George Lucas, and it starred Lea Thompson (the mom from *Back to the Future*) and Jeffrey Jones (the principal from *Ferris Bueller's Day Off*). Some of the effects were cool, but the duck looked like Gary Coleman covered in papier-mâché, and the whole thing just stunk.

See also ISHTAR; STAR WARS; THX 1138

HUDSON, ROCK

In 1985, he was the first celebrity to die after contracting AIDS . . . or at least the first to do it publicly.

See also AIDS; PATIENT ZERO

HUEY LEWIS AND THE NEWS

A bluesy, smiley band out of San Francisco that bordered on—but never achieved—megastardom. Between 1983 and 1986 they always seemed to have at least one song in the Top 10, and almost everybody had their third album, *Sports*. But their videos sucked, their fourth effort (cleverly named *Fore*) flopped, and they instantly became an easy-listening station favorite. Lewis did have quite a fashion impact, though, making it hip to wear skinny vinyl ties. And, of course, to be square.

See also NERD; SKINNY VINYL TIES

HUGHES, JOHN

The first man who cared to tell a story of our generation on film, mixing the right amount of adolescent angst with humor and basic mismatched-couple plotlines. *Sixteen Candles*, *The Breakfast Club*, *Weird Science*, *Pretty in Pink* (for which he only wrote the script), and *Ferris Bueller's Day Off* are all classics. Unfortunately, it all went downhill after *Planes, Trains and Automobiles*, and John has been recycling the *Home Alone* plot with ever-younger stars.

See also BREAKFAST CLUB, THE; BUELLER, FERRIS; HALL, ANTHONY MICHAEL; RINGWALD, MOLLY

HUMAN LEAGUE, THE

This English band, with their 1982 single "Don't You Want Me," will be remembered as the one who took the soul out of rock music and turned it over to machines, signaling the full arrival of New Wave on popular radio.

See also NEW WAVE

HUNGRY HUNGRY HIPPOS

A silly game (featuring plastic hippos you controlled to try to gobble marbles) with a great name.

See also CONNECT FOUR; ELECTRONIC BATTLESHIP

HYPER-

Fairly modern prefix used to describe a concept taken to a higher level. It's almost interchangeable with "super-," except "hyper-" applies to something more intense. Superman, for example, would be no match for Hyperman. A hypermall is bigger than a supermall. Hypergrody is grodier than grody to the max. The rapidly evolving language of computers has brought this prefix into common usage with stuff like Hypercard and hypertext.

See also CYBER-; GRODY; MEGA-; SUPERMAN: THE MOVIE

I

IACOCCA, LEE

He led Chrysler out of bankruptcy, became a household name in the process, then left and wrote a book. A great icon for the Reagan years and hero to the little Alex P. Keatons out there.

See also FAMILY TIES; KEATING, CHARLES; MINIVANS; TRUMP, DONALD; TZU, SUN

IBUPROFEN

Just when planet Earth needed more pain-reliever commercials, this little non-aspirin wonder drug emerged from the prescription world during the '80s. It took the form of Advil and Nuprin, which was, if you remember, "little, yellow, different, better."

See also TYLENOL SCARE

ICE PIRATES, THE

This 1984 movie sucked, but when we were 12, we thought it was hilarious. The story followed a space rebel (Robert Urich) who steals the water supply—in frozen form—of the evil guy. The scenes we liked best involved the castration conveyor belt and space herpes.

See also BATTLESTAR GALACTICA; STAR WARS

"IKO IKO"

For some reason, remakes of this traditional Cajun tune figured prominently in at least four '80s movies. *Rain Man* opened with a version by the Belle Stars; *K-9* (with James Belushi) closed with another; the '60s recording by the Dixie Cups made it into *The Big Easy*; and Justine Bateman and her "band" did something horrific to it in *Satisfaction*. Also, Cyndi Lauper remade it on *She's So Unusual*, but Dr. John still does the song best.

See also FAMILY TIES; LAUPER, CYNDI

"I'LL BE BACK"

Tied with "Go ahead, make my day" for most-quoted movie line of the 1980s.

See also "GO AHEAD, MAKE MY DAY"; TERMINATOR, THE

ILLUMINATI, THE

An ancient, supersecret sub-sub-sub-sub-sect of society that supposedly rules the world. It's so covert that even those in it don't know what's going on, especially since it probably doesn't exist. Most recent information/misconceptions about the Illuminati come from a satirical set of '70s sci-fi books, "The Illumuniatus! Trilogy," by

Robert Anton Wilson and Robert Shea. This work is considered a bible by many who coddle conspiracies about the government, drugs, aliens, Freemasons, pop culture, and absolutely anything else.

See also BRAZIL; ORWELL, GEORGE; SUBGENIUS, CHURCH OF THE

I'M GONNA GIT YOU SUCKA!

Homage to and parody of the blaxploitation movies of the '70s, done up hilariously by Keenen Ivory Wayans. Wayans starred as Jack Spade, an ex-football player and Army guy who tries to avenge the "OG" (over-gold) death of his brother Junebug at the hands of Mr. Big, played by Jack Vernon. Assisting him are fellow black heroes John Slade (Bernie Casey), Fly Guy (Antonio Fargas), Hammer (Isaac Hayes), and Slammer (Jim Brown). Chris Rock also cameos as the guy too cheap to pay for a cup with his Pepsi.

See also HOLLYWOOD SHUFFLE; IN LIVING COLOR

INCHWORM

Sort of a Big Wheel for sissies. This was a benign, green, smiley-faced, curled-up worm with a seat in the middle of its hump and two wheels at either end. You made it move by bouncing up and down on it.

See also BIG WHEEL

INCREDIBLE HULK, THE

The live-action show on CBS starred Bill Bixby as David Banner (Rumors

said his name was changed from Bruce in the comic book because network types thought Bruce was a "gay" name. Sheesh.) and Lou Ferrigno as his mean, green alter ego.

See also BATMANIA; CARTER, LYNDA; G.I. JOE; SUPERMAN: THE MOVIE

INDIAN WITH A TEAR IN HIS EYE

This image, of a Native American man standing on a hill overlooking a littered highway at sunset, became the symbol of an anti-pollution public service ad campaign in the mid- and late '70s.

See also HOW; THIS IS YOUR BRAIN ON DRUGS AD

INFORMATION SOCIETY

Lame-ass band that tried, and succeeded to some degree, to capitalize on the success of groups like Depeche Mode and The Cure and the general ascendancy of synthy music, with the song "Pure Energy (I Want to Know)."

See also ALL THE OTHER CRAPPY ENGLISH ONE-HIT WONDERS IN THIS BOOK; NEW WAVE; SYNTH-POP

IN LIVING COLOR

Early Fox show created by Keenen Ivory Wayans and significant for several reasons: It was an early Fox show; it showed a prime-time crowd that black people could do comedy on their own, not just as the sidekicks or comic relief for white folks; it proved that people would watch funny stuff, no matter who was delivering it, as long as the stuff stayed funny (see the show's last season and a half); and it was a mass audience's introduction to Jim Carrey.

See also Fox; *I'm Gonna Git You Sucka!*

INSIDERS, THE

Bad *Miami Vice* rip-off choked up by ABC. Stoney Jackson and Nicholas Campbell played way-too-hip magazine reporters on the trail of scoops, danger, and women.

See also Miami Vice; Outsiders, The

INSPECTOR GADGET

Cartoon about a bumbling crime fighter who, for reasons unexplained, had an arsenal of tools and appliances affixed to most of his body parts. But in his trench coat and hat, he looked fairly normal and sounded like Don Adams from *Get Smart* (who actually did the voice) when he said, "Wowsers!" Other players included evil mastermind Dr. Claw (of whom we only ever saw an arm and fist), his cohorts at M.A.D.D. (we'll make the parallel obvious: the bad guys in *Get Smart* worked for K.A.O.S.) and Gadget's preteen daughter Penny and dog Brain, who always solved the crimes.

See also Masters of the Universe; Thundercats; Transformers

INTELLIVISION

First-generation video game machine that boasted better graphics and cooler sports cartridges than the Atari 2600. But it had crappy controls with slick little circles that were impossible to move around. George

Plimpton pitched this in TV ads. Too bad none of us knew who he was.

See also Atari; Colecovision

INVASION USA

Testosterone-filled piece of crap in the *Red Dawn* mode that has Chuck Norris saving America after the Cubans, with much help from the hated Evil Empire, invade Florida and blow up a bunch of stuff for seemingly no reason other than they're Commies, and all Commies are bad.

See also Amerika; Evil Empire; *Iron Eagle*; Rambo; Red Dawn

INXS

If you were a record-company marketing person in the 1980s, you could not have created a band that better captured the zeitgeist. They were Australian. They had a lead singer, Michael Hutchence, who drove teenage girls loopy. They liked to make videos. They had a sax player. They had lots of hair, collectively and individually. Despite their cuteness factor, they had songs that frat boys could dig. And to top it all off, they did that cool "liberate-mediate-regulate" thing.

See also Aussiemania; Duran Duran; Jocko; *Mad Max*; Men at Work

I.O.U. CLOTHES

Available at Merry-Go-Round, Rave, and Chess King, the sweatshirts and rugby shirts that bore these insolvent letters were the hottest thing you could find down at your local mid-'80s mall and conferred instant status on the wearer, especially if worn in concert with a hip jean jacket.

See also Jean Jackets; Limited, The; Merry-Go-Round

"I PITY THE FOOL"

Catchphrase of one B.A. Baracus, and a surefire indication that a bad guy is about to get his ass whupped.

See also A-Team, The; Mr. T and the T Force; "Whatchootalkinbout?"

IRAN-CONTRA THING

Or, if you like, call it the Iran-Contra affair, Iran-Contra scandal, Iran-Contra incident, or Iran-Contra ordeal. Or just call it Irangate. The news media couldn't share a common name for this complex series of events, but everyone pretty much agreed that it was a bad deal. It embarrassed the government, tarnished the ever-godlike Reagan, and seeded enough semi-believable conspiracies to last for years.

Here's sort of what happened: Terrorists in Iran kidnapped some Americans, and the U.S. usually tells hostage-takers to screw off. So, at least publicly, they did. Meanwhile, halfway across the world, the anti-commie Contras in Nicaragua struggled against the Sandinistas and the U.S. decides not to send any more money to the "freedom fighters." OK. So, some government people—including, apparently, Gen. Richard Secord and Lt. Col. Oliver North—arranged to sell weapons to people in Iran, hoping to get the hostages out . . . and then they took that money and gave it to the Contras. Pretty illegal stuff. Some, however,

thought it was brave and daring and made North & Co. heroes.

And besides, how bad could a scandal be if it generated a couple of best-selling books (*The Tower Commission Report* and Ollie's *Under Fire: An American Story*) and a much-watched nonfiction miniseries (the congressional hearings)? The single most amazing fact surrounding the Iran-Contra thing is that nobody made a big-budget action movie about it.

See also Contras; -gate; North, Oliver; Qaddafi, Mu'ammar; Tower Commission Report, The

IRANIAN HOSTAGE CRISIS

The first big news event that had an impact on us. It was kind of confusing at the time, and remains that way. The Shah of Iran got sick in 1979 and came to America for treatment, which was a perfect time for that wacky Khomeini to take over the country, so he and his militants did. They stormed the U.S. Embassy, took about 60 people hostage, and demanded that President Carter send back the Shah so they could kill him. OK. So our man in the White House tried a daring rescue and ended up crashing a bunch of helicopters in the desert. Then the Shah died and eventually Khomeini let everybody go, but not before Reagan used the whole situation to whoop Carter's butt and bring us Morning in America. The end.

See also Giant peanut with a big grin on its shell; Iran-Contra thing; Khomeini, Ayatollah Ruhollah; *Nightline;* Reagan, Ronald; Yellow ribbons

IRON EAGLE

Yet another in a string of '80s kids-can-do-anything movies. This time, a struggling high school student (Jason Gedrick) highjacks an F-16 and does what the U.S. government won't: He flies a daring mission to save his dad, an Air Force pilot held hostage by an evil Mu'ammar Qaddafi clone. Adding to the extreme '80sness of his character, Gedrick blasts Queen on his Walkman while bombing the living shit out of a desert nation.

See also IRANIAN HOSTAGE CRISIS; KADDAFI, MOHAMAR; NIGHT OF THE COMET; QUEEN; WALKMAN

IRON-ONS

When we had only plain T-shirts to wear, these oh-so-cool designs, often found inside a box of your favorite sugary cereal, would spice them up. At least until they faded out of sight or fell off after three trips through the washing machine.

See also ETCH-A-SKETCH; PRESTO MAGIX; SMURFBERRY CRUNCH

ISHTAR

After *Howard the Duck*, the most embarrassing bomb of the 1980s.

See also HOWARD THE DUCK; PAINTER'S CAPS

ISUZU, JOE

This guy was the No. 1 commercial sensation of the 20th century. (*He's lying.*) He sold Hondas (*Isuzus. He sold Isuzus.*) and his name was Charlton Heston. (*Make that David Leisure.*)

Before doing these ads, he directed and starred in *Taxi Driver*, (*Actually, he had a small part as a Hare Krishna in* Airplane *and then later played Charley on* Empty Nest.) His commercials featured him talking to his imaginary friend Vern. (*No they didn't. The ads had him making outrageous and apocryphal statements while subtitles set the record straight.*) He died along with Mikey from the Life cereal ads during a tragic Coke-and-Pop Rocks accident. (*He's lying again, somebody stop him. Please.*)

See also BLU-BLOCKERS GUY, THE; GUY WHO TALKS REALLY FAST, THE; THAT "HEY VERN" GUY

IT'S A LIVING

Sexual-tension sitcom about a bunch of waitresses (including Ann Jillian) and a slimy lounge singer (Paul Kreppel) working in a ritzy restaurant called Above the Top. This spent most of its time in syndication after a short run on a real network (ABC).

See also WAITRESSES, THE

IT'S GARRY SHANDLING'S SHOW

Garry Shandling played a guy named Garry Shandling, who had some friends who did stuff, and occasionally Garry would turn directly to the camera and talk to the audience. Call it the proto-*Seinfeld*.

See also FOX; HBO

IT'S YOUR MOVE

Short-lived show on NBC starring

Jason Bateman as a smart-ass con man, essentially a rewrite of his character from *Silver Spoons*. He lived across the hall from and constantly matched wits with Norman Lamb (Richard Garrison, Steve from *Married . . . with Children*), who had the hots for Jason Bateman's mom. Bateman's best friend was a Dumb Guy character named Eli. The series ended with a two-part episode about a nonexistent band called the Dregs of Humanity.

See also DUMB GUY; *HOGANS, THE*; *SILVER SPOONS*

I WOULD DIE 4 U SIGN LANGUAGE

1. Point to yourself.
2. Wave.
3. You can't really do anything for the word "would" so just keep going.
4. Point a finger-gun at your head.
5. Put up four fingers.
6. Point to anybody else. Repeat until Prince stops singing.

See also PRINCE; RISKY BUSINESS DANCE

IZOD

Clothing brand of choice for the Preppie crowd. Of particular interest were those short-sleeve shirts that came in pastel colors and had collars that you could flip up and that damn little green alligator over the left nipple.

See also COLLARS TURNED UP; MEMBERS ONLY JACKETS; YUPPIES

J

JACKSON, BO

He was, for the last part of the '80s, the most famous sports guy in the world. Not only was he the first man in a long time to play back-to-back pro sports—changing from his Kansas City Royals cap to an L.A. Raiders helmet in a matter of days—but he was good at both.

Nike made him the you-can-do-anything poster boy with a series of omnipopular "Bo knows" ads. Bo knows football. Bo knows weights. Bo knows having cross-trainers named after you kicks ass.

After an appearance on *Sesame Street*, the onset of parody ("Bo knows your mother" T-shirts), and a dislocated hip, Bo got to know how quickly a celebrity can disappear.

See also JORDAN, MICHAEL; NIKE; REEBOK

JACKSON, JANET

Michael's equally talented, far more normal little sister. She first appeared on the pop-culture landscape as Penny in the post–John Amos *Good Times* and later as Willis' girlfriend on *Diff'rent Strokes*. But her 1986 debut album, *Control*, made her as much a household name as her weirdo sibling, and her 1990 transformation from cute singer to goddess-like diva was stunning. Oh yeah, and she made a string of pretty funky hit songs, including "What Have You Done for Me Lately," "Nasty Boys," and "Rhythm Nation."

BONUS FACT: That's Paula Abdul, Janet's then-choreographer, as one of the two girls in the movie theater in the "Nasty Boys" video.

See also ABDUL, PAULA; *FAME; GOOD TIMES;* JACKSON, MICHAEL; VICTORY TOUR

JACKSON, JOE

Angry young man whose first couple of albums were directly influenced by punk rock, whose biggest hit was the jazzy ballad "Steppin' Out," and whose music pretty much covers everything in between those two styles.

See also PUNK ROCK

JACKSON, MICHAEL

We have watched him go from the beaming singer of the Jackson Five to the reclusive megastar whose face has been altered too many times to count. In between, we bought many copies of *Thriller*, the best-selling album ever, learned how to do the moonwalk, and watched him take Brooke Shields and Emmanuel Lewis to the Oscars. He had that whole thing going on with a monkey, too.

Nose no. 2, circa 1983.

BONUS QUERY: Where were you when his hair caught on fire?

See also MICHAEL JACKSON DOLL; MONKEY-MANIA; *THRILLER;* VICTORY TOUR; *WEBSTER*

JACKSON, REGGIE

Prodigious home-run hitter for the New York Yankees in the late '70s. More importantly, though, he was the first sports star since Babe Ruth to have a candy bar named after him.

See also BIG LEAGUE CHEW

JAMS

It's really hard to say what made us want to wear these knee-length, loud, and (let's face it) ugly brand of surfer-dude shorts for a while there in junior high, but we sure as hell did.

See also NEON CLOTHES; VANS (THE SHOES)

JANE FONDA'S WORKOUT

If the '60s weren't already dead before Jane released her aerobics video, they most certainly passed on after that first utterance of "Feel the burn!"

See also FONDA, JANE; TURNER, TED

JANE'S ADDICTION

Collection of freaks fronted by Perry Farrell who combined elements of punk, metal, the Doors, and lots of drugs to produce a couple of excellent albums at the end of the '80s. The band helped bridge the gap between the heavy metal of the previous decade and the grunge phenomenon to come.

BONUS FACT: Farrell founded the Lollapalooza traveling concert/freak show.

See also BUNDY, TED

JANUARY 20, 1981

Arguably the most significant day in our generational history. If you look back at newspapers from that day and the next day, you will see many huge headlines about the freeing of the 52 American hostages in Iran. Then, if you look at the bottom half of the page, you will learn that in Washington on that day, the 40th president of the United States, a former actor, was inaugurated. "Morning in America" officially began that day when Ronald Reagan took the oath of office.

BONUS AUTHOR-SHARING-WITH-YOU-MOMENT: One of the hostages, Steven Lauterbach, was from Rick's hometown of Dayton, Ohio, and Rick made a big sign that said "Welcome home, Steve," complete with yellow ribbon, and hung it in his bedroom window.

SUPER-EXTRA-SPECIAL BONUS FACT: Lauterbach was later a contestant on *Jeopardy!*

See also IRANIAN HOSTAGE CRISIS; KHOMEINI, AYATOLLAH RUHOLLAH; REAGAN, RONALD; YELLOW RIBBONS

JAZZERCISE

A progenitor of aerobics that involved more complex dance moves and more expensive classes.

See also AEROBICS

JEAN JACKETS

Probably the last vestige of the fascination with the '50s a lot of us had in the '80s. Just about every fashion-conscious ninth-grader had one (preferably blue or black, though on certain people white and gray were acceptable), properly festooned with buttons or pins announcing who we had seen in concert or what pithy sayings we lived by.

See also ACID WASH; FRIENDSHIP PINS

JEDI MASTER'S TRIVIA QUIZ BOOK

A best-seller by 15-year-old Rusty Miller containing *Star Wars* trivia more obscure than anything in this book.

See also STAR WARS; WEDGE

JELLIES

Cheap, plastic, translucent web-like

shoes worn by almost every girl in junior high. Available just down the mall corridor at Rave, Charlotte Russe, Fashion Bug, Fashion Bug Plus, and Fashion Gal.

See also LEG WARMERS; LIMITED, THE; NEON CLOTHES; SWATCHES; VANS (THE SHOES)

JELLY BELLIES

When President Reagan announced that he had a weakness for these things, this small company that made a seemingly endless variety of flavors skyrocketed to popularity. But, really, what's with the popcorn flavor?

See also REAGAN, RONALD; WHATCHMACALLIT

JEM AND THE HOLOGRAMS

Poorly animated cartoon about the adventures of an all-woman glam-rock band called the Holograms. The spiky-haired JEM sang lead with Shana and Osha behind her, and the bad guys—because it's just not an '80s cartoon unless you've got bad guys—were in a band called the Misfits.

See also BENETAR, PAT; GO-GOS, THE; JETT, JOAN; LAUPER, CYNDI

JENNER, BRUCE

Won the Olympic decathlon in 1976, then made his living doing Wheaties commercials in the barren sports-hero world of the late 1970s. Dr. J was still fearsome-looking with his Afro, Larry and Magic were three years from stardom, and the jogging boom was at its peak. So Bruce was

Joanie, loving Chachi.

pretty much the only game in town.

See also BIRD, LARRY; JACKSON, BO; JOHNSON, EARVIN "MAGIC"; JORDAN, MICHAEL; RETTON, MARY LOU

JETT, JOAN

She might fight Pat Benetar for the Rock 'n' Roll Bad Girl title, but the would-be punker only had one really huge hit ("I Love Rock 'n' Roll" with her band The Blackhearts). Jett, we think, played harder than Benetar and could probably take her down in a bout of fisticuffs.

See also BENETAR, PAT

J. GEILS BAND

Goofy, sleazy band who made a comeback in the early 1980s with their album *Freezeframe*. Hits included the title track and "Centerfold" (which had a *na-na-na* refrain eerily similar to the *Smurfs* theme song). Also one of the last hangers-on of the arena-rock crowd of the 1970s, they smoothed the transition between that era and New Wave.

See also ROLLER SKATING; SMURFS

"JINGLE BELLS" (ALTERNATIVE VERSION)

Somehow, we all know the lyrics: "Jingle bells, Batman smells, Robin laid an egg. / Batmobile lost its wheel, and the Joker got away."

See also ELMO AND PATSY; MIKEY; MONY MONY CHANT; RUMOR ABOUT RICHARD GERE, THE

"JINGLE BELLS" (ALTERNATIVE VERSION NO. 2)

Dogs barking: *Woof woof woof, woof woof woof, woof WOOF woof arf woof.*

See also ELMO AND PATSY; "JINGLE BELLS" (ALTERNATIVE VERSION)

JJ FAD

Female rappers (M.C.J.B., Baby-D, Sassy C) who crossed over to the pop charts around 1988 with "Supersonic," which featured lightning-fast delivery and unintelligible lyrics.

See also RAP

JOANIE LOVES CHACHI

Oh, this was bad. The folks at ABC didn't understand that you could not build a series around Erin Moran and Scott Baio. It didn't do nearly as well as the other *Happy Days* spin-offs: *Laverne and Shirley*, *Mork and Mindy*, and *Happy Days Again*, which starred Ted McGinley (*Revenge of the Nerds, Married . . . with Children,* and *Love Boat*).

See also BAIO, SCOTT; *FONZIE* CARTOON

JOBS, STEVE

The rebellious Geek God genius of the '80s. Along with Stephen Wozniak he founded Apple Computer and created the Macintosh. After Jobs' bitter walkout from Apple, he lost much of his following. Only hard-core buffs stuck with him through the birth and death of his bizarre-yet-neat NeXT computers.

See also BIG BROTHER AD; GEEK ERA; NERD; NeXT

JOCKO

Australian professional wrestler who broke into U.S. mass culture by doing a few annoying commercials and then vanished, presumably forever. Most notable among his efforts was an Energizer battery commercial in which he said, "It'll suh-prise ya! New En-ah-gize-ah!" He also did a song and video called "I'm an Individual," in which he pretty much just went around yelling and pumping his arms and going "Oi!"

See also Aussiemania; Hogan, Paul; *Mad Max;* Men at Work; Minogue, Kylie; Serious, Yahoo

JOHN CAFFERTY AND THE BEAVER BROWN BAND

For some reason, a lot of us knew that this band's name came from a can of paint.

See also Eddie and the Cruisers

JOHNNY DANGEROUSLY

Pretty stupid 1985 spoof of gangster movies starring Michael Keaton. We loved it because of its bevy of catchphrases: Bad guy Joe Piscopo's .88 Magnum could "shoot through schools." There were the annoying things that people did to Piscopo "once (pause for effect) once." Plus, the head bad guy had a funny accent (always a plus for a film looking to appeal to 13-year-olds) and called everyone "fargin iceholes" and "bastidges." Oh, and there was a sight gag involving large testicles. C'mon, admit it. You thought it was funny then, too.

See also Ice Pirates, The; Piscopo, Joe

JOHNNY HATES JAZZ

Band from Britain known for a little late '80s song called "Shattered Dreams."

See also Baltimora

JOHNSON, BEN

Olympic runner who, in 1988, ran the 100-meter dash faster than any human ever, but had his medals taken away after it was discovered he used steroids.

See also Olympics; Williams, Vanessa

JOHNSON, EARVIN "MAGIC"

Along with Larry Bird, with whom he entered pro basketball, Magic resurrected the NBA, turning sports into entertainment and bringing hordes of movie stars in to watch Laker games at the Forum in the 1980s. He was also arguably the greatest passer the game had ever seen up to that point and helped the Lakers win five titles while he was there. Then in 1991, he said he had HIV and made a lot of us realize that AIDS really could affect anyone.

See also AIDS; Bird, Larry; Hudson, Rock

JOHN 3:16 GUY

Loon who showed up at seemingly every televised NFL game in the '70s and early '80s wearing a rainbow wig and holding a sign with the name of the Bible verse on it. A few years ago, he was convicted of killing someone. Seriously.

See also SAN DIEGO CHICKEN, THE

JOLLY RANCHERS

The hard candy of choice for the discerning preteen. At first, they came in stick form, offering only a few standard flavors, including the super-hot Fire Stix. They cost between 10 and 15 cents at your local skating rink or convenience store. Later, they became small and individually wrapped and offered more flavors.

See also BIG LEAGUE CHEW; JELLY BELLIES

JOLT COLA

With "all the sugar and twice the caffeine," this wonder beverage promised that none of us would ever sleep again. While outliving a few other bright cola ideas (New Coke comes to mind), it failed to catch on with the mainstream like high-octane competitor Mountain Dew. A distinct connection to nerd culture was part of the cola's problem . . . and appeal.

See also LIKE COLA; MOUNTAIN DEW; NERD; NEW COKE

JONES, GRACE

Giant androgyne with deadly hair who terrorized Roger Moore in *A View to a Kill*, made some disco-techno music, showed up a lot in the Random Notes section of *Rolling Stone* between 1983–86, and then returned to her home planet.

See also NIELSEN, BRIGITTE

JONES, ORAN "JUICE"

Soul crooner/rapper who sang/said the 1986 sort-of ballad "The Rain," which was about getting dumped and taking revenge, and featured the memorable line, "You without me is like Corn Flakes without the milk!"

See also BALTIMORA

JONES, TOM

Welsh superstar, singer of the *Late Night* theme song, receiver of women's undergarments, coverer of Prince's "Kiss."

See also ART OF NOISE; HINDU LOVE GODS; LETTERMAN, DAVE

JONNY QUEST

Supercool Saturday morning cartoon about a kid, his Indian buddy Hadji, and his dog Bandit. They traveled the world with Jonny's scientist/adventurer/crime-fighter father and spent a lot of time getting lost in jungles and hiding from angry natives and crafty, technology-laden bad guys. All the things those kids watching it wanted to be doing.

BONUS FACT: Teen-romp film god Tim Matheson did the voice of Jonny in the original series that ran in prime-time ABC during the '60s.

See also ALSO CRIME FIGHTING; MATHESON, TIM

JORDAN, MICHAEL

The greatest player in the history of basketball and a man whose image as a genuinely nice guy made him the most ubiquitous pitchman in history. Basketball fans who saw him play in college at North Carolina knew he was a great player. But after the Chicago Bulls selected him with the third pick in the 1984 NBA draft (Portland had the second pick and chose, uh, Sam Bowie), Nike signed him to a contract. In his first commercial, you heard the sound of a jet engine revving as he ran the length of the court in funny-looking, red-black-and-white shoes named after him. As the jet took off, so did he (from around the foul line), and a legend was born. He blurred the line between sports star and media celebrity like no one else before him and became so famous that we now know him simply as "Michael."

See also BIRD, LARRY; JACKSON, BO; JOHNSON, EARVIN "MAGIC"; NIKE

JOUST

Weird video game in which you rode around on a giant flying ostrich, trying to knock others off their ostriches and picking up eggs that appeared on the various landing pads.

See also ATARI; BURGER TIME; FOOD FIGHT; PAC-MAN

JUDAS PRIEST

British metal band that reached the height of its popularity after two kids in Nevada blew their heads off and the parents blamed the music. The band members actually went to court and listened to a bunch of fundamentalist Christian types say that Judas Priest records, when played back-

ward, contained satanic messages, and, when played forward, masked the subliminal message: "Do it." It was argued that this urged kids to kill themselves, while most rational people realized that it was just a Nike ad.

See also DUNGEONS & DRAGONS; HEAVY METAL BOOM; *MAZES AND MONSTERS*; NIKE

JUICE BOXES

After Caprisun was introduced, it seemed as though the last frontier of beverage container technology had been breached. Not so. For not long after that, the folks at Hi-C and Mott's and Welch's began packaging their fruit drinks in little rectangular boxes, with little pointy straws vacuum-sealed to them. They were convenient for parents to throw in the lunch box or bag, and kids could both stab the boxes with the straw's pointy end and squirt their friends. God bless American ingenuity.

See also CAPRISUN

JUMP 'N THE SADDLE BAND

What can you say about these guys? We have three words for you: "The Curly Shuffle."

See also BALTIMORA; *3 ROBOTIC STOOGES, THE*

JUSTICE LEAGUE OF AMERICA

The official name of the organization the Superfriends belonged to. Key members were Superman, Wonder Woman, Green Lantern, Aquaman, Batman and Robin, The Flash, Apache Chief, Black Vulcan, Samurai,

Atom, Hawkman, and El Dorado. They were usually outmanned by the forces of evil but always emerged victorious—until next week. Some of the science experiments they did between episodes were pretty cool, too.

See also BATMANIA; GLEEK; LEGION OF DOOM; *SUPERMAN: THE MOVIE*

JUST ONE OF THE GUYS

Awful high school film about a girl who dressed up like a guy for a few weeks so she could write a newspaper article about it. She/he befriended a real loser character and transformed him, through superficial means, into a cool kind of rebel guy. The unwitting climax came when the loser got gussied up in a blazer and skinny vinyl tie, and the girl/guy proclaimed: "Welcome to the '80s!"

See also BREAKFAST CLUB, THE; *FAST TIMES AT RIDGEMONT HIGH*; NERD; SKINNY VINYL TIES

JUST SAY NO

Catchy motto of Nancy Reagan's antidrug campaign. Largely regarded as futile.

See also KELLY, KITTY; THIS IS YOUR BRAIN ON DRUGS AD

JUST THE TEN OF US

A *Growing Pains* spin-off with Bill Kirchenbauer (the doughy Coach Lubbock) as the father of six girls and two boys. The central joke was that five of the daughters were the only females in the all-boys Catholic school where Daddy coached. Laughs and underage sexual tension ensued.

See also GROWING PAINS

K

KADDAFI, MOHAMAR

See QADDAFI, MU'AMMAR

KAJAGOOGOO

More synth-poppy fun from Britain. They had a great name and sang about being "Too Shy," and apparently were, having vanished by the end of 1983.

See also BALTIMORA

KANGAROOS

Shoes fitted with a small zipper-and-Velcro pouch on the side, useful only if you didn't have pockets and wanted to carry around a key, some money, or maybe three Tic-Tacs.

BONUS FACT: NBA star Clyde "The Guide" Drexler had an endorsement contract with the company for a few years.

See also FAT SHOELACES; JELLIES; L.A. GEAR; LATCHKEY KID; VANS (THE SHOES); VELCRO

KARATE KID, THE

Perhaps *the* feel-good sporting event/coming of age film of our generation. Like *Rocky*, but funnier. (Pat Morita's Mr. Miagi, with his bonsai trees and J.C. Penney belt, was a pseudocomic character, whereas

Burgess Meredith's Mickey was a complete nurturing-patriarch symbol. This may be why Sylvester Stallone would whoop Ralph Macchio.) Bill "I did the music for *Rocky*" Conti did the music. Soundtrack also included Bananarama's "Cruel Summer."

See also NIGHT OF THE COMET

KATE & ALLIE

Mid-'80s CBS sitcom starring Jane Curtin (Kate) and Susan St. James (Allie) as two single moms with teenage kids.

See also BERT AND ERNIE; *CAGNEY & LACEY; DOUBLE TROUBLE; SIMON & SIMON*

KAUFMAN, ANDY

Weird comedian who first made a name for himself on *Saturday Night Live*, then got famous as Eastern European mechanic Latka on *Taxi*, then made fun of some pro wrestlers and got his ass kicked, then, in an unrelated incident, died.

See also HOGAN, HULK; *TAXI*

KEATING, CHARLES

Evil capitalist scum.

See also BOESKY, IVAN; EVIL EMPIRE

Movie lines we said a lot

"I can't believe I gave my panties to a geek."

—Spoken with perfect understanding of just how horrible the situation was by Molly Ringwald in *Sixteen Candles*.

KELLY, KITTY

Thanks to this gossip/biographer, we "know" that Nancy Reagan had sex with Frank Sinatra and asked an astrologer about Ron's policy decisions.

See also GOLDMAN, ALBERT; JUST SAY NO; REAGAN, RONALD

KERSHAW, NIK

The man asked "Wouldn't it be good?" in his song of the same title, and it wasn't too bad, really. The tune ended up on the *Pretty in Pink* soundtrack, and he helped out with Live Aid.

See also LIVE AID; *PRETTY IN PINK*

KHOMEINI, AYATOLLAH RUHOLLAH

The greatest Middle Eastern terrorist of the 1970s.

See also IRAN-CONTRA THING; IRANIAN HOSTAGE CRISIS; NIDAL, ABU; QADDAFI, MU'AMMAR; REAGAN, RONALD; RUSHDIE, SALMAN; TERRORISM; YELLOW RIBBONS

KICK!

You were a clown, see, and what you did was you used the joystick to move around on your unicycle, and the button to kick the balloons that fell from the top onto your head, where you balanced them and tried to keep them from breaking.

See also ATARI

KID 'N' PLAY

High-haired rap duo better known for their dancing and general goofiness,

not to mention the movie *House Party* and their cartoon, than any song they ever did. Can you name one?

See also SALT-N-PEPA

KIDS ARE PEOPLE, TOO

With *Those Amazing Animals* and *That's Incredible*, part of the multi-host, isn't-that-something show boom that occurred around the turn of the decade. This one starred Michael Young.

See also REAL PEOPLE

KID SISTER

A feminine answer to My Buddy, which was, in itself, a *masculine* counter to the entire doll industry. Represents somebody in the toy industry thinking a little *too* much. These didn't really do anything, but on the strength of catchy commercial jingles became big sellers.

See also MON CHI CHIS; MY BUDDY

KIHN, GREG

Leader of a New Wave band bearing his name. The group's album titles all had the word "Kihn" in them, as in *Rockihnroll* and *Kihnspiracy*. Their best-known song is "Jeopardy," which is even better known as a "Weird" Al Yankovic parody.

See also YANKOVIC, "WEIRD" AL

KILLER BEES

For decades now we've been hearing that a pack of these is on their way to the U.S. border. They were accidentally shipped from Africa to South America and, naturally, want to relocate to Quebec. The first Mexican attack caused all kinds of minor hysteria, and so did the first spottings in the U.S. Now they're in Texas or California or somewhere.

See also FRUIT FLIES; SWARM, THE

KING, STEPHEN

Perhaps the ugliest human to achieve superstardom in America. Also known for writing huge, scary books and a lot of them. As a general rule, his books don't make for good movies, with the exception of *Stand by Me, Misery,* and *The Shining.* Even the one movie he directed, *Maximum Overdrive* (featuring AC/DC's "Who Made Who?"), sucked. King's submersion in the rest of '80s media includes a mini-series based on the superseller *It* and the obscure movie *Cat's Eye,* adapted from short stories.

See also BARRYMORE, DREW; CLANCY, TOM; STAND BY ME

KINISON, SAM

This loudmouthed ex-preacher became a genuine phenomenon in the late 1980s, taking vulgar comedy to new heights (depths?), making videos, and elevating anger to an art form.

See also CLAY, ANDREW "DICE"; *DELIRIOUS;* HAHN, JESSICA; STAND-UP BOOM

KINSKI, NASTASSJA

Eastern-bloc beauty most famous for being naked in *Cat People* and on a pinup poster that showed her wearing only a giant boa constrictor.

See also BARYSHNIKOV, MIKHAIL; FARRAH POSTER, THE; GORBACHEV, MIKHAIL S.; SMIRNOFF, YAKOV

KISS

A lot of parents got really upset when this band got popular in the '70s. But after you got past the satanic imagery (their name was rumored to mean Knights In Satan's Service), the S&M costumes, the evil face paint, and the blood-spitting, you could see that Paul Stanley, Gene Simmons, Ace Frehley, and Peter Criss were really nice boys. After all, they did "Beth," didn't they?

See also HEAVY METAL BOOM

KISSING POTION

The first makeup that many girls were allowed to wear. It was a clear and kind of watery lip gloss that came in flavors like grape and cherry. Most girls first wore it around age 10 or 11, and we're told it made them feel quite sexy.

See also MAKEOVER BARBIE

KLEIN, CALVIN

Take some designer jeans. Put them on Brooke Shields. Instant fashion empire.

See also SHIELDS, BROOKE

KNEE SOCKS

Big in elementary school, especially if you were in a Catholic school (as a way to quietly express your individu-

Movie lines we said a lot

"Does Barry Manilow know you raid his wardrobe?"

—A nice putdown for out-of-touch adult authority figures gleaned from Bender in *The Breakfast Club.*

ality). Available just down the mall corridor at Rave, Charlotte Russe, Fashion Bug, Fashion Bug Plus, and Fashion Gal.

See also JELLIES; LEG WARMERS; MALLS

KNEIVEL, EVIL

Motorcycle daredevil who jumped over lines of buses, cars, senior citizens, whatever, in the 1970s and was famous enough to have action toys made in his likeness. Broke every bone in his body, too. Or so we heard.

See also SUPER DAVE OSBORNE; *THAT'S INCREDIBLE!*

KNIGHT RIDER

The show that made David Hasselhoff

Michael and his machine.

a star and gave him the bankroll to do *Baywatch.* The rest of the cast included Edward Mulhare as Devon (head of the privately financed crime-fighting gang called the Foundation for Law and Government), Patricia McPherson as Bonnie (the lovely mechanic), and William Daniels as the voice of KITT (the talking super-car). Together, they fought crime. Then-head of NBC Brandon Tartikoff called the concept "casting-proof." He was right.

BONUS FACT: KITT stands for Knight Industries Two Thousand.

See also A-TEAM, THE; AUTOMAN; MANIMAL; TARTIKOFF, BRANDON

KOOP, C. EVERETT

The Surgeon General's Surgeon General. The man with the beard (not to be confused with fellow whiskered Reagan-era guy Robert Bork) told us about condoms and AIDS and how smoking was bad for us. Amazingly, he got away with telling us this without raising too many hackles among Christian fundamentalists or tobacco-company lawyers. That's how good he was at his job.

See also AIDS; BORK, ROBERT

KOOSH BALLS

Made of a whole lot of stringy rubber knotted in the middle by, we assume, gravity. You couldn't really do anything with these, but they felt cool in your hands. About the same size as a Rubik's Cube.

See also RUBIK'S CUBE

KOREAN AIRLINES FLIGHT 007

A part of the Cold War that, to listen to the news at the time, nearly touched off a real war with the Soviet Union. Soviet fighters shot down the plane over Siberia on a rainy night in 1983. They claimed the jetliner was in Soviet airspace and refused to identify itself. We claimed it was deliberate because so many Americans were aboard. Almost overlooked was the fact that more than 100 people died in the crash.

See also GORBACHEV, MIKHAIL S.; *RED DAWN*; STEALTH

KRAZY GLUE

Bonding agent so strong that just one drop can hold a construction worker, outfitted with a flat block on top of his hard hat, to a steel beam in midair. Answer to the prayers of all people who had construction workers suspended from steel beams in their homes who kept falling and making a mess on the carpet.

See also BLU-BLOCKERS GUY, THE; MR. MICROPHONE

KROFFT SUPERSHOW

A Saturday-morning bonanza that featured the cartoons "Jabberjaw" and "Speed Buggy" and had a theme song by the Bay City Rollers.

See also BARBARA MANDRELL & THE MAN-DRELL SISTERS; *LAND OF THE LOST*

KRULL

In 1983, this was supposed to be a big deal, a hot epic film with a whole line of action figures. But the only thing anybody can remember (if anything) about this nasty hybrid of medieval fantasy and futuristic space wars is a cool spiraling star weapon thing.

See also DARK CRYSTAL; *ICE PIRATES, THE*; NINJA THROWING STARS

K-TEL

Record label of the infinitely recycled. Hard-rocking hits from about six years before ended up on K-Tel compilations, as did instrumental remakes of easygoing favorites from the past 60 years. Actually, it seems that all music sold on TV during the past two decades came from these people, including Zamfir.

See also ZAMFIR

Another big moment in our lifetimes

In April 1986, a combination of bad design, inadequate safety measures, and human error causes a full meltdown at the Chernobyl nuclear power plant in Ukraine.

L

LAFF-A-LYMPICS

Cartoon show in which three teams composed of Hanna-Barbera characters competed against each other in various events. We were divided between fans of the Scooby Doobies and the Yogi Yahooies, but we all were sure that we wanted the Really Rottens to lose.

See also BATTLE OF THE NETWORK STARS; GRAPE APE; SCOOBY DOO

L.A. GEAR

When this footwear first appeared on the scene, many of us believed they were just another cheap, poorly made attempt to capitalize on the Reebok phenomenon. But gradually, they gained acceptance in stores like Foot Locker, and now they are considered just about as good as any other mid-priced athletic shoe.

BONUS FACT: Houston Rockets star Akeem Olajuwon (before he added the "H" to his first name) was the first well-known professional athlete to sign an endorsement deal with the company.

See also AEROBICS; NIKE; REEBOK

LAID BACK

Synth-pop band that had one very odd little hit in 1984 called "White Horse." It had only a few lyrics that were repeated over and over again and went a little something like this: "If you're gonna ride, don't ride the white horse." We think it had something to do with drugs.

See also BALTIMORA; DOBBS, J.R. BOB; HARDCASTLE, PAUL

L.A. LAW

A little serial that hit the spot just as America absorbed a massive lawyer boom in the '80s. The attorneys (played by many, many people such as Susan Dey, Blair Underwood, Jimmy Smits, and Harry Hamlin) all brought their personal problems to the offices of McKenzie-Brackman and the clients brought in cases remarkably similar to recent headlines. Sort of like *Hill Street Blues* in better suits. Key moments from the nine-year run include: Senior partner Douglas Brackman, Jr., (Alan Rachins) dating Vanna White; a segment on midget bowling; another on the Venus Butter-fly, a mysterious sexual maneuver; the ongoing romantic tension between weasel Arnie Becker (Corbin Bernsen) and his secretary Roxanne (Susan Ruttmen); anything involving Benny, the mentally handicapped office gofer (Larry Drake); and the scene where superbitch/partner Roz

(Diana Muldaur) falls down an empty elevator shaft and dies.

See also BOCHCO, STEVEN; *HILL STREET BLUES;* THURSDAY NIGHT LINEUP; WHITE, VANNA

LAMAS, LORENZO

With the name he was given, he was destined to be a prime-time soap hunk, and he was for several seasons on *Falcon Crest.* It probably didn't hurt that his dad is Fernando Lamas.

See also DALLAS; DYNASTY

LAMBADA!

The dance craze that went *beyond* dirty dancing, inspiring two films (one eponymous and the other called *The Forbidden Dance*) and thousands of lonely people to sign up for lambada classes in hopes they would meet that saucy lover the dance required as a partner. Dead six months after it was born.

EXTRA-SUPER-SPECIAL BONUS FACT: The guy who directed *Lambada*, one Joel Silberg, also directed *Breakin',* and both films feature Adolfo "Shabba-Doo" Quinones.

See also BREAKDANCING; *DIRTY DANCING;* ELECTRIC BOOGALOO

LANDIS, JOHN

Comedy/horror/kitsch director and genius. Responsible for *Animal House, An American Werewolf in London, The Blues Brothers, Kentucky Fried Movie, Amazon Women on the Moon,* and the "Thriller" video. He was also the first Holly-wood director to be charged with a felony in connection with on-location deaths. During the 1982 filming of his *Twilight Zone: The Movie* segment, a helicopter crash killed actor Vic Morrow and two kids. This created some grisly PR for a film already dipped in otherworldly weirdness, but Landis was found innocent of manslaughter.

See also AMAZON WOMEN ON THE MOON; DANTE, JOE; *THRILLER*

"LAND OF CONFUSION" VIDEO

A shining moment in the history of the dreary but decade-infusing band Genesis, only because the video featured Spitting Image puppets of world leaders like Reagan and Gorbachev and Khomeini—all dancing and surrounded by fire. Any serious rock-political "commentary" value this may have had was disqualified by the involvement of puppets.

See also "SLEDGEHAMMER" VIDEO; SPITTING IMAGE

LAND OF THE LOST

Sid and Marty Krofft's live-action show about a family of archaeologists whose raft somehow gets swept into a place where dinosaurs still exist. The special effects were really awful.

See also BARBARA MANDRELL & THE MANDRELL SISTERS; KROFFT SUPERSHOW

LAST EPISODE OF *M*A*S*H*

When this aired on February 18, 1983, it was the most-watched single show in the history of television, beating the "Who shot J.R.?" episode of *Dallas*.

See also Aftermash; Cheers; Dallas; Police Academy

LAST STARFIGHTER, THE

A combination of trailer-park life, video games, and aliens, three important themes that had been explored before but never connected. The movie suggested that if you're good enough at what you love (like, say, for instance, playing a video game about an interstellar war), your skills can take you wherever you want to go (like, oh, the other side of the galaxy to fight in an interstellar war). Lance Guest and Catherine Mary Stewart starred as kids stuck in small-town America, and Robert Preston was the alien who got them out.

See also Atari; Flo; Star Wars

LAST TEMPTATION OF CHRIST, THE

A long, boring film that pissed a lot of people off. Picketers surrounded theaters and cursed the name of director Martin Scorsese for this, perhaps the least disturbing of all his movies.

The debate pretty much boiled down to this:

Against the movie: *There's naked people involved. Jesus was the son of God, and he was perfect. No way did he have a sexual fantasy before being crucified for all of our sins. Didn't and couldn't happen. And so nobody should make a movie about it. It's not funny or*

entertaining or whatever. And people might believe it. Amen.

For the movie: *Jesus was just a guy who looked like Willem Dafoe and, sure, he might have had an erection once. What's wrong with that? But that's only about 30 seconds of a three-hour movie, most of which isn't nearly so entertaining. And it's a movie, for chrissakes. If you're worried about people believing this stuff, go picket Monty Python. The Life of Brian was a hell of a lot more blasphemous. But thanks for all the free publicity, you Bible-hugging freaks!*

See also Christ, Jesus; God; Monty Python and the Holy Grail

LATCHKEY KID

Academic sociological term used to describe youngsters whose parents were hardly ever home. The so-called latchkey kids had to let themselves in after school and hold down the house until Mom and Dad, both reaping their cut of the fountains of money everyone made in the '80s, got home.

The phrase was meant as a tragic description of a growing generation of neglected youth, another sign of declining civilization brought about by the working woman. But, from the kid's point of view, what could be better than a few parent-free hours with the Intellivision or Lazer Tag or Cinemax? One question remains, though: What the hell is a latchkey?

Bonus author-sharing-with-you moment: Rick used to get a piece of string, thread it through the key, then tie it around his neck, just like Tom Hanks in *Big*.

See also Big; Cable; Greed; Intellivision; Kangaroos; Lazer Tag; Microwave

LAUPER, CYNDI

Her career peaked with her first single, "Girls Just Wanna Have Fun" from the album *She's So Unusual*. She could have been bigger than Madonna had she not fallen in with the wrong crowd.

See also Albano, Capt. Lou

LAZER TAG

The Future of Toys . . . at least for a few months there in 1986. You and your friends could wear vests and hats outfitted with heavy red sensors and shoot at each other with infrared-spewing pistols—just like Han Solo! These looked and sounded cool and were all the rage. You could even get sniper rifles and hats fitted with sensors. Then people realized the game was clumsy and difficult. Sold primarily through places like Service Merchandise and The Sharper Image until the bust. Then you could pick up a set anywhere. And now you can find Q-Zar and Ultrazone in malls everywhere, being played by kids who never heard of Lazer Tag.

See also Photon; *Star Wars*

LEAD OR LEAVE

Perhaps the first political organization to focus on problems unique to our generation. It started just about

the time when many of us came of voting age, surged to a million-strong a few years later, and then just fizzled. In what they called grassroots manner, Lead or Leave tried to raise awareness of such things as the slow growth of the economy and the government investing too much money in old people and not enough in us: you know, the Future.

See also Amnesty International; Ban the Box; Rock the Vote

LEE PRESS-ON NAILS

A friend to every girl who's ever broken a tip. Came with or without nail polish already applied.

See also Colored hair spray

LEGION OF DOOM

The bad guys on the best episodes of the *Superfriends*. They were led by Lex Luthor, evil genius. Other members were Scarecrow, Sinestro (the anti-Green Lantern), Cheetah, Brainiac, Grod (the big, hyperintelligent ape), Black Manta, Toyman, the Riddler, Bizarro, Giganta, Solomon Grundy (the swamp zombie), and Captain Cold. The LOD hung out at the Hall of Doom, which bore a striking resemblance to Darth Vader's head and rested at the bottom of a swamp. They received occasional help from Mxylplyk, who came over from the Fifth Dimension and had to be tricked into saying his name backward to be returned there.

See also Justice League of America

LEGO

The most durable of all the small-scale analogies for construction materials with which we could play. Erector sets and Capsela and Tinker Toys just couldn't compete with these nubby blocks from Scandinavia. A colorful bucketful of Lego could create everything from spaceships to cars, gas stations to tow trucks, helicopters to cabins, robots to human beings. Notable in the Lego universe are the name-brand stickers (various gas station sets included Shell, Exxon, and British Petroleum), the people (they have cylindrical heads topped with a single nub), and Duplo blocks (for the tykes, bigger and presumably inedible).

See also CAPSELA; SLIME

LEG WARMERS

These multicolored knit tubes were worn by women between their ankles and knees—nobody really knew why. The rage for these coincided with aerobics, Jane Fonda, and Reeboks. Available just down the mall corridor at Rave, Charlotte Russe, Fashion Bug, Fashion Bug Plus, and Fashion Gal.

See also CARA, IRENE; JELLIES; KNEE SOCKS; MALLS

LENNON, JOHN

Shot and killed on December 8, 1980. Another one of the few "Where were you when it happened?" events in our lifetime.

See also CHALLENGER; CHAPMAN, MARK DAVID; JACKSON, MICHAEL; REAGAN, RONALD

LENNON, JULIAN

Son of John and Cynthia Lennon (John's pre-Yoko wife) who recorded his own album in the '80s and had sort of a hit with "Too Late for Good-byes" and sung with the remaining Beatles at Live Aid.

See also BAND AID; LENNON, JOHN; REAGAN, RON, JR.

LE SAC

Little rectangular purse made out of nylon, duffel-bag like material that came in bright, primary colors. Were all the rage for the hip teen girl round about 1983 or '84. Many girls who had these graduated to Louis Vuitton bags later in life.

See also LEG WARMERS; NEON CLOTHES

LESS THAN ZERO

Life sure did suck for grown-up young people. If you believe the movies, we moved right from smoking dope in the library during Saturday detention to doing cocaine in our parents' Los Angeles mansions and New York nightclubs. This 1987 movie (based on Bret Easton Ellis' second novel) and its kind may be responsible for at least some of the nihilism and directionless associated with Baby Buster types.

See also BREAKFAST CLUB, THE; BRIGHT LIGHTS, BIG CITY; HEATHERS

LETTERMAN, DAVE

The man from Indiana has only become a megastar in the last few years, but since 1982, he has been defining the way many of us act, talk, and look at the world. He is a sarcastic fatalist who has little respect for the people who pay him, and his style has had a direct or indirect influence on the way much of our generation looks at life. The Top Ten list has become a national cliché, largely because no one can make one as funny as Dave's. He started doing much of what he does because when he was on at 12:30, no one much cared. Now, because Dave didn't care, a whole bunch of us do.

See also CARLISLE, BELINDA; JONES, TOM; *PAT SAJAK SHOW, THE*

LEWIS, CARL

The dominant track star of the 1980s. He was so good, in fact, that regular people, and not just runners, knew who he was, and he even did an endorsement or two. His breakout came at the 1984 Olympics in Los Angeles, where he won four gold medals, something no sprinter had done since Jesse Owens in 1936.

BONUS FACT: Lewis was drafted by the NBA's Chicago Bulls in the 10th round in 1984.

See also RETTON, MARY LOU

LIBYA

In between Soviet crises of the 1980s, and when Iran and Iraq were too busy fighting among themselves to pay much attention, this North African nation, run by cut-rate dictator Colonel Mu'ammar Qaddafi, served as a mini–Evil Empire for the kids in the Pentagon. With its support of various terrorist causes and the colonel's fervent anti-American rhetoric, the nation practically begged the United States to kick its ass, which the U.S. Navy did in the spring of 1985.

See also EVIL EMPIRE; GREAT SATAN; QADDAFI, MU'AMMAR; REAGAN, RONALD

LIKE

Word that can be used instead of commas. When used as every third or fourth word, it turns you into a teenage girl from the '80s: *She like wanted to go see that like new Cher movie, and I was like, "Yeah like Eric Stoltz is so hot," and she goes, "And like Cher is rad."*

See also GO; *MASK;* RAD; WAS LIKE

LIKE COLA

7-Up's brown beverage, or, more technically, caramel-colored beverage. Another casualty of the 1983–84 Cola Wars.

See also NEW COKE; PEPSI LITE; 7-UP GUY, THE

LIKE FATHER, LIKE SON

Worst of the parcel of kid-inhabits-parent's-body movies of the late '80s, probably because it starred Dudley Moore and Kirk Cameron.

See also BIG; CAMERON, KIRK; *FREAKY FRIDAY;* SWITCHAROOMANIA; *VICE VERSA*

LIMITED, THE

Little young-women's clothing store from Columbus, Ohio, that took over every shopping mall in America in the mid-1980s on the strength of really

They're not booing, they're saying "Da-a-ve."

cool, affordable jewelry and clothes that were trendier and nicer than that IOU and Generra crap down the hall, but not so cutting-edge that they looked weird. The Limited empire now also includes Express, Victoria's Secret, Structure, and Abercrombie & Fitch, to name a few.

See also IOU; MALLS; MERRY-GO-ROUND

LIN, MAYA

Young architecture student who won the right to design the Vietnam Memorial in 1982. Her design, and the fact that she is Asian, caused a lot of protests by veterans' groups, until it was finished and became a very powerful symbol of the lives lost in the war.

See also VIETNAM-MANIA

LITE BRITE

It was a box, and you had to put a lightbulb in it. It came with a bunch of colored pegs and some patterns that showed you where to put them. Insert pegs, turn on light, and Presto! Fun for the whole family.

See also SHRINKY DINKS

LITTLE HOUSE ON THE PRAIRIE

Popular show based on the Laura Ingalls Wilder books about a pioneer family in the late 19th century, starring Melissa Gilbert and Michael Landon, pre-angel. A Monday night staple for almost a decade.

See also CHILD STARS GONE BAD; HOGANS, THE

LITTLES, THE

Mid-'80s cartoon about a family of tiny people who lived in a house with a family of regular-sized people. They did this in secret, and only the kid from the big family knew what was up.

See also SMURFS; SNORKS, THE

LIVE-ACTION SUPERHERO SHOWS

There were several of these around the turn of the decade, when *Superman: The Movie* was a big hit on the silver screen. The most successful were *The Incredible Hulk* and *Wonder Woman*, which each ran for a couple of seasons. There was also a Spiderman show that ran on and off for about a year and a couple of Captain America TV movies. A few years later, *The Flash* was a mid-season replacement on CBS but lasted only a couple of episodes.

See also BATMANIA; CARTER, LYNDA; *INCREDIBLE HULK, THE*; *SIX MILLION DOLLAR MAN, THE*; *SUPERFRIENDS*; *SUPERMAN: THE MOVIE*; WAGNER, LINDSAY

LIVE AID

Huge concert to benefit hungry people, particularly those in Ethiopia. Like Band Aid, this was put together by Boomtown Rat Bob Geldof and involved pretty much anybody who was anybody in the rock 'n' roll world of 1985. There were two simultaneous all-day concerts, one in London and one in Philadelphia, and Phil Collins even Concorded across the Atlantic to play in both. Climax of the whole mid-

'80s feed-the-world pop activism thing, and kind of a rip-off of George Harrison's Concert for Bangladesh.

See also BAND AID; FUN DIP; HANDS ACROSS AMERICA; USA FOR AFRICA

LIVING COLOUR

Loud, aggressive, very cool rock group whose first album, *Vivid*, from 1989, might have been a huge success if people had been able to get past the fact that the band members were black but weren't rappers or R&B singers.

See also RAP

LIVING IN A BOX

Almost forgettable English band, except for the fact that they had a single that got some MTV play in 1987 that was called "Living in a Box," from their album *Living in a Box*. The long awaited follow-up, "Still Living in a Box," never materialized.

See also ANYTHING BOX

L.L. COOL J

He's going back to Cali. He's going back to Cali. He's going back to Cali. No, he doesn't think so.

BONUS THOUGHTFUL ANALYSIS: The man successfully adapted to the changing style of rap. He used boastful rhymes and heavy scratch-and-synth music on his first couple of albums, then moved into more sparse arrangements and smooth Mack-daddy vocals, then into more funk-driven beats. This has allowed him to have a much longer career than his Old School counter-

parts from the mid-'80s. Historically significant for recording the first rap ballad, "I Need Love."

BONUS FACT: The name, as we all know, stands for Ladies Love Cool James.

EXTRA BONUS FACT: His real name is James Todd Smith, but people in-the-know just call him Todd.

See also JONES, ORAN "JUICE"; *LESS THAN ZERO*; RUN-D.M.C.

LOC, TONE

Girthsome, gravelly voiced rapper who sampled Van Halen's "Jamie's Cryin'" on his own "Wild Thing" and sashayed off into hip-hop history.

See also CLINTON, GEORGE; RAP; SAMPLING; VAN HALEN; YOUNG MC

LOGGINS, KENNY

King of the movie soundtrack, lending his vox humana to *Footloose* ("Footloose" and "I'm Free [Heaven Helps the Man]"), *Top Gun* ("Danger Zone" and "Playing with the Boys"), *Caddyshack* ("I'm Allright"), *Caddyshack II* ("Nobody's Fool"), and *Over the Top* ("Meet Me Halfway").

See also CADDYSHACK; CARA, IRENE; FOOTLOOSE; TOP GUN; WILLIAMS, JOHN

LONE JUSTICE

Country and folk-influenced band, fronted by the beautiful and wild Maria McKee, who made a minor ripple on college and AOR stations in the mid-'80s with their songs "Shelter" and "Ways to Be Wicked."

See also BALTIMORA

Yikes.

LOOK WHO'S TALKING

Cloying, sickeningly cute movie from 1989, starring Kirstie Alley as a single mom and John Travolta as her would-be beau. It purported to show what babies think about before they can talk, with the little kid's voice provided by Bruce Willis. Yeah, we saw it, too.

See also CHEERS; DIE HARD; MOONLIGHTING; RETURN OF BRUNO, THE; SATURDAY NIGHT FEVER

LORD OF THE RINGS

Dark, weird animated movie about the hobbits and ogres and wizards and stuff living in Middle Earth and fighting for the power that the rings will give them. Directed by Ralph *"Fritz the Cat"* Bakshi and adapted from J.R.R. Tolkien's dark, weird books.

See also BLACK CAULDRON, THE; SECRET OF NIMH.

LOVE BOAT, THE

Aired back-to-back with *Fantasy Island* on ABC's Saturday night in the late '70s and early '80s and epitomized the creative black hole of the time. It featured a bunch of romantic losers who always left the ship hooked up with a fellow passenger. It made stars out of such dim lights as Bernie Kopell, Jill Whelan, Ted Washington, and Fred Grandy, and every other show seemed to have Betty White as a guest star.

See also DALLAS COWBOY CHEERLEADERS; FANTASY ISLAND; SPELLING, AARON

LOVE, SIDNEY

Sitcom about a gay bachelor (Tony Randall) who lived with a single mother and her daughter (Swoosie Kurtz and Kaleena Kiff).

See also DYNASTY

LUCAS

Few people saw this movie in theaters, but when it hit the video stores and came on cable, it became a favorite among the sensitive-teen set. It's the story of a mussy-haired, skinny kid (a still-adorable Corey Haim) who tries to impress an older girl (Kerri Green) by going out for football, even though he's never played and is half the size of everyone else. In a nice twist on the standard teen film, the older girl and her boyfriend (Charlie Sheen) are actually nice to Lucas. Also one of Winona Ryder's first big movie roles, in which she's a friend who Lucas doesn't notice but who has a mad crush on him.

See also COREYS; HEATHERS

LUCAS, GEORGE

If he had only worked as often as Steven Spielberg did in the 1980s, he could have had an even more profound effect on film and popular culture than he did as the director of *American Graffiti*, the creator of *Star Wars*, and the producer of *Raiders of the Lost Ark*. To see how brilliant this man is, try the following test. Rent *Logan's Run* and *Star Wars* some night. Watch them back-to-back, *Logan's Run* first, noting the differences in the quality of the film-making and, especially, in the visual effects. Then sit back and consider that the two films came out in consecutive years, *Logan's Run* in 1976, "Star Wars" in '77.

See also FORD, HARRISON; *HOWARD THE DUCK*; *JEDI MASTER'S QUIZ BOOK*; MAKING OF . . . SHOWS; *MILLENNIUM FALCON*; *RAIDERS OF THE LOST ARK*; SPIELBERG, STEVEN; *STAR WARS*; *THX 1138*

LUKA

Lives up on the second floor.

See also *DUKES OF HAZZARD, THE*; *STAR WARS*; 2 LIVE CREW

LUKE AND LAURA

Their wedding on *General Hospital* was just about the biggest thing ever to happen on daytime television, and ABC ran a contest to choose a couple whose wedding would be just like that of their two stars. An uproar ensued when they left the show, but when they came back, hardly a peep was heard.

See also STEFANO DiMERA VS. ROMAN BRADY

LUNDGREN, DOLPH

Say it to yourself a couple of times: Dolph. Dolph. Dolph. Can we really put our faith in an action hero named Dolph? Even if he is the largest, baddest man to come from Sweden? No. No we can't. Plus he killed Apollo Creed in *Rocky IV*. We can never forgive him for that.

See also MASTERS OF THE UNIVERSE; MR. T AND THE T FORCE; SCHWARZENEGGER, ARNOLD

M

MA BELL BREAKUP

A big news event that we knew about but couldn't quite grasp.

See also AMERIKA; IRANIAN HOSTAGE CRISIS

M.A.C.H. 3

Introduced right after Dragon's Lair, this second laser video game made you a fighter pilot or bombardier (your choice) and took you into battle with digitized, animated photos of enemy planes and bombing sites.

See also DRAGON'S LAIR

MacGYVER

TV action hero who was more Mr. Wizard than Magnum P.I. He never carried a gun and so had to rely on his smarts. Good thing, then, that he always carried a roll of duct tape and could make a bomb out of Bubble Yum and a packet of ramen noodles. He worked for yet another '80s secret society bent on righting the wrongs of the world (the Phoenix Foundation), was played by Richard Dean Anderson, and hung out on ABC for about seven years.

See also A-TEAM, THE; CRIME FIGHTING; EQUALIZER, THE; MR. WIZARD; SELLECK, TOM

MacKENZIE, SPUDS

Just another pit bull until 1987, when Budweiser put him (technically a her) in a commercial and dubbed him "The Original Party Animal." Soon, the little mutt's mug was everywhere, including on T-shirts that some grade schools banned because they supposedly endorsed underage drinking.

See also MIKE THE DOG

MacLAINE, SHIRLEY

A woman who transformed from a fairly distinguished actress to a New Age creature living on either the fringes or cutting edge (depending on your opinion) of consciousness and communication with aliens. Her book, *Out on a Limb*, detailing past lives and bodyless experiences, made her a best-selling author and favorite of tireless stand-up monologuists. And, oh yeah, don't tell anyone: She was in *Cannonball Run II*.

See also CANNONBALL RUN; E.T.; KELLY, KITTY; STAND-UP BOOM

MADD

Acronym for Mothers Against Drunk Driving, which was started in the late 1970s by a woman whose young daughter was killed by an intoxicated motorist, and which grew to be a powerful lobbying organization for tougher DUI laws, the raising of the drinking age to 21, and the force behind countless public service campaigns in the '80s.

See also GRANDFATHER CLAUSE; JUST SAY NO; THIS IS YOUR BRAIN ON DRUGS AD

MADISON, DOLLY

Competitor to Hostess in the snack-cake and individual pie arena. The Peanuts gang was the symbol of the product, and about the only time you ever saw a Dolly TV ad was when a Charlie Brown special was on.

See also TWINKIE THE KID

MAD LIBS®

These were _____ (adjective) and had just as many _____ (pl. noun) as _____ (proper noun). But nonetheless, we _____ (adverb) _____ (verb) them.

See also _____ (ENTRY IN THIS BOOK)

MAD MAX

In 1979 this Australian oddity defined the genre of postapocalyptic films, in which chaotic societies in the middle of deserts are ruled by gore-hungry bikers.

See also AUSSIEMANIA; *DUDES*; MEN AT WORK

MADNESS

Cool ska band whose one hit was a tame New Wave sort of thing called "Our House," but was still a lot cooler than just about every other New Wave song.

See also MODERN ENGLISH; NEW WAVE; YOUNG ONES, THE

MADONNA

When she appeared on Dick Clark's *American Bandstand* in the early 1980s, she told Dick her goal was to "rule the wold." She has gotten closer to that than probably any female performer in history, certainly in our lifetimes. She has successfully altered her public image many times, going from dance queen to "boy toy" to Material Girl to slut to god knows what, influenced fashion with each change, and strung together a huge collection of hits that span several styles of pop music. The woman has been a constant in our popular culture ever since the first strains of "Holiday" floated across the airwaves.

See also "BORDERLINE"; LAUPER, CYNDI; MTV; PENN, SEAN; REAGAN, RONALD

MAGIC SAND

At last! We could make sand castles underwater! And they were blue! This substance came in a little genie bottle and behaved just like sand . . . until you got it wet. Then it turned into some sort of atomically bonded concrete.

See also MAGIC SHELL; SLIME

MAGIC SHELL

Revolutionary new chocolate gunk that would get all hard when you put it on ice cream.

See also MESSY MARVIN

"Demented and sad, but
social."

—Another *The Breakfast
Club* classic, this one
from Judd Nelson, who
along with Molly Ring-
wald, Anthony Michael
Hall, Ally Sheedy, and to
some extent Emilio
Estevez, never really
escaped the '80s.

MAGNUM, P.I.

Tom Selleck had a good setup: He was the private security guy for a Hawaiian gazillionaire who was always out of town. He lived on the beach, retired from working in naval intelligence, and had lots of free time on his hands. So, naturally, he fought crime. Along with a gang of island regulars, he solved mysteries and preserved justice.

See also HARDCASTLE & McCORMICK; MATT HOUSTON; MOONLIGHTING

MAKEOVER BARBIE

This wasn't a regular Barbie, but rather a life-sized head made in the image of the blond vixen, upon which aspiring teenage girls could practice their makeup and coifing skills without damaging the skin or hair of a friend or relative.

See also BARBIE; CABBAGE PATCH KIDS

MAKING OF . . . SHOWS

These became a Hollywood cottage industry in the few years after *Star Wars* came out, and every filmmaker seemed to want to tell us how this or that scene was done. At any rate, because of these programs, we now know what a "blue screen" is.

See also STAR WARS

MALLS

As strange as it may seem, we're the first mass of Americans to be raised in a mall-dominated society. Malls as we know them didn't exist before the 1970s, a decade that saw thousands of the indoor mini-cities built in sub-

urbs. The mall became the center of all culture. Teenagers found their every need filled: record stores, clothing stores, fast food, movie theaters . . . and all their friends.

What this means is that we spent many of our formative years in the same place, no matter where we lived. A girl in Ohio had similar experiences, friends, and problems as a girl in Colorado. Not only was all of our art and entertainment imported from Hollywood, but our homes and neighborhoods and malls—where we spent a lot of time *growing up*—were almost identical.

See also FAST TIMES AT RIDGEMONT HIGH; I.O.U. CLOTHES; JELLIES; KNEE SOCKS; LEGWARMERS; LIMITED, THE; MERRY-GO-ROUND; SKINNY VINYL TIES; VALLEY GIRLS

MAMA'S FAMILY

Bad sitcom involving Vicki Lawrence (from the *Carol Burnett Show*) dressed up as the aging, nagging Mama Harper and yelling a lot. The whole show revolved around the fact that nobody got along. Mama was always tiffing with the handful of relatives living in her house, especially her locksmith son (Ken Berry) and his wife (Dorothy Lyman). This ran for more than two years ('83–'85) on NBC and then for another four in syndication.

See also IT'S A LIVING; NIGHT THE LIGHTS WENT OUT IN GEORGIA, THE; SMALL WONDER; WE GOT IT MADE

-MAN

Suffix that, when added to the name of an electronic appliance, makes it instantly portable. Usage began in

1979 with the Walkman, and it technically belongs to Sony, which also made the Watchman (television), Discman (a CD player), and Reporterman (a microcassette player). But the suffix can be generically applied, as in Blenderman and Fridgeman.

See also WALKMAN

MANDELA, NELSON

Leader of the African National Congress in South Africa. He spent all of the 1980s (not to mention the '70s and most of the '60s) in jail for rebelling against apartheid. "Free Mandela" was as popular a political statement as "Boycott Coke" in the U.S. rallying against racism in a foreign country. He got out in the spring of '90.

See also AMNESTY INTERNATIONAL; APARTHEID; FREE JAMES BROWN

MANHATTAN PROJECT, THE

Yet another kid-empowerment movie with a message. Our hero, an archetypal mid-'80s nerd (except he's got a girlfriend), wows the judges at a science fair by building an atomic bomb. As usual, the military gets involved and tries to kill the kid, who remains defenseless except for the power to destroy New York.

See also GEEK ERA; NERD; *NIGHT OF THE COMET*; *WARGAMES*

MANHUNTER

More cool stuff from producer/director Michael Mann, best known for *Miami Vice*. In 1986, this was a slick-and-sanitary look at mass murder, and

featured Hannibal "The Cannibal" Lecter in one scene.

See also BUNDY, TED; *CRIME STORY*; *MIAMI VICE*

MANIMAL

A very short-lived, Tartikoff-era NBC series about a doctor (Simon Mac-Corkindale) who could change into animals. He somehow gained this power and learned martial arts by watching the motions of forest creatures. He changed (or as we would say today, "morphed") into panthers and owls to fight crime, but the effects were low-grade and nobody watched it. Had this been a hit in 1983, technology and better writers could have made it one of the greatest shows in the history of television.

See also AUTOMAN; TARTIKOFF, BRANDON

MANNEQUIN

Worst movie ever.

See also RAISING ARIZONA

MAPPLETHORPE, ROBERT

Artist and photographer who really shocked people and started the downfall of the National Endowment for the Arts when, in 1989, the city of Cincinnati tried to have a show of his explicit, sometimes homoerotic work closed as a violation of local obscenity laws.

See also HARING, KEITH; 2 LIVE CREW

MARCOS, FERDINAND

President of the Philippines who

embezzled something like $300 million from the government and fled to the United States with his wife Imelda in 1986. He spent most of the time in the hospital and died a few years later.

See also BOESKY, IVAN; MARCOS, IMELDA; NORIEGA, MANUEL

MARCOS, IMELDA

She had a lot of shoes.

See also MARCOS, FERDINAND

MARRIED . . . WITH CHILDREN

One of the first Fox shows, and one that sort of came to define themes in the rest of the network's sitcoms: a put-upon lead character, raunchy jokes, and women not wearing much clothing. But for the talents of Ed O'Neill, this would be unwatchable.

See also FOX; *TRACEY ULLMAN SHOW, THE*

M.A.R.R.S.

Faceless one-hit wonder band responsible for "Pump Up the Volume."

See also BALTIMORA; JONES, ORAN "JUICE"

MARTIKA

More-anguished-than-thou teen-girl singer who had us crying in our Pepsis with her song "Toy Soldiers." For some of us, though, they were tears of pain caused by her plaintive wailing. In 1989 she released an even more moving, even less successful Prince-scripted tune, "Love Thy Will Be Done."

See also I WOULD DIE 4 U SIGN LANGUAGE; PRINCE

MARTIN, STEVE

Comedian/genius who has at least two late '70s catchphrases ("We are two wild and crazy guys" from his *SNL* Festrunk Brothers bit with Dan Aykroyd and "Excuuuuuse me!" from his stand-up act) to his credit, as well as a list of movies that run the gamut from stupid (*The Jerk*) to literary (*Roxanne*) to Baby Boomer angstfest (*Parenthood*).

See also TUTANKHAMEN

MARX, RICHARD

Big-haired singer from Chicago who first had a hit around 1987 or '88, and managed to hang around long enough to become a staple of lite-rock stations everywhere. His song "Hold on to the Night" was the theme for many a high-school dance in 1989.

See also HART, COREY; YOUNG, PAUL

MASH GAME

Another pen-and-paper game played during class, except this one not only wastes time but determines your future. What you did was this: You took a sheet of paper, drew a box on it and wrote at the top "M A S H," which stands for Mansion, Apartment, Shack, House. You ask your friend for four boys' names (usually three she likes and one she hates) and write those down one side of the box. Down the other side you write four cities. Across the bottom, four occupations (the last one should be something like "bum"). In the middle, write four numbers. Now you're ready to play.

Cup your hand so that your friend can't see the spiral you're drawing and say, "Tell me when to stop." When your friend says "stop," you count the rings in the spiral (let's say it's 4) and you start counting around the box—one, two, three, *four*—crossing out wherever you land on four. Do this until there's one thing left in each category and reveal to your friend her future: "You're going to marry Rick, be a veterinarian, live in an apartment in Berlin and have 25 kids." And, as your friend digests this news, somebody else who was watching yells, "I'm gonna tell Rick!"

See also NINJA THROWING STARS; PAPER FOOTBALL

MASK

Perhaps the harshest how-kids-can-be-cruel-when-you're-different movie ever made. And it was based on a true story. Not only was our struggling teen hero (a budding Eric Stoltz with lots of makeup) massively deformed, but his mother was Cher.

See also STOLTZ, ERIC

M.A.S.K.

Would-be G.I. Joe cartoon about a bunch of good guys and a bunch of bad guys who only get to act like good guys and bad guys when they have these big helmets with opaque visors and lots of gadgetry inside them on their heads.

See also G.I. JOE; MASK

MASTERS OF THE UNIVERSE

Yet another gang of heroes and villains we were invited to follow by watching their cartoon and buying their action figures. The story of He-Man's ongoing tiff with Skeletor had a vaguely medieval tone (swords, castles, black magic) with a futuristic edge (robots, spaceships, lasers, other planets). The action figures had huge bulky muscles, and some had a cool chest plate that, when struck, flipped over to look dented. Swedish android Dolph Lundgren tried his best to speak English as He-Man in the major motion picture.

See also ADVENTURE PEOPLE; COX, COURTENEY; G.I. JOE; *KRULL*; TEENAGE MUTANT NINJA TURTLES

MATHESON, TIM

King of teenage sexploitation films. He defined the quick-witted-sleazy-guy-who-spends-entire-movies-in-pursuit-of-untouchable-women archetype in *Animal House*, and then played almost identical characters in *1941*, *Up the Creek* and *Speed Zone*.

See also FLETCH; PORKY'S

MATT HOUSTON

Essentially an ABC rip-off of *Magnum, P.I.* with Pamela Helmsley (Princess Drago from *Buck Rogers*) and Lee Horsley as the title character.

See also FALL GUY, THE

"MAY THE FORCE BE WITH YOU"

Winner of the "Most Quoted Movie

Line" award for the '70s.

See also "Go ahead, make my day"; "I'll be back"; Star Wars

MAZES AND MONSTERS

TV movie made in 1982, during the height of the craze/concern over Dungeons & Dragons, about a bunch of college students who become obsessed with a role-playing game and lose their grip on reality.

BONUS FACT: Tom Hanks was in it.

See also Bosom Buddies; Dungeons & Dragons

Mc-

The prefix of the bourgeoisie. Putting this in front of any noun makes it cheap, disposable, and dumbed-down for the common people. The concept behind *USA Today*, for example, was largely referred to as McNews. Much of what's in this book could be described as McCulture, and this very entry belongs to a category called McLanguage.

See also -man; McDonald's in Moscow; USA Today

McAULIFFE, CHRISTA

Probably the most tragic part of the *Challenger* disaster was the fact that McAuliffe was on it. She was a teacher who had been chosen from a bunch of applicants to accompany the astronauts on their mission, and she would have been the first civilian in space. This also added a level of sad irony, since we were in school on January 28, 1986, and heard the news from our own teachers.

See also Challenger

McDLT

A most illogical sandwich that was only sold for a few years. It was basically a Quarter Pounder with Cheese split into two parts and served in a segmented Styrofoam container. One half housed the top bun with mayo, tomato, mustard, pickles, onions, ketchup, and cheese, while the bun bottom and the beef patty sat in another compartment. What this meant, according to the ads, was that the hot side stayed hot while the cool side stayed cool. But this arrangement provoked a few questions: How did the cool side stay cool underneath a heat lamp? Why was the cheese on the cold side? And who wants *any* part of a burger to be cold, anyway?

See also Happy Meals; Herb; Peller, Clara

McDONALD'S IN MOSCOW

A big deal. The opening of the Soviet Union's first McDonald's in 1990 was followed with a lot of talk about Planet Earth's bright future and also about how many rubles it took to buy a Big Mac.

See also Evil Empire; Gorbachev, Mikhail S.; Mc-

McDONALD'S MANTRAS

Chant along with us: "Big Mac, Fillet-o'-Fish, Quarter Pounder, french fries. Icy Coke, thick shakes, sundaes, and apple pies."

And don't forget how to assemble

the immortal Big Mac: "Two all-beef patties, special sauce, lettuce, cheese, pickles, onions, on a sesame-seed bun."

See also HERB; McDLT; MEOW MIX THEME, THE; PELLER, CLARA

McENROE, JOHN

Sure, he was a great tennis player, but his nastiness on the court and his love of the limelight (not to mention the fact that he was in a band with his doubles partner, Peter Fleming) made him a lot more recognizable than your average serve-and-volleyer.

BONUS FACT: In a tournament in 1987, Mac was the first professional athlete to wear the original Nike cross-training shoes (the gray and black, midcut ones) in an actual sporting event. His explanation: They're comfortable.

See also BO; NIKE

McFERRIN, BOBBY

This jazzy, rubber-voiced singer had a little advice for all of us: "Don't worry, be happy." He also did one season's version of *The Cosby Show* theme.

See also COSBY SHOW, THE; WILLIAMS, JOHN

McKENZIE, BOB AND DOUG

OK, like they were these two guys, eh? And they were these hosers from the Great White North, eh, whose, like, real names were Dave Thomas and Rick Moranis. Like,

they just used those other names to get beer, eh. So they made a movie called *Strange Brew*, eh, and it was, you know, a fine piece of film-making, and the basis for one of the most deadly drinking games ever conceived.

Also, these guys did a well-known cover of the "Twelve Days of Christmas" that ends every verse with " . . . and a beer!"

See also ELMO AND PATSY; HOSER; *STRANGE BREW*

McNICHOL, KRISTY

Adorable sprite of an actress we sort of remember from early '80s heart-tuggers like *Only When I Laugh* and *Just the Way You Are*, and the odd musical *The Pirate Movie*.

See also NIGHT THE LIGHTS WENT OUT IN GEORGIA, THE

MEAN PEOPLE SUCK

Another in a line of "be nice to people" bumper stickers to become popular in the late '80s, very likely a descendent of the Grateful Dead-inspired "Are you kind?" and "Practice random acts of kindness" stickers.

See also BABY ON BOARD; SHIT HAPPENS; VISUALIZE WORLD PEACE

MECHANICAL BULL

When Texas ruled the earth, Gilley's nightclub in Pasadena was its Coliseum, the competitions aboard this motorized bovine its chariot races, as sturdy warriors from across the prairie came to do battle with the mechanized beast.

See also TEXAS

MECHANICAL PENCILS

Cool-looking but less than fully functional writing utensils. The replacement leads broke pretty easily, and you couldn't use them on standardized Scantron tests because they weren't "No. 2."

See also ERASABLE-INK PENS; STA-SHARP PENCILS; TRAPPER KEEPER

MECO

Disco DJ who mixed a groove-worthy beat into the *Star Wars* theme and made it a No. 1 record.

See also HOOKED ON CLASSICS; STAR WARS; WILLIAMS, JOHN

MEESE, ED

Another one of those political names, like Caspar Weinberger and Tip O'Neil, that a lot of people remember but can't place. This Meese guy was attorney general under Reagan and commissioned a big report on the dangers of pornography in the mid-1980s, leading to much sniggering among comedians as to just how much research Ed did on his own for the report.

See also MAPPLETHORPE, ROBERT; PARENTAL ADVISORY LABEL; STAND-UP BOOM

MEGA-

Prefix that can be added to any word to increase its potency, as in: *"That, like, megasucks."* Can also be used by itself to describe an event of importance: *"You and Duke broke up?! Why didn't you tell me?! That's mega!!"*

See also HYPER-; VALLEY GIRLS

MELLENCAMP, JOHN

Birth name of the rock star from Seymour, Ind., who was first known to us as John Cougar. When, at first, he added "Mellencamp" to his stage name, then dropped the "Cougar" altogether, he was telling us that he was actually a serious artist, and not the skinny, leather-clad biker *poseur* from the "Hurts So Good" video. The break came with *Scarecrow*, his mid-'80s album that featured a title track about the plight of Midwestern farmers and some nice, down-home love songs.

See also FARM AID

MELLO YELLO

It took twentysomeodd years for Coca-Cola to knock off the elusive-tasting Mountain Dew (owned by Pepsi) with a yellow fluid of their own. Many people have associated Mello Yello with a particular part of the country, largely because it was available only in the Midwest and South for many years. And while Mountain Dew nurtured the "extreme sports" demographic, Mello Yello stuck with the NASCAR racing crowd.

See also JOLT COLA; MOUNTAIN DEW; YELLO

MEMBERS ONLY

Purveyors of the superhip Members

Only jacket, a must-have item for any mall-hanger worth his salt before jean jackets became the outerwear of choice in the mid-'80s. Available at Merry-Go-Round or down the corridor at Chess King. These were particularly cool if you hiked up the sleeves, and especially uncool if you had an imitation brand. We have a question, though: What were those little straps-with-snaps on the shoulders for?

See also I.O.U. CLOTHES; JEAN JACKETS; MALLS; MERRY-GO-ROUND

MEMOREX

Tape company that asked the age-old question "Is it live? Or is it Memorex?" and gave us the much-lampooned ad of a guy sitting in a chair, getting blown away by the sound coming from the tape in his stereo.

See also THIS IS YOUR BRAIN ON DRUGS AD

MEN AT WORK

The first of the hot Australian bands to hit the States, they paved the way for INXS and Midnight Oil. Their album *Business As Usual*, which featured the singles "Down Under" and "Be Good Johnny," was, for many of us, the first LP we bought. This was in 1983, the same year that hunky Aussie Mel Gibson also became a star.

See also AUSSIEMANIA; *MAD MAX*

MENUDO

Recyclable Puerto Rican teen idols who had their own video segments between Saturday morning cartoons on ABC.

See also SCHOOLHOUSE ROCK

MEN WITHOUT HATS

The album was *Living in China*, the

Movies That Won Best Picture in the '80s and Those That Should Have

Won		Really Shoulda Won
1980	*Ordinary People*	*Airplane!*
1981	*Chariots of Fire*	*Raiders of the Lost Ark*
1982	*Gandhi*	*Fast Times at Ridgemont High*
1983	*Terms of Endearment*	*The Right Stuff*
1984	*Amadeus*	Tie: *Brazil, Beverly Hills Cop*
1985	*Out of Africa*	*The Breakfest Club*
1986	*Platoon*	*Ferris Bueller's Day Off*
1987	*The Last Emperor*	*Raising Arizona*
1988	*Rain Man*	*Die Hard*
1989	*Driving Miss Daisy*	*Heathers*

song was "Safety Dance," and the craze had everyone spelling "S-S-S-S-A-A-A-A-F-F-F-F-E-E-E-E-T-T-T-T-Y-Y-Y-Y" and looking at our hands.

See also TIANANMEN SQUARE

MEOW MIX THEME, THE

Sing along now: "Meow meow meow meow. Meow meow meow meow. Meow *meow* meow *meow* meow meow meow meow. Meow meow meow meow . . . "

See also MCDONALD'S MANTRAS; MORRIS THE CAT

MERLIN

Those of us who had parents that wouldn't let us have Atari likely settled for this little handheld number, or its second-generation cousin Split Second, that let you play several games like tic-tac-toe, getting through a maze, and stuff like that.

See also SIMON

MERRY-GO-ROUND

Clothing store famous for faux-hip clothing lines like Generra and I.O.U., its location almost exclusively in malls, loud music to appeal to the young kids, and salesfolk who will tell you that everything you try on looks great so they can get their commission. Founded by Baltimore entrepreneur Boogie Weinglass, who was also the basis for Mickey Rourke's oversexed character in *Diner*.

See also I.O.U. CLOTHES; MALLS; ROURKE, MICKEY

MESSY MARVIN

That kid who sold us Hershey's Chocolate Syrup in TV ads. The accident-prone Messy Marvin (played by Peter Billingsley) had mussed-up blond hair, thick glasses, and a knack for spilling everything he touched—except, of course, that delicious Marvin-proof Hershey's goo.

See also CHRISTMAS STORY, A; MAGIC SHELL; REAL PEOPLE; RUSSKIES

METRIC SYSTEM

A logical and unified standard of measurement that would have us drive kilometers instead of miles and fill our tanks with liters instead of gallons. We learned all the units and conversions in school because we thought the whole country was going to go metric one day—just like Europe. But nothing ever came of the plan and we forgot most of it.

See also BETAMAX; DAT; HDTV

MIAMI VICE

Michael Mann's masterpiece of color and style created more national trends than episodes per year: shoes without socks, pastels, NBC, stubble, Glenn Frey and Jan Hammer and Phil Collins, cocaine and Colombia. Don Johnson and Phillip Michael Thomas were hothothot.

See also COCAINE; CRIME STORY; ESCOBAR, PABLO; INSIDERS, THE; MANHUNTER; NORIEGA, MANUEL

MICHAEL, GEORGE

He left Wham! so he could expand his

creative horizons and make the music he really wanted to make, which he did on *Faith*. Or so he said. We think it was just so his butt wouldn't have to share screen time in videos with Andrew Ridgeley.

See also WHAM!

MICHAEL JACKSON DOLL

Released at the height of the Strange One's popularity after *Thriller*, much was made about the supposed "anatomically correct" features of the figure. Of course, it was about as anatomically correct as any other doll out there, which made for a really funny Eddie Murphy bit on *SNL*.

See also MURPHY, EDDIE; *THRILLER*

MICRO MACHINES

Large numbers of small cars, trucks, planes, and other vehicle-type things that came in briefcase-style containers, which opened out to make a complete playset. Part of the miniaturizing trend in toys in the mid-'80s. Their pitchman was John Moschitta, Jr., the Federal Express guy.

See also GUY WHO TALKS REALLY FAST, THE; SMALL STUFF

MICROWAVES

These amazing machines invaded the kitchens of America at the same time VCRs took over the living room, making sure that nobody ever had to wait longer than 20 seconds for gooey Velveeta again. A favorite appliance of single folks, latchkey kids, and their

parents. Just don't put metal or poodles in them.

See also LATCHKEY KIDS; VCR

MIKE AND THE MECHANICS

Feeble attempt at a supergroup organized by Mike Rutherford of Genesis round about 1986. Basically, the songs ("Silent Running," "Taken In," "All I Need Is a Miracle") sounded just like Genesis, but without the nasal vocals of Phil Collins.

See also "LAND OF CONFUSION" VIDEO; *MIAMI VICE*

MIKE THE DOG

Fluffy black-and-white border collie who outacted Bette Midler in *Down and Out in Beverly Hills*.

See also DOWN AND OUT IN BEVERLY HILLS; MACKENZIE, SPUDS; MORRIS THE CAT

MIKEY

The kid from the "Mikey likes it" Life cereal ads who died after washing down a handful of Pop Rocks with Coke. Or so went the wholly untrue myth that spread through our elementary schools.

See also CAP'N CRUNCH; POP-TOP COLLECTING; RUMOR ABOUT RICHARD GERE, THE

MILKEN, MICHAEL

Another evil capitalist scum.

See also BOESKY, IVAN; KEATING, CHARLES

MILLENNIUM FALCON

This smuggler's ship, when the light-speed drive was working, did the

---

Movie lines we said a lot

"I've got a trig midterm tomorrow, and I'm being chased by Guido, the Killer Pimp."

—Theoretically, none of us was old enough to see *Risky Business,* but we all did. This line, along with the image of Tom Cruise in his underwear and Rebecca DeMornay out of hers, stuck with a lot of us.

Kessel Run in less than 12 parsecs. Or so Han Solo would have us believe.

See also Jedi Master's Trivia Quiz Book; Star Wars; Wedge

MILLER, DENNIS

The man who made sarcasm cool again as the anchorperson on "Weekend Update" during the brief renaissance of *SNL* in the late 1980s.

See also Saturday Night Live

MILLER LITE

The beverage that forever wedded the notion of sports and beer together with its ads featuring a bunch of old athletes getting into heated discussions over whether the brew tasted great or was, in fact, less filling. Didn't they realize it was both?

See also Beerland; MacKenzie, Spuds

MINIDISCS

Variety of compact disc that didn't last but a few years. They measured 3 inches across and held maybe three or four songs each, usually a single and its dance/house remix. You needed a plastic adapter to play these on most machines, and music labels started putting singles on full-size CDs anyway, making the minidisc virtually worthless.

See also CD Longboxes; Compact discs

MINISERIES

A surefire ratings smash for sweeps month. Big ones were *The Thorn Birds*, *Amerika*, *Shogun*, *V.*, *North and South*, *North and South Part II*, *Winds of War*, *War and Remembrance*, *A.D.*, *Pompeii*, *Roots*, *Space*, and *Billionaire Boys Club*.

See also Amerika; Roots; V.

MINIVANS

Machine in which we were too old to ride as kids, and are too young to drive as parents. Exceptions to this include anyone who has or whose parents had a VW microbus. Modern-day minivans were introduced in 1984 (as the Dodge Caravan and Plymouth Voyager) and pretty much killed both the van and the station wagon.

See also Iacocca, Lee; Vans (the vehicles)

MINOGUE, KYLIE

Bubbly, toothy Australian chanteuse who managed to take every last drop of soul out of "Locomotion" when she covered the song in 1988.

See also Aussiemania; Gibson, Debbie; Martika; Tiffany

MIRACLE ON ICE

The 1980 U.S. Olympic hockey team that won the gold medal in Lake Placid, N.Y. Only a few of its players lasted longer than a season in the NHL, and no one gave them any chance of winning anything. But their victory over the Soviets in the semifinals (punctuated by Al Michaels' famous call that gave the team's run its name) was a great moment, genuinely for most people and cynically for people who made a Cold War metaphor of it. The movie of the same name starred Karl Malden as hard-bitten coach Herb Brooks.

See also BAD NEWS BEARS, THE; EVIL EMPIRE

MISFITS OF SCIENCE

What would you do with a group of teenagers with psychic superpowers living in Los Angeles? Right. You'd have them fight crime and combat evil, just like in this one-season (1985–86) series on NBC. A scientist leads a band of junior-mutants in a quest for justice and world peace. One channels electricity through his finger, one can shrink to 6 inches, and another (Courteney Cox) can make stuff levitate. A familiar plot to those who read *The Uncanny X-Men* comic book.

See also Cox, COURTENEY; CRIME FIGHTING; WHIZ KIDS

MISSILE COMMAND

Before the kids at Atari learned how to make characters move on a video screen, they had this game, where you shot your lines at the lines advancing from the top, hoping they didn't reach your blobs first and make big circles.

See also ATARI

MISS LUCY

A clever hand-clapping game song that went a little something like this: "Miss Lucy had a steamboat and the steamboat had a bell (ding ding)/Miss Lucy went to heaven and the steam-

boat went to/Hell-o operator, please give me No. 9, and if you disconnect me I will chop off your/Behind the 'frigerator there was a piece of glass, Miss Lucy sat upon it and it went right up her/Ask me no more questions, I'll tell you no more lies, the boys are in the bathroom, zipping up their/Flies are in the city, the bees are in the park, and the girls and boys are kissing in the D-A-R-K, D-A-R-K, D-A-R-K dark dark dark."

See also CHINESE JUMP ROPE; "JINGLE BELLS" (ALTERNATIVE VERSION)

MODERN ENGLISH

English (duh) New Wave band who scored a hit twice with their song "I'll Melt with You," once when it was released in 1982 and featured in the end credits of *Valley Girl*, and again in 1990, when some nostalgic DJ started to play it again and it caught on. The band even remixed the song a little and released a new single and video.

See also DUH; *VALLEY GIRL*

MOHAWK

Hairstyle that only caught on among punkers and people who wanted to look dangerous. Mr. T did more than anyone to further the style—a straight-up streak of hair surrounded by a sea of baldness—but you could hardly call the Mohawk a rage.

See also A-TEAM, THE; HOW; PUNK

MON CHI CHIS

These ambiguous fuzzy creatures didn't really do anything, but on the strength of catchy commercial jingles ("Mon Chi Chi, Mon Chi Chi, oh so soft and cud-dle-ee!"), they became big sellers. You could, as the ads said, stick their thumbs in their mouths and wiggle their little feet.

See also KID SISTER; MY BUDDY; SHIRT TALES, THE

MONDALE, WALTER

Got beat like a rented mule in the 1984 election.

See also DUKAKIS, MICHAEL; FERRARO, GERALDINE; REAGAN, RONALD

"MONEY FOR NOTHING" VIDEO

One of the most memorable videos ever. Funky computer-animated appliance deliverymen griped along with Dire Straits and Sting about how those punks on MTV make their money for nothing and get their chicks for free.

See also MTV; "SLEDGEHAMMER" VIDEO

MONKEYMANIA

An unexplained phenomenon in the '70s and early '80s when producers and writers everywhere concluded (incorrectly) that monkeys were hilarious. Some fruits of this include Clint Eastwood's *Every Which Way but Loose* and *Any Which Way You Can; Mr. Smith*, a show about an orangutan on Capitol Hill; *B.J. and the Bear*, about interspecies truckin' buddies; *Lancelot Link: Secret Chimp*, a live-action, all-monkey spy show. Cartoons have always had a monkey mascot, too: *Space Ghost, Super-*

friends, *Speed Racer*, and *Grape Ape*.

See also BEDTIME FOR BONZO; GLEEK; JUSTICE LEAGUE OF AMERICA; MR. SMITH

MONOGRAMS

What every preppy boy and girl had to have on at least two sweaters, if not shirts as well.

See also IZOD; PREPPIES

MONTY PYTHON AND THE HOLY GRAIL

Great movie that many guys know by heart. You have to watch it over and over again just to catch all the jokes and to figure out what the bloody hell those Brits are really saying.

See also BRAZIL; HBO; HEADROOM, MAX; SPITTING IMAGE; VCR

"MONY MONY" CHANT

Anybody who has heard Billy Idol's version of "Mony Mony" (originally released in 1981, hit No. 1 in 1987) at a dance or club or any public place probably knows the supplementary lyrics. They're chanted between lines of the verses, and they go a little something like this:

BILLY: "Here she comes now, say Mony Mony."

CROWD: "Hey. Hey what? Get laid. Get fucked."

BILLY: "Shoot 'em down, turn around, come on Mony."

CROWD: "Hey. Hey what? Get laid. Get fucked."

Variations include, "Hey motherfucker. Get laid. Get fucked." We have no explanation for why we know this or what it has to do with the song. In interviews, Idol has said that he grooved on the Tommy James and the Shondells version of "Mony Mony" because it accompanied one of his first sexual experiences in the '60s. This may or may not explain things.

See also "Jingle Bells" (alternative version); Mikey

MOON BOOTS

Big-ass boots we had to wear in the snow as kids. They were made from seemingly radiation-proof plastics and created footprints that looked like tire tracks. Some even had zipper/Velcro pouches on the side.

See also Fat shoelaces; Jellies; Kangaroos; Vans (the Shoes)

MOONLIGHTING

Almost everybody watched this. For three years it had the most inspired writing on television, as David Addison (Bruce Willis) and Maddy Hayes (Cybill Shepherd) bickered and almost-got-it-together through some pretty good mysteries. But the last several seasons had some of the most insipid writing on television, after Dave and Maddy did the deed and Herbert Viola (Curtis Armstrong) and Agnes DiPesto (Allyce Beasley) started towing the plotline more. Overall, the most memorable episode was the spoof of Shakespeare's *Taming of the Shrew.*

See also Armstrong, Curtis; *Remington Steele*; *Return of Bruno, The*

MOPEDS

When you considered yourself too old for bikes, but weren't old enough yet to get a motorcycle license—around age 13 for most boys and some girls, too—these contraptions, especially those made by Puch, were the ticket to Shangri-La.

See also Green Machine; Yugo

MORK FROM ORK SUSPENDERS

People actually *wore* these thick, rainbow-colored fashion accessories in public.

See also Nanu-Nanu; Shazbot!

MORNING IN AMERICA

That would be the 1980s.

See also Reagan, Ronald

MORRIS THE CAT

Longtime spokesmammal for 9-Lives brand cat food. This rust-colored, finicky tabby said it was OK to be big, lazy, and a little bit flabby. Even if you're a TV star. America choked on a collective hairball of sympathy when he (actually played by a she) used the last of his own allotment of lives.

See also MacKenzie, Spuds; Mike the Dog

MOTHERFUCKER

In the modern common language of the United States, this word has developed as the single most vulgar expression. It came to common usage in popular media during the 1980s through movies and rap, industrial and metal music. The saturation of this once-unthinkable word is such that one day we'll surely hear it on network television.

See also FUCK

MÖTLEY CRÜE

One of the most respectable of the '80s big-hair, tight-pants, three-riffs-and-a-video bands to seep from the edges of heavy metal, largely because they were one of the first. Between "Smokin' in the Boys Room" ('85) and "Don't Go Away Mad (Just Go Away)" ('90), Vince Neil and Tommy Lee and the boys had become elder statesmen of the genre.

See also BILLY AND THE BOINGERS; BON JOVI; GREAT WHITE; POISON; RATT; WARRANT

MOUNTAIN DEW

A mysterious yellow beverage that, more than any other fluid on the planet, has been marketed at our generation. Pepsi bought the regional southern drink (originally designed as a nonalcoholic moonshine whiskey) in the early '70s and, almost a decade later, decided the market would be the youngsters of America. After several successful ad campaigns featuring thrill-seekers ("Dewin' it country cool!"), the tart sugar-water has come to symbolize energy, youth, vitality, and an inherent adventurousness.

It is also widely known that the semi-fizzy liquid has more caffeine than most sodas, which made it popular among those who like to stay up and stay hyper, particularly students and nerds. Two questions remain:

What flavor *is* it anyway? And why is it yellow?

See also BEERLAND; JOLT COLA; LIKE COLA; MELLO YELLO; NERD; NEW COKE; TAB

MOUNT SAINT HELENS

A volcano in Washington that erupted in 1980, filling much of the western United States sky with bits of dust. Many of us remember some weird, hazy days right after this happened. If you somehow got hold of a little container of the ashes from the explosion, you were cool.

See also BERLIN WALL; *CHALLENGER*; UNION CARBIDE

MOUSETRAP

Whoever came up with the design for the trap in this board game was an engineering genius and the bane to all adults whose 8-year-olds made them play it more than twice in one week.

See also ELECTRONIC BATTLESHIP; TRIVIAL PURSUIT

MOUSSE

Word that, before the 1980s, you rarely saw without "chocolate" in front of it. Then it came to mean a kind of foamy goo that you used to make your hair bigger, and which no high-banged teenage girl headed to the mall or young stock trader on the make could do without.

See also GEL; *WALL STREET*

MR. BILL

Made-of-clay *SNL* character who always seemed to find himself, with a fateful cry of "Oh noooo!" on the flattened end of some wacky situation or other.

See also S<small>ATURDAY</small> N<small>IGHT</small> L<small>IVE</small>

MR. DO!

Weak rip-off of the subterranean Atari classic Dig Dug.

See also A<small>TARI</small>; D<small>IG</small> D<small>UG</small>

MR. MICROPHONE

You talk into this wireless black tube, see, and your voice comes out of a nearby radio. Pretty cool, huh? Ad god Ron Popiel thought so. His mid-'80s TV spots featured people who looked absolutely *thrilled* to hear their own voices, including a carload of guys who used Mr. Microphone to inform a nearby pedestrian beauty: "Hey, Good Looking. We'll be back to pick you up later!"

See also P<small>OPIEL</small>, R<small>ON</small>

MR. MOUTH

Tiddlywinks for the Mechanized Age, with a giant, Pac-man looking thing that rotated in the center of the board, awaiting your flipped chips.

See also H<small>UNGRY</small> H<small>UNGRY</small> H<small>IPPOS</small>; P<small>AC</small>-M<small>AN</small>

MR. SMITH

A surreal Tartikoff-era NBC show about an orangutan named Cha-Cha with an IQ of 256 and a job as a U.S. government advisor. Ran in a nightmare lineup with *We Got It Made* and *Manimal.*

See also M<small>ANIMAL</small>; M<small>ONKEYMANIA</small>; T<small>AR-</small>TIKOFF, B<small>RANDON</small>; *W<small>E</small> G<small>OT</small> I<small>T</small> M<small>ADE</small>*

MR. T

Mohawked former bar bouncer and

One-man marketing empire Mr. T.

professional badass who first hit our consciousness as Clubber Lang in *Rocky III*, went on to *The A-Team,* and soon became a multimedia (and multigrain) star.

See also A-*Team; The*; "I pity the fool"; Mohawk; *Mr. T and the T Force*; Mr. T cereal; Pee Wee Herman; *Rocky*

MR. T AND THE T FORCE

Saturday morning cartoon in which Mr. T leads a bunch of teenage gymnasts in crusades against evildoers.

See also F<small>ONZIE</small> <small>CARTOON</small>; G<small>ILLIGAN'S</small> P<small>LANET</small>

MR. T CEREAL

Part of a nutritious breakfast . . . if you included eggs and toast and orange juice and Wheaties and a Flintstones vitamin. Featured in *Pee-Wee's Big Adventure.*

See also A-TEAM, THE; CAP'N CRUNCH; C-3POS; G.I. JOE CEREAL; MOHAWK; *MR. T AND THE T FORCE*; NERDS CEREAL; OJS; PEE-WEE HERMAN; SMURFBERRY CRUNCH; WAFFLE-OS

MR. WIZARD

Smart old science guy who, through his constant gee-whiz demonstrations of gravity, fire, and volatile-substances-dissolved-in-water on Nickelodeon's *Mr. Wizard's World*, inspired an entire generation of amateur pyromaniacs and explosives experts.

BONUS FACT: His real name? Mr. Don Herbert.

See also MACGYVER; 3-2-1-CONTACT!

MS-DOS

Or Microsoft Disk Operating System to you and me. Only real computer geeks knew about this in the early days, when most of us played games on our Apple IIes or Commodore 64s. But these five letters made all those IBMs and clones get up and go before something called Windows, and most people eventually had to learn a few of the funky DOS commands, like "dir" and "cd.." and "autoexec.bat." This was also what made Bill Gates the richest man in the world.

See also COMMODORE 64; EPCOT; GATES, BILL; SALT II

MTV

Perhaps no other single entity has influenced us more than this little enterprise that started on Aug. 1, 1981, and grew into the monster it is today. Original veejays J. J. Jackson, Martha Quinn, Alan Hunter, Nina Blackwood, and Mark Goodman guided us through the early years and were as recognizable to us as Dan Rather, Barbara Walters, and Peter Jennings. MTV has influenced the rest of television, too; rapid-fire editing and jumpy cameras have their roots in music video. Unfortunately, a lot of TV execs think the only way to get our attention is to imitate MTV's style, and the network has become self-important and rarely plays videos anymore. But, unlike anything else on TV, this station is ours.

See also "ADDICTED TO LOVE" GIRLS, THE; BUGGLES; *FRIDAY NIGHT VIDEOS*; HOT FOR TEACHER/JUMP/PANAMA; "LAND OF CONFUSION" VIDEO; "MONEY FOR NOTHING" VIDEO; *NIGHT TRAX*; PUTTIN' ON THE HITS; *REMOTE CONTROL*; "SLEDGEHAMMER" VIDEO; *SOLID GOLD*; THRILLER

MTV GENERATION

Another in a long line of labels that failed to stick to us for very long.

See also GENERATION X; YUPPIE PUPPIES

MUPPET MOVIE, THE

Similar in style to the old Hope-Crosby *Road to . . .* pictures, this film centered on the dreams a young frog and his bear friend have of making it to Hollywood. Along the way, though, they have to do battle with an evil proprietor of fast-food frog-leg joints and meet a lot of wacky characters, both Muppet and human. The songs, including "Moving Right Along," are classic.

See also HENSON, JIM; MUPPET SHOW, THE

MUPPET SHOW, THE

Jim Henson's prime-time variety show starring his creations and some cheesy celebrity guest host such as Dudley Moore and C-3PO. Some of the characters were truly funny, like Animal, Gonzo, Beaker and Dr. Bunsen Honeydew, Dr. Teeth (leader of the show's house band, The Electric Mayhem), the Boomerang Fish Act guy, and the geezers in the balcony.

See also DARK CRYSTAL

MURPHY, EDDIE

The biggest, funniest comedian of the 1980s.

See also DELIRIOUS; HINCKLEY, JOHN; MICHAEL JACKSON DOLL; SATURDAY NIGHT LIVE; STAND-UP BOOM

MURRAY, BILL

The king of self-aware sleaze. From the first time he did his lounge singer bit on *Saturday Night Live* ("Sta-ar, Wars! Every-thing's . . . *Star* Wars!"), he has made a career of playing guys who, if you knew them in real life, you'd hate, but on screen are some of the funniest people you'll see. His two classics are *Caddyshack* and *Stripes*.

See also CADDYSHACK; GHOSTBUSTERS; REITMAN, IVAN; SATURDAY NIGHT LIVE; STAR WARS

MUSCLE SHIRTS

Trendy garments that fell somewhere between T-shirts and tank tops and took hold of summertime fashion in the early '80s. They looked like T-shirts with no sleeves. Some came snug around the armpit (in order to make skinny guys look even ganglier), others had the appearance of having the sleeves violently ripped off. Way too many of these came in pastel colors.

See also MIAMI VICE; OP; PAINTER'S CAPS; PANAMA JACK; RIPPED SWEATSHIRTS

MY BUDDY

These dolls-built-for-guys didn't really do anything, but on the strength of catchy commercial jingles, they became big sellers.

See also CABBAGE PATCH KIDS; KID SISTER; MON CHI CHIS

MY LITTLE PONY

Cartoon and line of toys that featured horses with long, multihued manes and starry eyes. Little girls loved it, but most people over 10 found it nauseating.

See also CARE BEARS; RAINBOW BRITE; STRAWBERRY SHORTCAKE

MY SISTER SAM

CBS sitcom that starred Pam "*Mindy*" Dawber and Rebecca Schaeffer. Famous mostly, and unfortunately, because Schaeffer was killed by an obsessed fan who had been stalking her.

See also CHAPMAN, MARK DAVID; HINCKLEY, JOHN; MORK FROM ORK SUSPENDERS

N

Lines we said a lot

"Mr. McGee, don't make me angry. You wouldn't like me when I'm angry."

—Yes, there was a period when the Hulk was cool and you could buy inflatable green muscles and "Hulk out." Immortal line by Bill Bixby from *The Incredible Hulk*.

NANU-NANU

An omnifunctional word, sort of like *aloha* and *shalom*. In its Orkian context, it meant "hello," "good-bye," "nice shoes," "my refrigerator's broken," and pretty much anything else.

See also **How; Mork from Ork suspenders; Shazbot!**

NENA

Serious one-hit wonder from Germany who sang about 99 red, or *luft*, balloons.

See also **Falco**

NEON CLOTHES

In junior high, these were bigger than Menudo, especially in hues of pink and green. A neon sweatshirt worked best with a pair of two-tone jeans and those superhigh Converse Chuck Taylors that you could fold over and reveal yet another color.

See also **Jellies; Ripped sweatshirts; Swatches; Two-tone jeans**

NERD

A character that didn't have a defined image or recognizable stereotype until the early '80s. Thanks to the popularity of home computers and the creative efforts of Hollywood in the Geek Era, the nerd emerged as a cultural icon.

Just look for a few unmistakable characteristics: Skinny. Or fat. Male. Socially awkward, almost to the point of being a recluse. Unkempt, often with either greasy hair and/or severe acne. Fashionably challenged, wearing suspenders and polyester and short sleeve button-up shirts with—this is key—pocket protectors lined with pens and mechanical pencils. Laughs funny, often in a snorting manner. Has superhuman math/science/computer skills.

We usually explore the nerd's plight in a high school or college setting, where he can easily reveal the faults of more shallow social stereotypes like dumb jocks and hot women.

Some actors (Eddie Deezen) got typecast as nerds, while others (Val Kilmer in *Real Genius*, Anthony Michael Hall in *The Breakfast Club*) broke the geek mold and later played hunky cool Men. The "nerd" stereotype eventually broke down and diversified into hip subgroups like "hackers" and loser subgroups like "grown men who never have sex and die alone."

See also **Armstrong, Curtis; *Breakfast Club, The*; Commodore 64; Deezen, Eddie; Dungeons & Dragons; Edwards, Anthony; Geek Era; Jolt Cola; *Real Genius*; *Revenge of the Nerds*; *Riptide*; *Square Pegs***

NERDS CANDY

Tiny, sour pellets that looked like brightly colored pebbles and came in boxes divided up for two flavors. The mascots were cartoon versions of the candy pieces with eyes and frog-like legs, but that didn't keep kids from putting handfuls of friendly little Nerds in their mouth.

See also NERD; NERDS CEREAL

NERDS CEREAL

Gross.

See also CAP'N CRUNCH

NERF

Along with Wham-O, this company has to be the all-time why-didn't-I-think-of-that enterprise. Their idea: Take soft foam and shape it into balls that could be used indoors but wouldn't break anything. This eventually expanded from the amorphous Nerf Ball to Nerf footballs, Nerf basketballs, Nerf soccer balls, even Nerf dart guns and cross-bows.

See also CAPSELA; HACKY SACK; LEGO

NEUROMANCER

Essentially the Bible for cyberpunk, a fairly new subgenre of science fiction. William Gibson's dark novel of computer hacker thugs in the Future can take full credit for coining the phrase "cyberspace" and predicting the way we view the Internet (Gibson called it the Matrix) and virtual reality. And all this back in 1984.

See also *BLADE RUNNER*; CYBERPUNK; HEADROOM, MAX

NEW COKE

Easily the most colossal mistake in the history of beverages. In 1985, the formula to Coca-Cola, just about the most popular beverage on the planet, was changed. It wanted to be sweeter, like Pepsi. And this came right after Coke ran a big ad campaign with Bill Cosby saying it wasn't so sweet as that nasty Pepsi. Anyway, New Coke was pitched by the computerized noggin Max Headroom ("C-c-c-c-catch the wave!" he beckoned), but people just simply didn't like it. Or maybe they didn't like the idea. The beverage overlords brought back old Coke as Coca-Cola Classic and sold it alongside the new stuff (later named Coke 2 and then discontinued). And soon, life on Earth returned to normal.

See also APARTHEID; HEADROOM, MAX; JOLT COLA; LIKE COLA; PEPSI LITE

NEW EDITION

A hot collection of young R&B talent, all of whom are still around: Bobby Brown, Johnny Gill, Bell Biv Devoe, and Ralph Trevesant.

See also MENUDO; NEW KIDS ON THE BLOCK

NEW KIDS ON THE BLOCK

The white version of New Edition. These five boys—Donnie Wahlberg, Danny Wood, Joe McIntyre, and Jordan and Jon Knight—simultaneously pulled off being thuggish yet sweet, tough yet sensitive, annoying yet popular, wholesome yet pantsless. As expected, they had an army-sized following of young females. NKOTB put

ANOTHER OVERUSED CATCH-PHRASE: *"Who you gonna call?"*

Year: 1985

SOURCE: *Ghostbusters*

COMMON USAGE: Often said at the end of conversations instead of saying "call me."

ADVICE FOR PEOPLE WHO USED IT: You need, very badly, to stop doing that.

out a few albums (including a Christmas record) and toured with Tiffany. Donnie's brother, one Marky Mark, eventually took over the "being famous" part for a while.

See also DURAN DURAN; MENUDO; NEW EDITION; TIFFANY

NEW ORDER

Groundbreaking British band that almost got lost in the '80s synth-pop scene, largely because it kind of pioneered the music being made popular by lesser musicians (Real Life and Information Society). The only two songs of theirs that most people know, anyway, are "True Faith" and "Bizarre Love Triangle." Both were high school dance favorites.

See also DEPECHE MODE; "PARADISE BY THE DASHBOARD LIGHT"; SYNTH-POP

NEWTON-JOHN, OLIVIA

She made roller skating both hip and ethereal in *Xanadu*, and her song "Physical" was No. 1 for, like, a record 10 weeks in '81 and '82. But most of us remember her best as Sandy from *Grease*, which we've all seen a few dozen times.

See also GREASE 2; POLICE, THE; *XANADU*

NEW WAVE

A generic term that could be applied to most early '80s music—except R&B and heavy metal. Groups ranging from Madness to Erasure to the Talking Heads to Duran Duran to the Dead Milkmen were described as New Wave, but the term applied mostly to

synthesizer-driven European dance bands.

See also DURAN DURAN; HEAVY METAL BOOM; SYNTH-POP; WAVERS

NeXT

A computer that lacked popular appeal but made up for it in cool design. The main unit was a matte-black cube that looked like it might, if cracked open, reveal the infant Superman. But boy genius Steve Jobs' 1988 follow up to the Macintosh was almost too powerful and definitely too expensive for the general public, so those who cared either chalked it up as a flop or gathered all the equipment they could and called it a collector's item.

See also BIG BROTHER AD; JOBS, STEVE; *SUPERMAN: THE MOVIE*

NIDAL, ABU

Most dangerous and sought-after terrorist in the world. And, after Carlos the Jackal, the one with the best name. He and his anti-Israel gangstas (a group also called Abu Nidal and thought to be centered in Libya or Syria) were behind the 1985 airport bombings in Vienna and Rome that killed 16 people. Plus a whole lot of car bombings and assassinations. Pretty evil stuff.

See also ESCOBAR, PABLO; GOTTI, JOHN; KHOMEINI, AYATOLLAH RUHOLLAH; QADDAFI, MU'AMMAR; REAGAN, RONALD

NIELSEN, BRIGITTE

Gargantuan blonde who dated Sylvester Stallone, starred in *Beverly*

Hills Cop 2, *976-EVIL II*, and *Rocky IV*, made all sorts of star-worshiping headlines and then evaporated.

See also LUNDGREN, DOLPH; RAMBO

NIGHTLINE

A late-night ABC newsfest that started during the Iranian hostage crisis and opened up host Ted Koppel to decades of bad hair jokes.

See also IRANIAN HOSTAGE CRISIS

NIGHTMARE ON ELM STREET, A

Multi-sequel horror series that hit theaters about once a year beginning in 1984. The premise was simple: Freddy Krueger, a child murderer who was killed by a mob of parents, returns from the dead to kill those parents' children. It was the way he did it—invading their dreams to kill, and using a glove made of sharp knives—that made the first few interesting. Unfortunately, later installments were less creative, and Freddy was reduced to just saying "Bitch" before he cut someone. Johnny Depp got iced in the original.

See also FRIDAY THE 13TH; 21 JUMP STREET

NIGHT OF THE COMET

The least appreciated but most obvious of the kids-can-do-anything-by-themselves movies that fed on our imaginations and egos, and showed us all the wonderful things we wished we could do without our parents. This was the we-can-rule-the-world-all-by-ourselves movie where everybody on Earth dies except a handful of teens and preteens. (*A dream come true! We can play our music loud! We can screw all day long! Now, if only those zombies would leave us alone . . .*)

The moviemaking trend was guided by the whims of Steven Spielberg and peaked with *E.T.* (we can hide aliens all by ourselves), *Gremlins* (we can hide morphing Asian creatures all by ourselves), and *The Goonies* (we can explore caves all by ourselves). Also notable: *Stand By Me* (we can find dead bodies and learn about ourselves all by ourselves), *Explorers* (we can build a spaceship and meet aliens all by ourselves), *WarGames* (we can start World War III all by ourselves), and *Red Dawn* (we can fend off the commies all by ourselves).

See also CLOAK AND DAGGER; E.T.; EXPLORERS; GOONIES, THE; GREMLINS; KARATE KID, THE; MANHATTAN PROJECT, THE; RED DAWN; SPIELBERG, STEVEN; STAND BY ME; WARGAMES

NIGHT RANGER

Definitive proof that the years 1981–85 were among the most creatively bankrupt in the history of American popular music. Most Night Ranger songs featured a verse or two about young love, a repetitive chorus, and some very, very long guitar solos. Their hits included "Sister Christian," "Don't Tell Me You Love Me," "You Can Still Rock in America," "Secret of My Success," and "When You Close Your Eyes (Do You Dream about Me)," the video for which featured a monkey. The boys are still, we're sure, playing county fairs somewhere in this land of ours.

See also HEAVY METAL BOOM

NIGHT THE LIGHTS WENT OUT IN GEORGIA, THE

A 1981 movie about country singers and backwoods Southern lawmen, only sort of based on the 1973 Vicki Lawrence song. Starred Dennis Quaid, Mark Hamill, and Kristy McNichol.

See also DUKES OF HAZZARD, THE; MAMA'S FAMILY; MCNICHOL, KRISTY; STAR WARS

NIGHT TRAX

Another late-night video show (this one syndicated) meant to squeeze some viewers from the new MTV audience.

See also FRIDAY NIGHT VIDEOS; MTV

NIKE

Greek goddess of victory, she symbolized . . . oh, *that* Nike. The shoe company with the laid-back corporate culture, the one that first started to prosper during the jogging boom of the 1970s, then signed John McEnroe to its first big endorsement deal, then developed Air shoes, then signed Michael Jordan, then pioneered the idea of self-actualization and achievement through athletic apparel and advertising, and then took over the world. Yeah, we heard of that, too.

See also JACKSON, BO; JORDAN, MICHAEL; L.A. GEAR; MCENROE, JOHN; REEBOK; VANS (THE SHOES)

1984

Pretty big year.

See also ORWELL, GEORGE; VAN HALEN

9 TO 5

Depending on whom you ask, this 1980 movie starring Dolly Parton, Jane Fonda, Lily Tomlin, and Dabney Coleman was either a rallying cry for the women's movement or a silly update on *How to Succeed in Business Without Really Trying* and an excuse for Parton to cash in on the title song. There was also a TV series starring none of the principals.

See also COLEMAN, DABNEY; *HARPER VALLEY PTA*

NINJA THROWING STARS

Objects made by folding two sheets of notebook paper in a certain way and tucking them together. It had four corners and could be decorated and thrown across the elementary school or junior high classroom at your buddy, who probably had a few of his own. These were popular during the height of ninja fascination among the youngsters of America (notable role models were the ninja from G.I. Joe, the Teenage Mutant Ninja Turtles, and Wolverine from the X-Men). Some guys even had real, metal throwing stars they kept in little boxes and talked about in hushed tones.

See also PAPER FOOTBALLS; TEENAGE MUTANT NINJA TURTLES

NIXON, MOJO

Songwriter/maniac/genius responsible for the cautionary tune "Elvis Is Everywhere" and the tender ballad "Debbie Gibson Is Pregnant with My Two-Headed Love Child."

See also ELVIS HAS LEFT THE BUILDING; GIBSON, DEBBIE

NOID, THE

Psychotic Claymation creature who wanted nothing more than to stomp all over your pizza and delay the delivery guy. Domino's claimed they could keep this skinny red freak at bay.

See also CALIFORNIA RAISINS; COOKIE CRISP

NORAD

Another alphabet-soup defense agency that protected us from those big, bad Soviets during the Cold War.

See also SALT II; *WarGames*

NORIEGA, MANUEL

A bad guy with a bad complexion. Usually referred to as "Panamanian strongman Manuel Noriega," he was actually the country's president and was also apparently involved in all sorts of bad-guy stuff, like running drugs and laundering money and (as the rumors went) working for the CIA. So in 1990 and in the interest of ridding the world of drug-dealing heads of state, President Bush sent troops down to nab him. Manuel hid out in a Vatican mission and requested asylum from the Pope, while Marines tried to annoy him out of hiding by blasting very loud, very

bad '80s music at him (like Guns 'N Roses). Eventually, he gave up and came to the U.S. for trial and lots of publicity.

See also BREZHNEV, LEONID; COCAINE; GOTTI, JOHN; GUNS 'N ROSES; QADDAFI, MU'AMMAR

NORTH, OLIVER

A former U.S. Marine who came to celebritydom by being the most visible bad guy in the Iran-Contra Affair. He handled himself so well in front of a congressional committee (and on live television) that he turned his image around, crafting himself as a superpatriot who struggled against the evils of communism and intrusive government and stuff like that. But the record still showed that he was a weasel.

See also CLANCY, TOM; HALL, FAWN; IRAN-CONTRA THING; REAGAN, RONALD; STONE, OLIVER

NORTHERN LIGHTS

The Canadian version of Band Aid.

See also BAND AID; LIVE AID; USA FOR AFRICA

NORVILLE, DEBORAH

Perky blonde who worked the early-early-morning news on NBC for a while in the mid-'80s and moved in on Jane Pauley's perky blond monopoly of the *Today Show*. The tabloid press painted her as a conniving, backstabbing tart, and, eventually, she left the show to work for the tabloid press as host of *Inside Edition*.

See also SAVITCH, JESSICA

NOT NECESSARILY THE NEWS

A rip-off of Britain's *Not the Nine O'clock News*. The American version starred Rich Hall and Harry Shearer, aired on HBO, and is best known for the "Sniglets" feature.

See also SNIGLET; SNIGLETS

NÜSHOOZ

Man-woman duo who used the latest recording technology to make like they had a full band backing them on the 1986 single "I Can't Wait." The video featured a bunch of shoes moving around by themselves.

See also BALTIMORA; MÖTLEY CRÜE

NUTRASWEET

Artificial sweetener that appeared in 1983 and has all but eliminated the need for saccharin. A massive marketing campaign got us all used to the name (much friendlier than its technical moniker, aspartame) and logo.

See also IBUPROFEN; SACCHARIN

NWA

When these rough-mouthed, raw-ass, straight-up, gun-to-your-head-so-you-best-listen motherfuckers started selling *Straight Outta Compton* in 1988, the easy-going world of Young MC and D.J. Jazzy Jeff and the Fresh Prince vanished. Members included, among others, Dr. Dre, Ice Cube and Eazy-E.

See also D.J. JAZZY JEFF AND THE FRESH PRINCE; MOTHERFUCKER; RAP; YOUNG MC

O

OAKLEY STICKERS

Giant adhesive signs that came free with a $90 pair of trendy late '80s Oakley shades and which many people secured on the upper edge of their front windshield. Apparently, the sticker indicated how cool you were. The glasses themselves boasted scratch-proof lenses made from something called Uridium™, which would probably kill Superman, and the sticker said, "Thermonuclear Protection," which was probably a lie.

See also Hart, Corey; *Risky Business* dance; Shit Happens; *Superman: The Movie*; Vuarnet

OAK RIDGE BOYS, THE

Harmonizing country band who had a big hit on both the country and pop charts with a song called "Elvira." (C'mon, sing along in your best fake bass voice: "Giddy up, ah-oompah-pah, oompah-pah mau-mau.")

See also Dukes of Hazzard, The

OAT BRAN

A scientist somewhere declared that this mysterious substance might help stop heart disease, and so oats started showing up everywhere: Cereal, muffins, pills, whatever. Prepacked foods started sprouting little yellow starbursts: "Contains oat bran!" Hell, somebody could have even made money with a chewing gum called "Oat Blow."

See also Big League Chew; Rice Cakes

OCEAN, BILLY

Smooth crooner who had several hits in the 1980s, including "Caribbean Queen" and "Get Out of My Dreams, Get into My Car," the theme song from that Coreys movie, *License to Drive*.

See also Coreys, The

O'CONNOR, SANDRA DAY

Her 1981 appointment to the Supreme Court was hailed as a major advance for women everywhere, but something tells us that the fact that Reagan appointed her tempered the feminist joy a touch.

See also Bork, Robert; Dallas Cowboy Cheerleaders

OCTOBER 19, 1987

Black Monday, as it was called. The Dow dropped something like 500 points that day, and a few stockbrokers reportedly did similar things from their office windows. That sad spectacle gave rise to the *SNL* falling-stockbroker cuckoo-clock gag. Quite

---

Between March 20 and May 8, 1987, two of the best sex scandals of the decade erupted. First, tearful televangelist Jim Bakker admitted his dalliance with church secretary Jessica Hahn. He would later go to prison for stealing funds from his PTL ministry. And then on the second date, leading Democratic presidential contender Gary Hart dropped out of the race after the *Miami Herald* caught him with model Donna Rice the previous weekend.

possibly signaled the death knell for the yuppie life and conspicuous consumption that marked the decade.

See also BOESKY, IVAN; KEATING, CHARLES; MILKEN, MICHAEL; TRUMP, DONALD; TZU, SUN; *WALL STREET*; YUPPIES

OFFICER AND A GENTLEMAN, AN

Movie about Navy officers-in-training that had Richard Gere for the ladies to eye and Louis Gossett, Jr. (as a true badass) for the guys to enjoy. If only that song "Up Where We Belong" hadn't ruined everything. Imitating the final scene, in which Gere sweeps Debra Winger off her feet and hauls her away, has been a sitcom staple ever since.

See also GOSSETT, LOUIS, JR.; RUMOR ABOUT RICHARD GERE, THE

OH MY GAWD

Popular Valley Girl variation on the standard "oh my god" phraseology used to denote disgust. For maximum effect, a pause should be inserted between each word: "*Oh (pause) my (pause) gawd! That Wacky Wall Walker is, like, sooooo grody.*"

See also OMIGOD; VALLEY GIRLS; WACKY WALL WALKERS

OJs

A short-lived cereal that looked like little oranges but tasted like Apple Jacks, which don't taste like apples at all.

See also CAP'N CRUNCH; C-3POs; G.I. JOE CEREAL; MR. T CEREAL; NERDS CEREAL; SMURFBERRY CRUNCH; WAFFLE-OS

OMD

This stands for Orchestral Maneuvers in the Dark, a band best known for doing "If You Leave," which is best known as "that song from *Pretty in Pink.*"

See also PRETTY IN PINK

OMIGOD

Common among Valley Girl types as a way of expressing excitement: "*Omigod! Jack Wagner just, like, looked at me!*" This phrase is said very quickly and should not be confused with "oh my god" or "oh my gawd."

See also OH MY GAWD; LIKE; WAGNER, JACK

O'NEAL, TATUM

Daughter of Ryan who starred in *The Bad News Bears* and hung with John McEnroe for a while.

See also BAD NEWS BEARS, THE; FOSTER, JODIE; MCNICHOL, KRISTY; NIKE

ONE CENT

What 13 records or tapes would cost you if you joined Columbia House through a magazine ad in the late '70s. You just taped your penny to the order card and mailed it in.

See also K-TEL; TROLL/SCHOLASTIC PRESS

$1.98 BEAUTY PAGEANT, THE

Humiliation TV at its, uh, finest.

See also BLOOPERMANIA; GONG SHOW, THE

O'NEIL, TIP

Speaker of the house during much of the Reagan Era. He looked sort of like W.C. Fields and did commercials for computers after retiring.

See also COMMODORE 64; MEESE, ED; REAGAN, RONALD

OOKLA THE MOK

Furry sidekick in postapocalyptic Saturday morning show *Thundarr the Barbarian*. This character's resemblance to Chewbacca the Wookiee from *Star Wars* would be easier to forgive if the rest of the show wasn't also an obvious rip-off. (The Sunsword wasn't *exactly* a lightsaber. And Princess Ariel wasn't *quite* a Princess Leia clone; she had one more letter in her name.)

See also STAR WARS

OP

Brand of clothing that was hot around the same time as Jams and Panama Jack stuff. Ocean Pacific T-shirts, muscle shirts, and shorts came mostly in bright and pastel colors, featured icons from surfing culture (beaches, boards, silhouettes of attractive people), and could be bought at a mall near you.

See also JAMS; MALLS; MUSCLE SHIRTS; PANAMA JACK; VANS (THE SHOES)

OPERATION

From Milton Bradley. You know, the wacky doctor game. Where you remove his spare ribs for one hundred dollars. As the ads said, "It takes a very steady hand."

See also CONNECT FOUR; ELECTRONIC BATTLESHIP; HUNGRY HUNGRY HIPPOS; MOUSETRAP

ORWELL, GEORGE

Dead author who made a huge comeback in, of course, 1984. His pseudo-prophetic *1984*, written in 1948, topped best-seller lists and stirred up all kinds of societal self-analysis about how far we've come and where we're going and so on. "Big Brother" became a buzz phrase. Many mistook the growing omnipresence of cameras, computers, television sets, phones, and other smart technologies as markers on the road to Room 101. And while these are now seen more as a leap *away* from the Thought Police, toward freedom of movement and personal control of information, the paranoid view of technology persisted for a while.

A lot of us just had to read the book for English class and didn't think about that stuff at all. The movie (released in—*duh!*—1984) flopped, despite a cool soundtrack by the Eurythmics.

See also BIG BROTHER AD; *BRAZIL*; HEADROOM, MAX; VAN HALEN

OSBOURNE, OZZY

Bit the heads off live bats in concert.

See also KISS

OSMOND, DONNY AND MARIE

This brother-sister team and the rest of their large Mormon clan had a variety show in the '70s that was so clean you could see your reflection in it. Other things we know: Donny wore purple socks and attempted a comeback in the late '80s and early '90s. Things we don't know: What happened to Marie, and why anyone watched the show.

SEE ALSO BARBARA MANDRELL & THE MANDRELL SISTERS; *GREAT BRAIN, THE*

OUTLINER PENS

A fairly useless writing utensil that, for some reason, became popular in early '80s elementary and middle schools. These made thick lines of metallic silver or gold with very thin color borders, which, for some reason, was cool. The main part of the pen had one of those spray-paint pellets inside (it rattled when shaken) and the tip retracted back into the body if you pressed too hard. These would bleed through a sheet of paper, write on almost any other surface—Trapper Keepers, balloons, your arm—and never came off.

See also ERASABLE-INK PENS; STICKERS; TRAPPER KEEPER

OUTSIDERS, THE

This 1983 social yarn (from the S. E. Hinton book) essentially created the Brat Pack, along with *St. Elmo's Fire* and *The Breakfast Club*. The Greasers and Socs included: Tom Cruise, Leif Garrett, Matt Dillon, C. Thomas Howell, Ralph Macchio, Patrick Swayze, Emilio Estevez, Rob Lowe, and Diane Lane. Francis Ford Coppola directed, and Stevie Wonder wrote the theme song, "Stay Gold."

See also BRAT PACK, THE; *INSIDERS, THE*

P

PAC-MAN

A little yellow circle that ate dots, went "wakka wakka wakka," and became the first superstar of the video game age. Pac-man's simplicity (eat the dots, avoid the ghosts unless they're blue) and addictiveness drew millions of kids into the arcade habit. He eventually had a cereal, a Saturday morning cartoon, and a series of sequels, including Ms. Pac-man (with moving fruit bonuses) and Pac-man Jr., the first combination pinball-video game.

BONUS FACT: The ghosts in the original game were Pinky, Blinky, Inky, and Clyde.

See also ATARI; BUCKNER AND GARCIA; PATTERN, THE; SATURDAY SUPERCADE

PAINTER'S CAPS

A baffling '80s fashion phenomenon. These white cloth cylinders-with-brims resembling baseball caps have traditionally been worn by people *painting houses*. But the caps started showing up on teenagers' heads (many stamped with the OP logo) and a trend was born. Some had two cloth flaps hanging down the back, giving the owner that stranded-in-the-desert, or "*Ishtar*," look. Complete the outfit with a pastel muscle shirt, a Swatch (with Swatch Guard), Jams, Vuarnet shades (with fluorescent Croakies) . . . and you'll look just like a guy from the '80s!

See also CROAKIES; *ISHTAR*; MUSCLE SHIRTS; OP; PANAMA JACK; SWATCH; SWATCH GUARDS; VUARNET

PANAMA JACK

A brand of sun-tanning products better known for promotional paraphernalia than oils. Most popular were T-shirts decorated with the mug of Mr. Jack, a smiling and well-tanned gentlemen wearing a Panama hat. Often worn with Jams.

See also JAMS; OP

PAPER FOOTBALL

First you fold up a piece of notebook paper into a tight little triangle (most boys knew the pattern). Then you use it to play football across the lunchroom table or with the guy in the desk in front of you. You alternate turns pushing the triangle, trying to make it stop with just a corner off the edge of the table, thus scoring a touchdown and allowing you to kick for a bonus point by flicking the football through a goalpost your friend made with his fingers, hopefully hitting him in the face.

See also NINJA THROWING STARS; SUPER BOWL SHUFFLE

PARACHUTE PANTS

Slick and baggy and covered in zippered pockets, these were a staple of the "breakdancing look." Also cool because they looked like you could wear them in outer space or, of course, when parachuting.

See also Bandannas; Breakdancing; Ripped sweatshirts; Vans (the Shoes)

"PARADISE BY THE DASH-BOARD LIGHT"

Operatic ode to teenage love as sung by a big fat guy named Meat Loaf. Many of us know all the words to this lengthy piece (including the baseball-sex analogy play-by-play from Phil Rizzuto), even if we never owned Meat Loaf's *Bat Out of Hell* or saw *Rocky Horror*. This was a favorite at high school dances.

See also Americathon; Rocky Horror Picture Show, The

PARENTAL ADVISORY LABEL

Yet another attempt to regulate the ever-growing, ever-accessible content of media available to kids. This black-and-white rectangle containing the warning "Explicit lyrics" started showing up on CDs and tapes and albums in the late '80s, signifying bad language or sex or violence or some other force of evil. This, of course, had the opposite effect intended by proponent Tipper Gore, and made CDs with the label way cool.

See also Fuck; Gore, Tipper; PG-13; 2 Live Crew

PARTON, DOLLY

Country superstar and subject of about one third of all jokes made by smart-mouthed 10-year-old boys in the late 1970s.

See also 9 to 5

PARTS IS PARTS

When the Great '80s Burger Wars turned into the Chicken Nugget Wars, Wendy's ads attacked McNuggets on the grounds of the meat's unclear origins. The campaign, a weak follow to the "Where's the Beef" series, had a pseudo-McDonald's cashier explaining that "parts is parts" and that it doesn't matter what's in the nugget and the angry customer declaring that Wendy's nuggets had nothing but breast meat and were, therefore, better.

See also Chicken McNuggets

PATIENT ZERO

Most people have heard about this guy, who is credited with single-handedly spreading the AIDS epidemic to the North American gay community. One of the first people known to die of the disease, Gaeton Dugas was a particularly horny Canadian airline steward who had sex with thousands of men in the late '70s.

See also AIDS

PAT SAJAK SHOW, THE

This, an attempted bridge between the worlds of late-night and game shows, died quickly. (*Audience reac-*

We all loved Pee-Wee's Big Adventure, and in a way, it prepared us for the whole masturbating-in-a-theater thing.

tion: "Awwwwww!") A Guy Smiley show would have been much cooler.

See also **SESAME STREET; WHITE, VANNA**

PATTERN, THE

If you didn't know it, there was pretty much no way that you were going to get on that high-score list on Pac-man down at the local arcade.

See also **PAC-MAN**

PC JR.

A tiny machine IBM created to compete with the Commodore 64 and Apple IIe, which dominated the growing early '80s home PC market. Notable for the ad campaign, which featured Charlie Chaplin look-a-likes.

See also **ALSO APPLE IIE; COMMODORE 64; GATES, BILL**

PEBBLES

Very un-Flintstone-like singer who asked us if we wanted to ride in her Mercedes, boy. Not heard from since, so we assume the car's been repossessed.

See also **BALTIMORA**

PEE-CHEE FOLDERS

Cheap, semi-generic folders that were sort of yellow and decorated with simple drawings of people playing sports.

See also **TRAPPER; TRAPPER KEEPER**

PEE-WEE HERMAN

You can look at this character created by Paul Reubens in two ways: a grown man who acts like a little kid, or just an eccentric with super-sophisticated taste and mannerisms.

All these guys are famous now. Who'd a thunk it?

Either way, the man is a freak. For some reason he was all-the-rage for a few years between the Tim Burton-directed *Pee-wee's Big Adventure*, the Saturday morning goof-fest *Pee-wee's Playhouse*, and Reubens' arrest for jerking off in a public porn theater.

See also BURTON, TIM; *EMMANUELLE*

PELÉ

The only bona fide superstar to emerge from the world of soccer. He helped Brazil win the World Cup three times, joined the New York Cosmos in '75 as the highest paid athlete on the planet, and then starred in the absurd Nazi-soccer-action film *Victory* with Sylvester Stallone.

See also MIRACLE ON ICE; SOCCER

PELLER, CLARA

The lovely little old "Where's the Beef?" lady, bless her soul. We're sure she didn't mean to, but she started a national craze and a fast-food ad war with her commercial for Wendy's. The creative spree ended about a year later with the ill-fated unveiling of Herb by Burger King. Peller's quip also spawned T-shirts, bumper stickers, beef patty–oriented school cafeteria pranks, and presidential-election taunts.

See also HERB; McDLT; PARTS IS PARTS; WACKY WALL WALKER

PENN, MATTHEW

This songwriter (and brother of Sean) used a weird instrument called a

chamberlain in his song "No Myth," which, despite its obscure literary references, enough people understood to make the tune popular.

See also PENN, SEAN

PENN, SEAN

Real quick, a few '80s highlights: Starred in *Fast Times* and *Colors*. Married Madonna. Beat up a photographer. Divorced Madonna. Became serious actor.

See also *COLORS*; *FAST TIMES AT RIDGEMONT HIGH*; MADONNA

PENN AND TELLER

Magic and comedy team that came from the '80s, making themselves famous by sheer force of will. Penn is the big one who talks, and Teller is the diminutive mute and straight man. Regulars on the late-night shows, the duo also appeared in the Run-D.M.C. video for "It's Tricky" as street hustlers.

See also LETTERMAN, DAVE; RUN-D.M.C.

PEPPER, A

It's what I am. It's what he is. It's what she is. It's what we all are. Wouldn't you like to be one, too?

See also MEOW MIX THEME; NEW COKE

PEPSI CHALLENGE

Sometime around the middle of the 1980s, the folks over at Pepsi made a startling revelation: Apparently, somebody *else* was out there selling *another* fizzy brown beverage loaded with sugar and caffeine. And this other company, called something like Coca-Cola, had been at it even longer. Imagine! So Pepsi, what they did was this: To fend off rumors that their fizzy brown beverage was exactly the same as Coke, and thus a rip-off, they staged something called "The Pepsi Challenge." They set up booths in malls and in front of supermarkets, and they gave people two little unmarked cups, one with Coke and one with Pepsi, and asked them which tasted better. We all drank, we all judged, we all continued drinking whichever one we drank before. Nobody really knows which beverage actually won the Challenge, despite the ubiquitous commercials featuring shocked fluid sipper after shocked fluid sipper deeming Pepsi the more delicious product.

BONUS MOMENT OF RAW, RAGING '80S TEENAGE REBELLION: Many raucous youngsters, sick of being told to take the Pepsi Challenge, sick of being told that Pepsi should and does taste better, fine-tuned their taste buds (Pepsi's sweeter, folks), flocked to the malls, and intentionally voted for Coke, hoping to tip the scales.

See also APARTHEID; NEW COKE

PEPSI FREE

Short-lived mid-'80s caffeine-free cola immortalized in *Back to the Future* when Marty McFly asks a 1955 soda jerk for a Pepsi Free, only to be told that if he wanted a Pepsi he was going to have to pay for it.

See also BACK TO THE FUTURE; JOLT COLA; NEW COKE; TAB

PEPSI LITE

Pepsi with a twist of lemon. Very short-lived. Its spokesmen were a bunch of NFL linemen. You figure it out.

See also JOLT COLA; NEW COKE

PERESTROIKA

The policy of implementing *glasnost*. Probably a made-up word.

See also EVIL EMPIRE; GLASNOST

PERFECT

The scene is the office of a Columbia Pictures executive, circa 1984. He is hearing a pitch from one-time *Rolling Stone* reporter Aaron Latham.

Latham tells him about this exposé he did on the aerobics fad. Not bad, the exec thinks, aerobics is hip, it's hot. His movie script, based on that story, is about how this reporter (who works, as luck would have it, for *Rolling Stone*) goes undercover to expose the aerobics fad. But he falls for this one instructor, see, one that he's going to thrash in the story. What should he do to resolve this dilemma?

Somehow, this story actually got made, with John Travolta as the intrepid journalist and Jamie Lee Curtis as the instructor. Shame on that Columbia executive.

See also AEROBICS; *STAYING ALIVE*

PETE'S DRAGON

Disney did this live-cartoon movie in 1977 about an orphan kid and his protective, some say imaginary, dragon buddy in a small seaside town. It also starred Mickey Rooney, who was doing just about every movie of this kind at the time, and Helen Reddy.

See also **Black Cauldron, The**; **Black Stallion, The**

PET SHOP BOYS

Was it us, or did the United States not produce any pop music in the 1985–86 fiscal year? Because these two guys, along with about 57 other thinly talented British groups, bands with names like Wet Wet Wet and Johnny Hates Jazz, all had hits around that same time. The Petters' were "Opportunities" and "West End Girls" from their album *Please*.

See also **Frankie Goes to Hollywood**

PETTY, TOM

When he came onto the scene around the turn of the decade, folks didn't know quite what to make of him. Was he New Wave? The skinny ties he and his band, the Heartbreakers, wore said yes. But wait . . . he drew influence from a lot of rock pioneers, and could even go a little country. Whatever, he has been around ever since, and most rock fans, regardless of their particular favorite subgenre, probably wouldn't switch the radio if one of his songs came on. Except maybe "Free Fallin'."

See also **Skinny vinyl ties**; **Traveling Wilburys, The**; **Valley Girls**

PG-13

The first new movie rating in recent history. The all-mighty Motion Picture Association of America made this up in 1984, right about the time that many of us were 13 or so. It followed a stink made about violent movies aimed at the younger set, particularly the PG-rated *Indiana Jones and the Temple of Doom*, which featured a guy ripping out another guy's heart and holding it up and laughing. The first official PG-13 films—*Red Dawn* and *Dreamscape*—came out the same week.

See also **Dreamscape**; **Parental Advisory labels**; **Red Dawn**

PHANTOM TOLLBOOTH, THE

A classic children's book by Norton Juster that was, when it came right down to it, about math and science. But the story of a kid lost in a strange world full of irrational numbers and silent valleys and big dog-like creatures seemed much cooler than geometry textbooks. A favorite read among the more "intellectual" kids in elementary school.

See also **Chronicles of Narnia, The**; **Wrinkle in Time, A**

PHILLIPS, LOU DIAMOND

There are only two ethnicities this guy hasn't played: black and white. He was a Mexican in *La Bamba* and *Stand and Deliver*, a Native American in *Young Guns*, an Eskimo in *Shadow of the Wolf*, and he could probably pass for Italian, Arabic, and Swedish—all at the same time.

See also **Young Guns**

PHOTON

The clumsy predecessor to Lazer Tag, where contestants paid to run around an arena with infrared guns and shoot at blinking plastic chunks on each other's bodies.

See also LAZER TAG

PICTIONARY

OK, so you picked a card that had a word on it, like "existentialism." Then you got a little pad, and you had about two minutes to draw what the word was, and your teammates had to guess what the word was. And you couldn't talk or use any numbers or letters in your drawing. What this usually boiled down to was: one person doodled something stupid-looking, while everybody else in the room yelled. Great fun.

See also ELECTRONIC BATTLESHIP; TRIVIAL PURSUIT; WIN, LOSE OR DRAW

PINCHOT, BRONSON

A perfectly normal-voiced actor whose only fame has come from playing dumb guys from far-off lands who have unplaceable accents, namely Balki in *Perfect Strangers* and Serge, the art gallery guy in *Beverly Hills Cop*.

See also DUMB GUY; MURPHY, EDDIE

PIONEER 11

Sent back really cool pictures of Saturn and its rings in 1979 and was the subject of many a show-and-tell for science-minded kids.

See also COSMOS; SKYLAB

PISCOPO, JOE

Funnier before he started working out.

See also SATURDAY NIGHT LIVE; JOHNNY DANGEROUSLY

PLAQUE

Did anybody get this before the '80s, when it became the topic of scary toothpaste commercials?

See also BALTIMORA; GINGIVITIS; PUMP TOOTHPASTE; TARTAR

PLATOON

Gruesome, violent, disturbing, and hugely popular film that, by winning a bunch of Oscars, begat Vietnam-mania. For two years there, just about every other movie had a 'Nam twist. Thank you, Oliver Stone, for sending late '80s moviegoers back into the jungle.

See also FULL METAL JACKET; STONE, OLIVER; VIETNAM-MANIA

PM MAGAZINE

Cutesy, post-evening news show that flourished for a few years around the turn of the decade, when everyone was doing Minicam reports. The show was a quasinational, syndicated thing that had the same logo in every market and some of the same stories. But the hosts (usually a perky male-female tandem) were local or regional folks, and they usually did one of their own stories.

See also NIGHTLINE

Another big moment in our lifetimes

On Nov. 9, 1989, East Germany allowed its citizens to move freely across the Berlin Wall to West Berlin. Euphoric Germans from both sides of Berlin took sledgehammers to the structure and danced on top of it.

PMRC

The Parents' Music Resource Center, a group founded in the mid-'80s by Tipper (Mrs. Al) Gore to combat all those smutty lyrics and evil messages in rock music. Succeeded in getting those advisory labels put on albums with lots of nasty language.

See also GORE, TIPPER; PARENTAL ADVISORY LABELS

POCKET PANTS

The big brother of parachute pants. Made by companies like Bugle Boy and Banana Republic, these pants featured usually two extra pockets sewn onto the legs, usually around the knee. A hip item from 1985 to 1987, after which it was cool to cut them off about a third of the way up on the leg pockets.

See also PARACHUTE PANTS

POINDEXTER

The nerdiest character in *Revenge of the Nerds* (played by Timothy Busfield, the redheaded guy on *thirtysomething*) or one of the central figures in the Iran-Contra scandal. Take your pick.

See also EDWARDS, ANTHONY; IRAN-CONTRA THING; NORTH, OLIVER; *REVENGE OF THE NERDS*

POINDEXTER, BUSTER

He had huge hair, a spiffy suit, and one song: "Hot! Hot! Hot!"

See also ERASERHEAD; FALCO

POISON

The catchiest, poppiest of the "hair metal" bands, they asked us to talk dirty to them while doing the unskinny bop and having nothin' but a good time. Then they reminded us that every rose has a thorn and that every cowboy sings a sad, sad song.

See also BON JOVI; CINDERELLA; RATT; VAN HALEN; WARRANT

POISON IVY

A TV summer-camp movie with NBC teen stars Nancy McKeon and Michael J. Fox. The pair also starred in another film, *High School USA* or something.

See also FACTS OF LIFE; FAMILY TIES

POLAROID

A brand name that quickly became a generic term for any picture taken with an instant camera. This emerged in the late '70s when people started clicking the amazing (if bulky) machines and developing film by waving little squares in the air and then peeling off the chemical-soaked cover sheet.

See also DISC CAMERAS; VELCRO; WALKMAN

POLE POSITION

Racing game from Atari that gave you a choice of tracks to run, provided you passed the time trial.

See also ATARI

POLICE, THE

One of the few popular bands of the early '80s to still be considered cool once the epoch expired. Ex-schoolteacher Sting and band mates Stewart Copeland and Andy Summers drew from a lot of other kinds of music to make their own songs and wrote some good lyrics to go with them. They eventually had one of the top-selling singles of the entire decade, "Every Breath You Take" (only three '80s songs spent more time as the Billboard No. 1 song: Olivia Newton-John's "Physical," Kim Carnes' "Bette Davis Eyes," and Lionel Richie and Diana Ross' "Endless Love"). The album *Synchronicity* was a big early music buy for a lot of us.

See also DUNE; DURAN DURAN; HYPER-; NEWTON-JOHN, OLIVIA; RICHIE, LIONEL

POLICE ACADEMY

The movie series that wouldn't end. OK, the first one, which came out in 1984, was watchable, but the subsequent five or six, or however many, were just so much charity for the likes of Bubba Smith and the guy who makes noises and the meek female officer and the guy who played Rizzo on *M*A*S*H*. Steve Guttenberg was smart enough to get out after four of these.

See also PORKY'S; SOUND EFFECTS GUY; ZUCKER BROTHERS

POLICE ACADEMY RIP-OFFS

The *Police Academy* formula of sex and general silliness in the otherwise stiff-backed law enforcement environment led to a series of shameless copycats, including: *Stewardess School* (with Donny Most), *Vice Acad-*

emy (parts 1–3), *Honeymoon Academy*, *Moving Violations*, *Feds!* (with Rebecca DeMornay), and *Speed Zone*.

See also MATHESON, TIM; *PORKY'S*

POLTERGEIST

Horror movies enjoyed a renaissance from the late '70s to the mid '80s, thanks in no small part to this film directed by Tobe Hooper, produced and written (in part) by Steven Spielberg, and starring Craig T. Nelson and JoBeth Williams. It was less downright scary and more spooky and eerie. For months after, saying "They're here" in a little-girl voice was a sure way to give someone the chills. Inevitably, there was a sequel, and inevitably, it wasn't as good.

Weird deaths involving cast members only made the movies spookier, though: Heather O'Rourke, the tiny Carol Ann, died of a sudden illness after making *Poltergeist III*, and Dominique Dunne, who played her sister, was strangled by an ex-boyfriend.

See also CALL TO GLORY; FRIDAY THE 13TH; NIGHTMARE ON ELM STREET, A; SPIELBERG, STEVEN

PONG

The innocent little game from Atari that started it all.

See also ATARI

POPEMOBILE

Strangely stylish semi-convertible car built to protect Pope John Paul II after a Turkish radical shot him in 1981. The pontiff, who previously

Why?

walked around towns he visited, had to start waving to fans from inside the bulletproof bubble thing in the back of the car. And, even though the Pope being shot isn't funny, the word "Popemobile" is, so people started using it.

See also DeLorean; *Knight Rider*; Yugo

POPIEL, RON

Advertising god behind products that cost $19.99 and were seen during daytime TV, like the Veggiematic and Pocket Fisherman and Mr. Microphone. But wait, there's more! He was also an important innovator in the genre of infomercials.

See also Mr. Microphone; Soloflex

POP ROCKS

Little bits of crystallized carbonation, sugar, and fake flavor that you put in your mouth so they could jump around. And no, no kid ever died from swallowing pop rocks and then drinking Coke, although he probably did get a tummyache.

See also Mikey; Nerds

POP-TOP COLLECTING

An inexplicable phenomenon in which most every school in America had one or two kids who collected the pop-tops from soda cans. Friends would know to save theirs for The Collector, who had a box or bag full of the things and said they would help a kid with leukemia or some other disease. Where these collectors got their information, and what good pop-tops

would do for this mythical Sick Child is unknown.

See also Fuck tab; Mikey; Mony Mony Chant

PORIZKOVA, PAULINA

Brunette supermodel familiar from mid-'80s overexposure, teenage boys' bedroom walls, and a 1989 Tom Selleck movie called *Her Alibi*. Inexplicably married to Ric Ocasek, gaunt singer for the Cars.

See also Kinski, Nastassja

PORKY'S

The first and most famous of the films in the early '80s teen-sex film pantheon, the one that was most talked about when guys spent the night with each other in fifth grade. Then, when we finally saw it, it was like, *So what?* The plot of this movie, and pretty much all the others like it, involved numerous sexually frustrated guys, a few peripheral loose women, and a seemingly unattainable Beautiful Girl. The good-natured working-class guys, one of whom was always dumb or fat or both, would compete against the rich snobs for the Beautiful Girl. The entire film would make references to "going all the way," but no one ever saw more than a pair of breasts and a few bare butts. These films were loosely based on, but not true to, the plot of *Animal House*. Others in the genre included the *Porky's* sequels, the *Hardbodies* movies, *Spring Break, Up the Creek, Private Resort, My Tutor, Hot Dog: The Movie, H.O.T.S., 1941, The Last*

American Virgin, and *Screwballs.*

See also MATHESON, TIM; *POLICE ACADEMY*

POST-ITS

One of the most significant advances in the area of communication since the invention of the intercom. According to the often-repeated legend, a young chap at 3M came up with an adhesive that would stick to paper without tearing it and could be reused, and he did it accidentally, while trying to create some other futuristic substance. The result is all those little squares of brightly colored paper all over your computer at work now.

See also KRAZY GLUE; VELCRO

POUND PUPPIES

Adorable stuffed critters with sad eyes and droopy, wrinkly skin that were sold under a cruel, if very subliminal, premise: *If you don't take this fuzzy guy home . . . well, you know what happens to unwanted dogs at the pound.* Kind of sick.

See also CABBAGE PATCH KIDS; SMURFS; STRAWBERRY SHORTCAKE; TEDDY RUXPIN

POUND SIGN, THE

That would be this thing: #

Before phone mail and voice mail, nobody knew what to call the thatch mark on telephone keypads. Now we know it's called the pound sign, but we don't know why.

See also ANSWERING MACHINES

POWER STATION

A minor incarnation of the very '70s phenomenon, the supergroup. This one consisted of two members of Duran Duran (John Taylor and Andy Taylor) and Robert Palmer. They had two big songs: "Some Like It Hot" and a remake of T-Rex's 1972 "Get It On (Bang a Gong)."

See also "ADDICTED TO LOVE" GIRLS, THE; ARCADIA; DURAN DURAN; *GONG SHOW, THE*

PREPPIES

Back in the early 1980s, tiny little alligators who lived just above the hearts of young humans ruled the planet, often taking over their hosts' minds and making them dress in such colors as pink and lime green, wear deck shoes without socks, and drape sweaters over their necks while they tooled about in their Alfa Romeos. Eventually, the alligators left, and their hosts grew up to become yuppies.

See also COLLARS TURNED UP; IZOD; YUPPIES

PRESLEY, ELVIS

Fat old drug addict who died on the john in 1977.

See also COSTELLO, ELVIS; ELVIS HAS LEFT THE BUILDING; NIXON, MOJO

PRESTO MAGIX

A step up from coloring books. Colorful characters were negatively attached to a piece of wax paper, and you created your own work of art by rubbing them onto the supplied cardboard background. Available in violent (for boys) and pretty (for girls).

See also Iron-ons

PRETTY IN PINK

Classic John Hughes–written romance that took teenage cliques to the extreme. Molly Ringwald lived in a working-class neighborhood and hung out with eccentric Duckie (Jon Cryer) and then fell for a guy from the rich side of the tracks, the adorable Andrew McCarthy, who got a lot of shit from his evil, classist buddy James Spader for liking a poor girl. Fun, fun, fun. Sort of like *The Outsiders*, except nobody died.

See also Hughes, John; OMD; *Outsiders, The*; Ringwald, Molly

PRINCE

When we stopped listening to *Thriller* and started to get interested in that sex thing, along came Prince, in his ruffly shirts, tight pants, and sparkly purple coat. He first entered our consciousness with *1999*—both the album and the song, and the single "Little Red Corvette." Then he went megasuperhuge with *Purple Rain*, and everyone knew his guitar player's name (Kamikaze) and the backup singers (Wendy and Lisa). He surrounded himself with kind of his own mini-movement, making The Time and Sheila E. successful acts and indirectly spawning bands like Ready for the World. His stage shows and those of his entourage played like an updated version of the best funk bands of the '70s, complete with

lasers and outrageous costumes. He had his own label, Paisley Park, and made a few movies, all of which sucked.

See also Art of Noise, The; Martika; Ready for the World; Sheila E.; Time, The; Vanity

PRINCIPAL, VICTORIA

Dallas vixen who quickened many a pulse when she appeared on screen or, later, in one of her exercise tapes. She was so hot, in fact, that the readers of *People* magazine said she had the best body of any female in March of 1983.

See also Dallas; Fonda, Jane

PRIVATE BENJAMIN

This 1980 film starring Goldie Hawn was among the first R-rated movies our parents would let us watch on HBO. Later a TV series.

See also HBO; *Red Dawn*

PUBLIC ENEMY

The years of 1987 and 1988 were nice times for rap. Run-D.M.C. were playing their role of elder statesmen well; the Beastie Boys, those obnoxious white kids from Brooklyn, had introduced hip-hop to a pretty wide audience; and artists like Rob Base, Biz Markie, and even LL Cool J were making basically fun, easy-to-swallow songs. Then came the release of *It Takes a Nation of Millions to Hold Us Back*, an incredible album put together by Chuck D and his crew, and rap was pretty much turned on

Chuck and Flav come correct.

neered the way human beings dispense toothpaste. The Tube would no longer do. Empty toothpaste containers should not look like curled-up, squeezed-up snakeskin. This idea erupted into a marketing frenzy as every major toothpaste maker tried to create the best Pump, the fluoride dispenser of the future. The results all resembled tiny missile silos: upright plastic cylinders with a trigger and nozzle on top. They defied gravity! They never shriveled up! They failed! This phase passed, the humans of Earth returned to their tubes, and the next big toothpaste crisis campaign, Tartar Control, began.

See also ALASKA PIPELINE; GINGIVITIS; PLAQUE; TARTAR

its ass. Chuck and whacked-out sidekick Flavor Flav rapped about a racist power structure in America, police abuse, and black people still fighting for rights that should have been theirs long ago. Most radio stations refused to play it because it wasn't "safe" enough; it didn't matter. *Nation of Millions* is one of the best-selling rap albums ever, and when someone looks back on the history of hip-hop years from now, its release will be a watershed moment.

See also BEASTIE BOYS, THE; RAP; ROB BASE AND D.J. E-Z ROCK; RUBIN, RICK; RUN-D.M.C.

PUMP TOOTHPASTE

Sometime in the mid-'80s, somebody *somewhere* decided that the world could not go on unless we reengi-

PUNCH-OUT

This boxing game was unique in that your point of view and that of the character you controlled were the same. Consequently, all you ever saw of yourself was your arms, and the opponent was always in front of you.

See also ATARI

PUNK ROCK

This music had been moping at the fringes of the record business since the early 1970s with bands like the Stooges and MC5, but it exploded with the 1977 debut of the Sex Pistols in England. Over here, the Clash was the best-known band, but they were disparaged as sellouts when they signed with a major label. Punk rockers generally didn't really know how to play their instruments, but they were

You're on your way to school in 1987. You're a guy. You have on a pastel pink Ocean Pacific T-shirt, a white linen jacket with the sleeves rolled up and matching pants with the *cuffs* rolled up. No socks. Top siders. Glenn Frey's "Smuggler's Blues" going through your head.

angry at what rock 'n' roll had become, and that anger went a long way. With the exception of the Clash, punk hardly made a blip on any '70s or '80s charts, but it has had more influence than any other kind of rock on today's monster that we call alternative music.

See also ATHENS, GA.; CLASH, THE; NEW WAVE; R.E.M.; SYNTH-POP

PUNKY BREWSTER

A perky little sitcom that emerged from the same brilliant mind as *Knight Rider*, *Manimal*, and *The A-Team*. Raging genius/NBC head Brandon Tartikoff must have pulled this tale about an abandoned girl (Soleil Moon Frye) living with a crusty landlord (George Gaynes) from the bottom of his heart. Indeed, the show was

named after a girl that Tartikoff knew growing up, and Punky's TV dog was even named Brandon. On the Saturday morning cartoon *It's Punky Brewster*, the sharp-witted orphan kicked around the neighborhood with a floating magical being called Glomer.

See also A-TEAM, THE; GLOMER; KNIGHT RIDER; MANIMAL; TARTIKOFF, BRANDON

PUTTIN' ON THE HITS

With music video came the inevitable idea of "Hey, let's have ordinary folks like you and me act like they're in a music video." The result was this relentlessly bad lip-sync show starring Allen Fawcett, who gave away cash and prizes to the people who could mouth the words and air-guitar better than all their competitors.

See also SOLID GOLD

Q

QADDAFI, MU'AMMAR

Nobody could figure out how to spell this swarthy Libyan dictator's name. The networks and major papers all had trouble: Was it Gadhafi? Qadhafi? Kadaphi? And was it Mohamar? Moammar? Anyway, Reagan made one of his most memorable speeches after we bombed Libya in retaliation for a number of suspected terrorist attacks. In his quickie tirade, the President actually said, "You can run, but you can't hide."

See also REAGAN, RONALD; TERRORISM

QADAFFI, MOHAMAR

See also QADDAFI, MU'AMMAR

QADDAFFI, MOHAMAR

See also QADDAFI, MU'AMMAR

QADDAFI, MOHAMAR

See also QADDAFI, MU'AMMAR

QADHAFI, MOHAMAR

See also QADDAFI, MU'AMMAR

A bad guy, no matter how you spell it.

Q-BERT

The game featured a little ball of fur, looking not unlike a McDonald's Fry Guy with a big schnoz, jumping on squares of a pyramid while avoiding the evil furballs and falling stuff. The cartoon featured . . . oh, come on, no one watched the cartoon.

See also ATARI; PAC-MAN; SATURDAY SUPERCADE

QUEEN

Along with Pink Floyd, The Who, Led Zeppelin, Rush, and Yes, these cool "older" bands somehow made us think our musical tastes were maturing beyond Quiet Riot, Skid Row, and New Edition. This stuff was, after all, the "roots" of real rock 'n' roll. Styx counts, too. Sort of.

See also DOMO ARIGATO; HEAVY METAL BOOM; IRON EAGLE; REMO WILLIAMS

QUEST FOR FIRE

Weird, no-talking (except in made-up languages) movie about a long-ago tribe that loses its fire and has to go find some more because it hasn't figured out how to make it yet. Kinda cool, actually, in a bizarre way.

See also CAVEMAN; CLAN OF THE CAVE BEAR

QUIET RIOT

A weak early '80s metal band whose only decent songs were covers of tunes by Irish rockers Slade, such as "Cum on Feel the Noize" and "Mama, Weer All Krazee Now." The lead singer wore a hockey mask in all the videos; nobody's sure why.

See also FRIDAY THE 13TH; TWISTED SISTER

QUIK RABBIT

An anomaly in the animated world of kid commercials, this bouncing rodent with a jones for powdered chocolate actually had access to the product he sold. All the while, the Trix rabbit, Fred Flintstone, and the Cookie Crisp thief couldn't get their hands on the sugary snacks they loved so much, being denied nourishment at every turn by spiteful kids. But the Quick rabbit and Lucky the Leprechaun (who turned the tables and kept the Lucky Charms all to himself) gave us confidence that not *all* cartoon characters starved to death.

See also COOKIE CRISP; FLINTSTONES CHEWABLE VITAMINS

R

RACQUETBALL

When fit Baby Boomers traded in their first jogging shoes in the late 1970s, they often chose to buy miniature versions of tennis rackets and hard, blue rubber balls, then head to the club to play this sport in glass-enclosed chambers. While it's enjoyable enough to play and a pretty good workout, we think the game's main attraction was that you could smack the shit out of the ball and not worry about it going out of bounds. That, and the modular, carpeted benches you sat on while waiting for your court.

See also AEROBICS; NIKE; REEBOK

RAD

Slang adjective that crossed all sorts of cultural borders. You'd find this in the Valley Girl lexicon, and you'd hear it from the mouths of Skaters and Wavers and even Nerds.

Rad, short for "radical" (more of a Bill&Ted-length word), was used to describe something that was not only cool, but over-the-top cool. A new haircut, for example, was only *rad* if it looked like John Taylor's or Grace Jones'—and not Michael J. Fox's.

See also BILL&TEDSPEAK; DURAN DURAN; FOX, MICHAEL J.; GRODY; JONES, GRACE; NERD; SKATEBOARDS; SKATERS; VALLEY GIRLS; WAVERS

RAIDERS OF THE LOST ARK

Along with *Die Hard*, this set the standard by which all action films are judged.

See also BRING 'EM BACK ALIVE; FORD, HARRISON; LUCAS, GEORGE; PG-13; SPIELBERG, STEVEN; *TALES OF THE GOLD MONKEY*; WILLIAMS, JOHN

RAINBOW BRITE

Saturday morning cartoon that obviously originated as a neat toy/character onto which a plot had to be forced. Rainbow Brite lived in a land of rainbows and sunshine and other happy creatures such as herself. But Murky, the bad guy, was always trying to bring everybody down.

See also CARE BEARS; *SHIRT TALES, THE*; SMURFS; STRAWBERRY SHORTCAKE

RAIN FORESTS

Phrase that took over when, at some point in the 1980s, the word "jungle" was deemed derogatory to wildlife.

See also BAN THE BOX; SEUSS, DR.

RAISING ARIZONA

One of the best movies ever made. Those who have seen it usually either agree or think it just really, really sucks. It's the story of an infertile white trash couple (Nicolas Cage,

"Two dollars!"

—Inspired by the psychotic but enterprising young paper boy from *Better Off Dead,* we used this line as a kind of universal mock-threat.

Holly "I'm barren!" Hunter) who steal a baby from an Arizona furniture tycoon blessed with quintuplets. The directing by Joel Coen is seamless, and there isn't a wasted line of dialogue in Ethan "Yeah, we're brothers" Coen's script. Plus, who can't love a movie when the soundtrack includes Beethoven's 9th Symphony as done by a banjo and yodeler?

See also SPOCK, DR.

RAMBO

Reagan with a better body and fewer (but not by many) weapons. Sylvester Stallone's character took on a very patriotic, very (we hate to say it) '80s attitude in *Rambo: First Blood Part II* and *Rambo III.* He went back to Vietnam to "win this time," and then he crawled in the sand with anti-commie rebels in Afghanistan. A nice cash-in on the peaking Cold War.

See also AFGHANISTAN; EVIL EMPIRE; REAGAN, RONALD; TERRORISM; VIETNAM-MANIA; *WARGAMES*

RAMPAGE

If you were in a bad mood, this was a great video game to play because what you did was pick a favorite giant monster, then roam the city destroying buildings and stuff.

See also ATARI

RANCH

Before the mid-1980s, this flavoring came only from a place called Hidden Valley, and only in little packets. Then someone at Frito-Lay spilled some on

his corn chip or something, and Cool Ranch Doritos were born. Soon, you couldn't get away from ranch if you tried.

See also DORITOS

RANKIN/BASS

The creative team responsible for all those stop-motion puppet holiday specials, including *Rudolph the Red-Nosed Reindeer, Rudolph's Shiny New Year, Santa Claus Is Coming to Town, Year Without a Santa Claus* (featuring Mr. Heat Miser and Mr. Cold Miser), and the tearjerker *Nestor.*

See also KROFFT SUPERSHOW; SPITTING IMAGE

RAP

The only form of music that we can really say is ours. Rap and hip-hop culture grew out of 1970s funk when DJs discovered they could mix beats and songs together and MCs started rhyming over them. Early rappers like the Sugarhill Gang and Grandmaster Melle Mel toiled in relative obscurity, but with Run-D.M.C.'s hybrid hit "Walk This Way," helped by extensive video rotation, the music gained mainstream (white) acceptance. Later, Public Enemy, NWA, and others brought some of the realities of inner-city life to people who otherwise wouldn't know or care, and now rap influences can be seen in the speech and fashion tastes of all of us. The genre didn't have a No. 1 album until 1986 with *License to Ill* by white guys the Beastie Boys. And it didn't have a

No. 1 song until 1990 with "Ice Ice Baby" by white guy Vanilla Ice.

See also BEASTIE BOYS; BEAT BOXING; BREAKDANCING; CLINTON, GEORGE; D.J. JAZZY JEFF AND THE FRESH PRINCE; LOC, TONE; MTV; PUBLIC ENEMY; ROB BASE AND D.J. E-Z ROCK; RUBIN, RICK; RUN-D.M.C.; SAMPLING; WOO-YEAH! SAMPLE; YOUNG MC

RATT

More bad '80s metal. They did "Round and Round" and some other stuff. When will it end? When will this madness stop!?! Oh yeah. It did. Great. OK. Phew.

See also POISON; SCORPIONS, THE; TWISTED SISTER

"READ MY LIPS"

What George Bush challenged us all to do during the 1988 campaign. But his lips were so dang thin, it was hard to tell from a distance if there was anything printed on them.

See also HORTON, WILLIE

READY FOR THE WORLD

Was it us, or did "Oh Sheila" sound just a wee bit like "When Doves Cry"?

See also PRINCE; SHEILA E.; TIME, THE; VANITY

REAGAN, RONALD

The most significant, visible, and influential pop culture figure of our generation. He might as well have been married to Madonna. Our ideas of politics, life, and sex formed during his rule. He set the standard for what a president should be in our lifetimes. He had very odd hair. And if John Hinckley would have been more accurate, Reagan may have attained the mythical status to which Boomers have elevated JFK.

See also BEDTIME FOR BONZO; BORK, ROBERT; GORBACHEV, MIKHAIL S.; HINCKLEY, JOHN; IRAN-CONTRA THING; KELLY, KITTY; KHOMEINI, AYATOLLAH RUHOLLAH; RAMBO; ROCKNE, KNUTE; SALT II

REAGAN, RON, JR.

Presidential son best known for doing the Risky Business dance around the White House on *Saturday Night Live*.

See also RISKY BUSINESS DANCE; REAGAN, RONALD

REAL GENIUS

Another product of the Geek Era. This movie about brainiac students at the fictional Pacific Tech celebrated the power and appeal of smart people. Val Kilmer, who later turned to hunkier roles as fighter pilots and superheroes, played the one guy who knew how to handle being a genius. The secret: relax and be a smart-ass.

The plot had something to do with the evil Professor Hathoway (William Atherton, the evil TV reporter from *Die Hard*) tricking his students into making a death-beam laser for the CIA and the students destroying his house with popcorn and said laser. But the subplots, about the trials of nerds (one of whom lived in the closet), made the movie.

BONUS FACT: Director Martha Coolidge also did the classic *Valley Girl*.

See also DIE HARD; GEEK ERA; NERD; TOP GUN; VALLEY GIRL

REAL GHOSTBUSTERS, THE

Cartoon series based on characters from the movie—plus Slimer, the friendly ghost. Through some sort of copyright loophole, another animation company put out a show called *Ghostbusters*, which had nothing to do with the film but came out before *The Real Ghostbusters*, hence the need for the word "real."

See also GHOSTBUSTERS

REAL LIFE

Crappy synth-poppers who noticed that Modern English and UB40 had hits by rereleasing songs they'd recorded several years earlier and decided to do the same. Thus came "Send Me an Angel '89," a remixed version of a song of theirs that barely made a blip the first time around.

See also MODERN ENGLISH

REAL PEOPLE

These were Skip Stephenson, John Barbour, Byron Allen, Sarah Purcell, Peter Billingsley (aka Messy Marvin and Ralph Parker in *A Christmas Story*) and the people they talked about.

See also BILLINGSLEY, PETER; *KIDS ARE PEOPLE, TOO*; *THAT'S INCREDIBLE!*

RED DAWN

A wholly unrealistic 1984 Cold War scare movie in which the Russians and Cubans take over Colorado. Spunky, armed youngsters (Patrick Swayze, C. Thomas Howell, Lea Thompson) from a Fort Collins high school lead the revolution as a gang of rebels called Wolverines. This was tied with *Dreamscape* for being the first movie released with the PG-13 rating.

See also AMERIKA; *NIGHT OF THE COMET*; PG-13

RED HEAT

Jim Belushi is a free-and-easy Chicago cop . . . *with an attitude*. Arnold Schwarzenegger is a strait-laced Russian narcotics officer . . . *with an attitude*. And together . . . *they fight crime*. Fill in the plot with cross-cultural drug dealers and dissolving 1988 Cold War tensions, and you've got yourself a movie!

See also *CITY HEAT*; *RED DAWN*

RED OCTOBER

A cool submarine that can't be detected by enemy sonar . . . because it doesn't exist.

See also CLANCY, TOM; STEALTH

REEBOK

In 1982, this company introduced something called "aerobic shoes" and changed the world of high-tops and tennies forever. These new creatures were white, soft, leather, and almost certainly responsible for the massive footwear buildup that led to hybrids like cross-trainers and shoes fitted with pumps.

See also AEROBICS; FONDA, JANE; L.A. GEAR; NIKE; VANS (THE SHOES)

REESE'S PIECES

Just like M&M's, except with peanut butter instead of chocolate. Also E.T.'s favorite candy.

See also E.T.; WHATCHAMACALLIT

REITMAN, IVAN

The best director in Hollywood at taking a seemingly flimsy premise and making an engaging, if not particularly deep, movie out of it. Responsible for both *Ghostbusters* films, *Stripes*, *Meatballs*, and *Twins*.

See also GHOSTBUSTERS

R.E.M.

Four guys in Athens, Ga., a couple of them from the art school there, got together in 1980 or '81 and formed a band. They recorded a five-song EP called *Chronic Town* that didn't sound like most of the other music out there. It wasn't punk, exactly, but it wasn't plain old rock either.

Then they did a few full-length albums for a little label called IRS Records. Jangly guitars and murky lyrics became their trademark, though with each album, their sound grew and changed some, and they made some videos, and word about these four guys started to get around.

Then, in 1988, they left IRS for Warner Bros., which had the publicity machine to make people notice these four guys, even if people didn't want to. They released an album called *Green*, and most of America noticed. MTV took videos by the four guys off

120 Minutes and put them into heavy rotation.

"Alternative music," in its true sense, died the day *Green* was released, because "alternative" was now cool in a mainstream sense. And all those big-haired pop-metal bands were given their walking papers.

See also ATHENS, GA.; HEAVY METAL BOOM

REMINGTON STEELE

This came out before *Moonlighting*, did the whole 1940s detective romance thing before *Moonlighting* and the veteran-P.I.-has-to-deal-with-pretty-face character structure before *Moonlighting*. Pierce Brosnan should have been James Bond years ago, yes?

See also MOONLIGHTING

REMOTE CONTROL

One of MTV's first forays into non-video programming. Host Ken Ober turned the game show on its side with categories like Alive, Dead, or Indian Food; Sing along with Colin; Beat the Bishop and Brady Physics. Adam Sandler got his start here as the Trivia Delinquent. This show was years ahead of its time, in that it was doing in 1987 what we're just getting around to now with this book, albeit for a slightly older crowd.

See also GAME SHOWS; MTV

REMO WILLIAMS

As in, *The Adventure Begins*. He's a modern initiate into an ancient line of assassins. He can dodge bullets and walk on water. He's so super-secret that everybody thinks he's dead. He's Remo Williams, kids, and he's the 1985 answer to James Bond. Or rather he would have been, if this film adaptation of the testosterone-soaked action book series called "The Destroyer" had been a hit. Instead, star Fred Ward moved on to a series of "also starring" roles. And the adventure ended.

BONUS FACT: Bleach-blond supergrouper Tommy Shaw (from Styx and Damn Yankees) did some songs for the soundtrack.

See also RIGHT STUFF, THE

REO SPEEDWAGON

Overwrought, overproduced band from Illinois that symbolized all that was bad about rock in the late 1970s and early 1980s.

See also HALL & OATES; NIGHT RANGER

RETARDED

A slang word that most people disposed of after gaining a social conscience. It can be used as an adjective for something or someone you don't like (i.e., "Tiffany is so *retarded*"), but it's so derogatory to handicapped people that usage is restricted to elementary and middle schools of the 1980s. Variations include *retard*, a noun (i.e., "Gimme back my joystick, you *retard*").

See also GAY; TIFFANY

RETTON, MARY LOU

America's Sweetheart, 1984 edition.

See also OLYMPICS; RIGBY, CATHY; SHIELDS, BROOKE

RETURN OF BRUNO, THE

If daytime hunks Rick Springfield and Jack Wagner could have hot rock albums, then so could prime-time timber like Bruce Willis. Right? Willis made it known—by the musical numbers on *Moonlighting* and his rootsy ads for Seagram's Golden Wine Coolers ("It's wet, and it's dry.")—that his real passions had something to do with singing the blues and breathing with a harmonica. Only one song from this album (a remake of "Respect Yourself" with the Pointer Sisters) got much airplay, and a lot of Bruce Willis fans who bought the album were embarrassed to listen to it.

See also BARTLES & JAYMES GUYS; *DIE HARD*; HEART BEAT; MOONLIGHTING; SPRINGFIELD, RICK; WAGNER, JACK

RETURN TO OZ

In 1985, Disney got the idea that it would be cool to make a sequel to *The Wizard of Oz* where Dorothy, in therapy for her "dream" of the far-off land, returns to it. The result was a dark, disturbing, not-very-good film: The Emerald City is in ruins, and weird thugs on unicycles have taken over. Some cool Claymation-type stuff, though.

See also BLACK CAULDRON, THE

REVENGE OF THE NERDS

If you wanted to do a dissertation on the pinnacle of the Geek Era, this 1984 film and its 1987 sequel, subtitled *Nerds in Paradise*, would be an excellent place to start. All the elements are there, from the nerd stars who are rather tool-like themselves (Robert Carradine, Anthony Edwards, Tim Busfield, Curtis Armstrong) to Ted McGinley as the head jock/bad guy, to the nerd-loves-and-eventually-wins-jock's-very-hot-girl-friend-but-only-after-initial-rejection-and-using-chicanery-to-get-her-in-bed-where-of-course-he-is-a-machine subplot, right down to the casting of John Goodman as the football coach who's got it in for nerds.

See also ARMSTRONG, CURTIS; EDWARDS, ANTHONY; GEEK ERA; POINDEXTER; *PORKY'S*; *THIRTYSOMETHING*

REYNOLDS, BURT

All that was sexy in the 1970s man was embodied by this former Florida State football player, even though he was short and was wearing a rug by the end of the decade. Inseparable from Dom DeLuise and Dolly Parton and Sally Field and Loni Anderson. Well, maybe not Loni Anderson.

See also CANNONBALL RUN, THE; FIELD, SALLY; PARTON, DOLLY; *SMOKEY AND THE BANDIT*

RICE, DONNA

Sometime-model and -actress who sank the hopes of presidential aspirant Gary Hart and the entire Democratic Party when she was photographed sitting on Hart's lap on a yacht called the *Monkey Business* outside Miami in early 1988. The Dems were left with Michael Dukakis, and well, you know the rest.

See also DUKAKIS, MICHAEL; HAHN, JESSICA; HART, GARY

RICE CAKES

A form of food resembling small Styrofoam Frisbees. These became a health-culture rage in the mid-'80s, most likely because the things have practically no calories, nutrients, or flavor. In order to get any nourishment from rice cakes, you have to load them up with so much peanut butter, cream cheese, or (insert your fatty spread of choice here) that you might as well have just eaten a Big Mac.

See also MCDONALD'S MANTRAS; OAT BRAN

RICH CORINTHIAN LEATHER

A nonexistent substance touted by Ricardo Montalban in a commercial for Chrysler. The thick-maned and always believable pitchman would sweep his hands across the seats and purr the praises of "r-r-rich Cor-r-*in*-thian leather," and later admitted that the stuff didn't exist, that it just sounded like a luxurious thing to say. That hasn't stopped the stuff from becoming a vital part of our textural vocabulary.

See also FANTASY ISLAND; IACOCCA, LEE; *STAR TREK II: THE WRATH OF KHAN*

RICHIE, LIONEL

One of the great mysteries of the '80s remains: Why was this man so popular? And why does it feel good to dance on the ceiling?

See also WHITE NIGHTS

RIDE, SALLY

The first woman astronaut, and the only one, male or female, to be named after a line from a blues song.

See also McAULIFFE, CHRISTA

RIGBY, CATHY

Before there was Mary Lou Retton, there was this little sprite of a gymnast who represented our country in the 1976 Olympics and appeared on a Wheaties box. All this enabled her to be the gymnastics analyst at the '84 games, where we heard her talk about the performance of her heir apparent, the aforementioned Ms. Retton.

See also RETTON, MARY LOU

RIGHT STUFF, THE

A book. A movie. A concept. A trendy phrase. The novel and film by this name chronicled the early years of the space race, but more important than that was author Tom Wolfe's attempt to define what makes the best pilots and astronauts able to speed through the air on top of a rocket day after day. He developed an ethereal, manly concept called the Right Stuff, and this caught on (headlines of the period include anything from *The Write Stuff* to *The Wrong Stuff*). The epic movie wasn't exactly a blockbuster, but a series of related books (*Yeager, The Wild Blue*) and movies

(*Top Gun, Iron Eagle*) followed.

Years later, the New Kids on the Block recorded a song called "You Got It (The Right Stuff)," which had nothing to do with any of this.

See also BONFIRE OF THE VANITIES, THE; CHALLENGER; IRON EAGLE; NEW KIDS ON THE BLOCK; STUFF, THE; TOP GUN; YEAGER, CHUCK

RINGWALD, MOLLY

She personified a lot of our hormonal angst in movies like *Sixteen Candles* and *Pretty in Pink*. She wasn't ultrabeautiful, and she whined a lot—and that made her seem all the more real.

See also BREAKFAST CLUB, THE; FACTS OF LIFE, THE; HUGHES, JOHN; PRETTY IN PINK

RIPPED SWEATSHIRTS

Fashion trend spawned from the movie "Flashdance," which soon crossed over into breakdance culture. A ripped-up, inside-out sweatshirt looked especially good with some parachute pants, a bandanna or two, and a pair of Vans.

See also BANDANNAS; BREAKDANCING; FLASHDANCE; PARACHUTE PANTS; VANS (THE SHOES)

RIPTIDE

An NBC series (aired right after *The A-Team*) about two cool private detectives (Joe Penny and Perry King) and one nerdy smart guy (Tom Bray). They lived on a boat (the *Riptide*), cruised around on a smaller boat (the *Ebbtide*), and had a helicopter called *Screaming Mimi*.

See also CANNELL, STEPHEN J.; CRIME FIGHTING; SIMON & SIMON

RISKY BUSINESS DANCE

1. Make sure your parents aren't home.
2. Strip down to your underwear, socks, and an oxford shirt.
3. Put on sunglasses, preferably Ray Bans.
4. Crank up Bob Seger's "Old Time Rock & Roll" on the 8-track or turntable.
5. Run around the house lip-synching the song, sliding across hardwood floors and jumping on the sofa.
6. Be Tom Cruise (optional).

See also CRUISE, TOM; I WOULD DIE 4 U SIGN LANGUAGE; REAGAN, RON, JR.

RIVERA, GERALDO

Did you watch his first live public embarrassment as he opened Al Capone's vault? How about his "investigation" into kids and Satanism? Or when somebody whooped up on his nose with a chair?

See also AL CAPONE'S VAULT

RIVER'S EDGE

Dark, dark teenage drama that hit theaters in 1986. Starring Keanu Reeves, Crispin Glover, Ione Skye, and Dennis Hopper, this was the anti-John Hughes movie: The opening scene shows a kid dismembering his sister's doll, then looking across the river and seeing a guy sitting with the body of his girlfriend, whom he just killed. These kids have serious problems, and they won't be resolved before the credits roll. Directed by Tim Hunter.

See also HUGHES, JOHN

RIVERS, JOAN

She catches a lot of flak, but you could argue (as we're about to) that she was the Woman of the '80s. Think about it: For the most part, she was famous for being famous. There was a lot of that going on then, and she was better at it than most. She made a big show about having nice stuff all the time, which was pretty much the theme of the decade. She had a catchphrase. And she had a talk show years before any other marginal celebrity did. If Nancy Reagan hadn't been first lady, she'd have been Joan Rivers.

See also "CAN WE TALK?"; COLLINS, JOAN

ROB BASE AND D.J. E-Z ROCK

They recorded the 1988 rap hit "It Takes Two," featuring one of the most famous samples in all of music. The song was relatively huge on both the rap and pop charts, and it was among the first rap songs to appeal to a large audience.

See also RAP; WOO-YEAH! SAMPLE

ROBERTS, TANYA

They say you can't trust redheads, and however much it isn't her fault, this actress, who went on to star in such gems as *The Beastmaster* and *Sheena*, will always be remembered as the woman who killed *Charlie's Angels*.

See also CHARLIE'S ANGELS

ROBOCOP

Gory movie about a cyborg Detroit cop that suggested, in 1987, that the police cruiser of the future would be a black Ford Taurus. But years later, police forces across the country decided that the Taurus-esque Chevy Caprice was the way to go.

See also TAURUS, FORD; *TERMINATOR, THE*

ROBOTECH

The most thoughtful, involved and intelligent of the '80s Japanese cartoons featuring big robots and spaceships. You had to watch it every morning for several months in order to catch the three different series, each with totally new casts of characters, ships and alien bad guys. The plot spanned several generations of deep-space explorers and defenders of the Earth, and, despite consistently first-rate battle sequences, often rambled on like a soap opera.

BONUS OBSERVATION: Be it coincidence or not, the space cruiser in the first *Robotech* series (*Macross*) usually looked like the ship in *Star Blazers*, but more resembled *Voltron* after transforming into battle mode.

See also STAR BLAZERS; *VOLTRON*

"ROCK LOBSTER"

Song by the B-52s that a lot of our older siblings had and played a lot in 1982, when Fred and the gang were just breaking out of Athens. At the time, few of us probably comprehended that we were hearing one of the songs that would come to define "alternative" music.

See also ATHENS, GA.; R.E.M.

ROCKNE, KNUTE

Legendary 1920s football coach who turned Notre Dame's program into a powerhouse. We only mention him here because the 1940 movie *Knute Rockne, All American* features Ronald Reagan as a young player named George Gipp who dies and inspires the rest of the team to "Win one for the Gipper!"

See also BEDTIME FOR BONZO; REAGAN, RONALD

ROCK THE VOTE

A pseudo-political movement devised to get all us kids to vote, appealing to us through our exposed pop-culture veins. Around the 1988 presidential campaign (the first in which a large number of us could vote), "Rock the Vote" ads on MTV explained that our generation could make a huge difference in the political process—if only we did something about it. Postcards to Congress—preaddressed and prewritten with complaints about environmental policy—were attached to the liner notes of some CDs (like R.E.M.'s).

See also BAN THE BOX; LEAD OR LEAVE; RAIN FORESTS; R.E.M.

ROCKWELL

Son of Motown legend Berry Gordy, Jr., he had two very paranoid hits: "Somebody's Watching Me" (with

Michael Jackson) and "Obscene Phone Caller."

See also ILLUMINATI, THE; JACKSON, MICHAEL

ROCKY

Small movie about a down-and-out boxer who gets the shot of a lifetime, starring and written by marble-mouthed pug Sylvester Stallone, that became a huge sensation, won the Best Picture Oscar for 1976, and, along with *Star Wars* a year later, signalled the end of the dark, edgy filmmaking of the 1970s in favor of more happy endings and less challenging stories. The myriad sequels took the charm out of the series, but the first film (and even *Rocky II* to some degree) are really pretty good.

See also MR. T; *RAMBO*; *STAR WARS*

ROCKY HORROR PICTURE SHOW, THE

A movie that has been playing in theaters since 1975, largely because that's the *only* way to see it. There's probably an estimate somewhere about what percentage of our generation has seen it . . . and we're sure it's pretty high. The plot (a sci-fi/horror spoof thing) and cast (Tim Curry, Susan Sarandon, Meat Loaf) take a backseat to the shadow actors/fans/freaks who—in every town in America where *Rocky Horror* plays at a midnight show—get up in front of the screen and take over acting and singing "Hot Patootie" and "Time Warp."

See also "PARADISE BY THE DASHBOARD LIGHT"

ROLLER SKATING

There was a point in elementary school when almost everything socially relevant in life happened at the skating rink. Friendships, rivalries, and romance all flourished beneath the disco ball of Skate World or Skate City or whatever it was called.

See also BUCKNER AND GARCIA; J. GEILS BAND; MALLS; *THRILLER*

ROOTS

Huge 1977 ABC series that taught us all about the slave trade by telling the story of an African family brought to America. Based on Alex Haley's book, this featured, among others, Louis Gossett, Jr., O. J. Simpson, Burl Ives, Ed Asner, and John Amos (the dad from *Good Times*). *Roots* was among the first movies to be shown as what came to be called a "miniseries," which became a sweeps-week-favorite format in the '80s. At the time, this received some of the biggest ratings in TV history and, of course, a sequel (*Roots: The Next Generations*) aired two years later.

How did we go from this to *V.* in such a short time?

See also AMERIKA; GOOD TIMES; IRON EAGLE; LAST EPISODE OF *M*A*S*H*; MINISERIES; THORN BIRDS, THE; V.

ROPERS, THE

Bad spin-off from *Three's Company.* But really, a good spin-off from *Three's Company* was mathematically impossible.

See also THREE'S COMPANY

The fairy tale, as seen on TV.

ROTH, DAVID LEE

Probably the only man who effectively pulled off the high-hair and leopard-skin Spandex look that '80s cheese metal required. He swung from the rafters and did splits as lead singer for Van Halen before going solo and remaking "California Girls" and "Just a Gigolo/I Ain't Got Nobody." His videos, packed with bikinied blondes and TV-show parodies, go down as classics.

***See also* Fat Boys; Heavy metal boom; Van Halen**

ROURKE, MICKEY

Someone, somewhere decided that he was to be a sex symbol. We just don't get that.

***See also* Angel Heart**

ROYAL WEDDING

When the entity known as "all three networks" broadcasts something, you know it's a big deal. The only wedding to receive such a programming endorsement united Charles and Diana, the prince and princess of Wales, Chuck and Di, the future King and his lovely country bride—a fairy tale come to life! She was only 20, her dress' train went on for 25 feet. These two dominated so much media time in the coming years—with kids, affairs, vacations, shopping, just sitting around the house,

Mr. Rubik and his cubes.

hairdos, and finally a breakup—that you might even be convinced that being British royalty actually meant something.

See also LUKE AND LAURA

RUBIK'S CUBE

Perhaps the only mentally stimulating trend of our era. America was transfixed with it, and anybody who could do it in 30 seconds got on national television. The puzzle trend also included the Missing Link, the Pyramid, the Snake, the Rubik's Cube key chain, Rubik's Revenge, the Orb, Alexander's Star, and a variety of imitating cubes (identified by the blue and green sides being opposite each other, rather than the blue-white dichotomy of the original). Many believed that this and Tetris were Soviet conspiracies to make all of us lazy slackers. Many others believe that it worked. And we were all better off without the

cartoon, *Rubik and the Amazing Cubes.*

See also EVIL EMPIRE; GORBACHEV, MIKHAIL S.

RUBIN, RICK

Founder of Def American records and producer who engineered the crossover success of Run-D.M.C. with "Walk This Way," and who came up with the idea of turning an obnoxious punk band from Brooklyn called the Beastie Boys into a rap act. He made hip-hop safe for white people, who in turn picked up the truer, more authentic product.

See also BEASTIE BOYS; RAP; RUN-D.M.C.

RUMOR ABOUT RICHARD GERE, THE

Did you hear? *Richard Gere checked into an emergency room to have a gerbil removed from his butt!* No matter where in America we lived, we heard about this piece of "news" (very likely a myth) from a friend or two. Some people named reliable sources, like a friend of a friend of theirs who knew a nurse who was working the ER that night. Variations included different rodents and celebrities.

See also MIKEY; "MONY MONY" CHANT

RUN-D.M.C.

The first true stars to emerge from the rap scene, aided by their willingness to make videos and their huge "Walk This Way," a hip-hop cover of the Aerosmith song that featured

"You using the whole fist there, Doc?"

—Fletch, *Fletch*

Steven Tyler and Joe Perry in both the song and the video.

See also BEASTIE BOYS; RAP; RUBIN, RICK; TOGETHER FOREVER TOUR

RUSHDIE, SALMAN

The only writer in modern times to receive a death threat from a head of state. Our buddy Ayatollah Khomeini didn't like Rushdie's book *The Satanic Verses* and requested that somebody kill the author. Every once in a while he showed up in London or on Letterman, but he achieved fame by rivaling J. D. Salinger for low profiles.

See also KHOMEINI, AYATOLLAH RUHOLLAH; LETTERMAN, DAVID

RUSSIANS

Sting hopes they love their children, too.

See also POLICE, THE

RUSSKIES

In 1987, the U.S.-Soviet relationship was getting friendlier on-screen, and buddy movies and human interest stories took over where kill-the-commie-bastard films left off. In this fuzzy little film, kids Peter Billingsley (aka Messy Marvin) and Leaf Phoenix help a downed Soviet pilot in Florida while the government hunts the commie bastard.

See also EVIL EMPIRE; *RED HEAT*

RUST, MATHIAS

The West German kid who flew a small airplane into the Soviet Union and landed in Red Square—completely undetected. In 1987, this was a bold and well-demonstrated political statement about communism sucking and how the USSR didn't scare anybody anymore. Of course, Mathias spent a little time in prison, but that's a small price to pay for a good practical joke.

See also GORBACHEV, MIKHAIL S.

RYDER, WINONA

Porcelain-skinned young actress who became the object of many amorous boys' desires in the late '80s. We first saw her in *Lucas*, where she played a mousy, somewhat geeky girl. She had grown up some by *Beetlejuice* two years later, but because of all the fright-night makeup she wore in that movie, it came as quite a surprise to us when *Heathers* came out and she was, well, a babe. But she also proved that she wanted to move beyond the teen-star bit by actually projecting intelligence on screen and taking roles in smaller, quirkier pictures like *Welcome Home, Roxy Carmichael* and *Mermaids*.

See also BEETLEJUICE; BURTON, TIM; HEATHERS; LUCAS

S

SACCHARIN

Potent sweetener that the FDA tried (and failed) to ban in 1977 for being unsafe and generally evil. Also responsible for creating the entire diet cola industry.

See also NUTRASWEET; TAB

SALT II

Yet another cool acronym we learned during the Cold War. This meant Strategic Arms Limitation Talks (part two), which took place in Iceland and involved two guys named Reagan and Gorbachev. Other all-caps favorites included DEF-CON (Defense Condition), NORAD (North American Air Defense Command), MAD (Mutually Assured Destruction), START (Strategic Arms Reduction Talks), SDI (Strategic Defense Initiative), and *D.A.R.Y.L.* (a bad movie about a robot-kid created by the government).

See also ADIDAS; AIDS; CNN; DAT; EPCOT; HBO; HDTV; MADD; MS-DOS; MTV; OMD; PMRC; SDI; VCR; WGN; WTBS

SALT-N-PEPA

First female rappers to have any real impact on the hip-hop scene. Their first hit, "Push It," was about what it sounded like it was about and intro-duced us all to the phrase "Yo-yo-yo baby pop!" They clowned around with Kid 'N' Play in some of their early videos.

See also JJ FAD; KID 'N' PLAY

SAMPLING

Practice of taking bits of previously recorded songs and incorporating them into your own songs, most often practiced by rap DJs. Sampling sparked some nasty finger-pointing and even a lawsuit or two when it was first practiced, but eventually everyone settled down and realized it was kind of cool.

See also CLINTON, GEORGE; LOC, TONE; RAP; WOO-YEAH! SAMPLE

SAN DIEGO CHICKEN, THE

Preeminent mascot of the 1970s and 1980s. The Chicken had very little to do with his home team, the Padres, but was a little wackier than all those other mascots, so he got a lot of air-time and appeared at a lot of other teams' games as a special attraction.

See also JOHN 3:16 GUY

SATURDAY NIGHT FEVER

Historically significant social drama about a guy and his need to dance,

dance, dance. We were never the right age to appreciate this film, so few of us ever will. Also, the Bee Gee-rific soundtrack was huge.

BONUS, PUTTING-IT-ALL-IN-PERSPECTIVE FACT: This came out the same year as *Star Wars*.

See also DISCO; SOLID GOLD; STAR WARS; STAYING ALIVE

SATURDAY NIGHT LIVE

More phrases and characters from this show have found their way into our speech and mannerisms than from any other show. Most of us started watching around the transition from the Joe Piscopo/Eddie Murphy cast to the Billy Crystal/Christopher Guest group. Classic era sketches came mostly from Murphy's brain, including "Buckwheat has been shot" and "I'm Gumby, dammit!" The show hit a low point in 1985–86 with Anthony Michael Hall, Robert Downey, Jr., and Joan Cusack.

See also DELIRIOUS; HALL, ANTHONY MICHAEL; KAUFMAN, ANDY; MILLER, DENNIS; MR. BILL; NOT NECESSARILY THE NEWS

SATURDAY SUPERCADE

CBS Saturday morning cartoon anthology taking its plots and characters from first-generation arcade games like Frogger, Q-Bert, and Donkey Kong. Pac-man had enough Hollywood clout to get his own show over on ABC.

See also ATARI; DONKEY KONG; PAC-MAN; Q-BERT

SATURDAY THE 14TH

Stupid parody (made in 1981) of the horror series based on the previous day. If the filmmakers had waited a couple of years, they could have saved some money, because the object of their derision became a self-parody round about part four.

See also FRIDAY THE 13TH

SAVITCH, JESSICA

She was the first woman ever to become a network news anchor, but her meteoric rise from local TV to the big time was accompanied by several abusive relationships and cocaine use, and she died in a car accident in 1983.

See also NORVILLE, DEBORAH

SAY ANYTHING . . .

This thinking teen's romance, from culture wizard Cameron Crowe, starred John Cusack as lovable blue-collar guy/aspiring kickboxer/philosopher Lloyd Dobler and Ione Skye as Diane Court, the upper-middle class girl/valedictorian/object of Lloyd's affections. Better than most of its kind because Crowe knows how people like us talk and think and was able to show just how uncomfortable love can be.

BONUS SOUNDTRACK NOTES: The film, which was released in 1988, made Peter Gabriel's song "In Your Eyes" a ubiquitous teen-love anthem and dance theme. However, the song was part of Gabriel's album *So*, which was released in 1986. The soundtrack also featured tunes by Fishbone ("Skankin' to the Beat," playing in the background at the party) and pre-*Mother's Milk* Red Hot Chili Peppers (on Lloyd's car radio as he and Diane are driving the drunk guy home after the party).

See also BOOM BOX; CROWE, CAMERON; DIRTY DANCING; PRETTY IN PINK

SCANNERS

Dumb movie, but it was cool when people's heads blew up.

See also EXPLORERS; HOOSIERS; INSIDERS, THE; OUTSIDERS, THE

SCHMOO

A big blob of protoplasm with a heart of gold, or something like that. Only the kids over at Hanna-Barbera know.

See also CAPTAIN CAVEMAN; SCOOBY DOO

SCHNEIDER

Building super/handyman on *One Day at a Time*, played by Pat Harrington. Though he started off as merely a Dumb Guy, he became, after a couple of seasons, a central character, an unprecedented move in sitcomdom.

BONUS FACT: His first name was Dwayne.

See also BERTINELLI, VALERIE; DUMB GUY

SCHOOLHOUSE ROCK

At first a sneaky way of making us learn stuff, ABC's short educational cartoons are now burned on our brains like cattle brands. They came on during the regular Saturday morning lineup, so we couldn't avoid them. The songwriting was usually pretty funny, and at our tender age, we didn't realize how much smarter we were getting. We learned fairly academic tidbits about verb forms, electricity, and American folk heroes. Favorites include the obscure "Mother Necessity" (about great inventors) and the catchy "Conjunction Junction." While these covered a breadth of subjects, nutritional know-how came from an unrelated singing red circle guy pitching good-for-you snacks like celery-and-sour cream "Saturdays" instead of ice cream sundaes. And NBC stars shared social wisdom (avoiding fights, not doing drugs, etc.) during "One to Grow On" segments.

Sadly, Schoolhouse Rock was yanked in 1985 and replaced by (gulp) Menudo videos.

See also KROFFT SUPERSHOW; MENUDO; SATURDAY SUPERCADE

SCHWARZENEGGER, ARNOLD

It was decided sometime between *The Terminator* and *Total Recall* that this hard-to-understand, Volvo-chested neohuman would be the first and last word in action-movie stars.

See also CONAN THE BARBARIAN; "I'LL BE BACK"; RED HEAT; STRETCH ARMSTRONG

SCOOBY DOO

Detective dog who, along with Fred, Daphne, Thelma, and Shaggy, sniffed out supernatural wrongdoings while riding around in the Mystery Machine. Of course, it always turned out that there never was a ghost haunting the house or a Bigfoot scurrying around the ski lodge. It was always just one of the story's minor characters (an owner, a disgruntled worker) going to extremes in order to seek revenge or scam some money.

Scooby was a lot better off without the relatives Hanna-Barbara created in the '80s to keep the show lively: Scooby Dee (a she!), Scooby Dumb (as if Shaggy wasn't dumb enough), and Scrappy Doo. This last member of the clan was the most offensive. He and his cute, squeaky puppy voice basically took over the show.

See also Laff-a-Lympics; Smurfs; Vans (the vehicle)

SCORPIONS

They came from Germany and sang about how they wanted to rock us like a hurricane. This didn't make a whole lot of sense, but we figured maybe something was lost in the translation.

See also Falco; Nena; Poison

SCOTT, RIDLEY

Widely regarded as one of the best directors around, he's most famous for bleak futuristic tales like *Blade Runner* and *Alien*. Also, he directed two commercials that ran once each during Super Bowls, one for Apple and another for Nissan.

See also Alien; Big Brother ad; Blade Runner

SCOTT, WILLARD

Friend to 100-year-old ladies everywhere, this jolly, corpulent forecaster on NBC's *Today* show is the original and still the best of the celebrity weathermen. Al Roker learned every-

thing he knows from Willard, and Willard only taught him half.

See also Norville, Deborah

SDI

Depending on who you listened to, the SDI (the Strategic Defense Initiative or Star Wars) was either the end of warfare or the beginning of interplanetary destruction. Basically, the plan was to put lasers on satellites so we could shoot down nuclear missiles and the lasers on other people's satellites. A lot of nerd types dug the idea because there's hardly anything cooler than lasers in space.

See also Cosmos; Nerd; Real Genius; Star Wars; WarGames

SELLECK, TOM

The man who booted Burt Reynolds off his throne as the most desirable guy in movies or on TV. Actually, he was a lot like Burt, only more so. He was taller and more laid-back, with more hair (both on top and on his chest). Plus, he didn't have Dom DeLuise hanging around him all the time, just T.C., Rick, and Higgins.

See also Magnum, P.I.; Reynolds, Burt

SECRET OF NIMH

One of the few decent big-screen cartoons made during the time we would have been interested in big-screen cartoons. Disney hadn't made a good animated movie in decades, and so a whole bunch of us went and saw Don Bluth's 1982 story of a mouse and some chemicals and a corporate conspiracy or something like that. More people remember Bluth's next movie, *An American Tail*, also about a mouse, a little more clearly.

See also BLACK CAULDRON, THE

SEPTEMBER 22–OCT. 3, 1982

In the span of these 12 days, eight television shows premiered. One is among the best ever; two are solid, one of those occasionally great; three were amusing and fun in a campy sort of way; one had the hottest young heartthrob of the time; and one just plain sucked. But taken together, you could argue that those 12 days were the 12 days that the '80s began on the small screen.

Here's the lineup: On Sept. 22, *Family Ties* premiered. Three days later, on the 25th, we saw the debut of *Silver Spoons.* The next night brought forth *Matt Houston* and *Knight Rider*, and the night after that, *Square Pegs* was on. Then came Sept. 30, bearing *Cheers. Remington Steele* followed on Oct. 1, and the extraordinary time ended on Oct. 3, with the first episode of *Voyagers!*

See also CHEERS; FAMILY TIES; KNIGHT RIDER; MATT HOUSTON; REMINGTON STEELE; SILVER SPOONS; SQUARE PEGS; TARTIKOFF, BRANDON; THURSDAY NIGHT LINEUP; VOYAGERS!

SERIOUS, YAHOO

Australian guy known for two things: big hair and the movie *Young Einstein.*

See also AUSSIEMANIA; HOGAN, PAUL; JOCKO; *MAD MAX;* MEN AT WORK; MINOGUE, KYLIE

SESAME STREET

Magical kids' show featuring Big Bird, his "imaginary" friend Snuffalupagus, Grover, Cookie Monster, Oscar the Grouch, Count le Count, game-show host Guy Smiley, and the rest of the original Muppets. We'd guess at least 80 percent of us learned our alphabet, numbers, and a little Spanish partly from this show. It got kind of old after age 6 or 7, but a lot of people gained a new appreciation for the Muppet sketches later in life, like after they start paying for cable themselves. Come on, sing the theme song with us: "Sunny day, wishin' the clouds away . . . "

See also DARK CRYSTAL; ELECTRIC COMPANY; KROFFT SUPERSHOW; MUPPET SHOW, THE; 3-2-1 CONTACT

SEUSS, DR.

Lyrical, whacked-out children's author who most people will never outgrow. Classics that everybody alive can remember include *The Cat in the Hat*, *One Fish Two Fish Red Fish Blue Fish*, *Green Eggs and Ham*, and *How the Grinch Stole Christmas*. Also, *The Lorax* was one of our first exposures to environmentalism. And tons of us got *Oh, the Places You'll Go!* for graduation and now know somebody who's got one of those silly Cat in the Hat hats.

BONUS FACT: His real name was Theodor S. Geisel, may he rest in peace.

See also BAN THE BOX; CLEARY, BEVERLY; PHANTOM TOLLBOOTH, THE

7-UP GUY

In between "Uncola" ad campaigns came this large, bald Caribbean man in a white suit, touting, in that wonderful deep-voiced island accent, the clean, crisp, refreshing taste of the clear beverage, punctuating it with a hearty "Ha ha ha!"

See also BLU-BLOCKERS GUY, THE; GUY WHO TALKS REALLY FAST, THE; ISUZU, JOE; THAT "HEY VERN" GUY

SHA NA NA

Sure, they went on right before Jimi Hendrix at Woodstock, but at the time, most of the people there just thought it was the brown acid from the night before. Ten years later, though, John "Bowser" Bowman and his merry band of greasers had themselves a syndicated TV musical-variety show (think *Hee Haw* with motorcycles) and Bowser was a favorite celebrity guest on such shows as *Match Game* and *The Hollywood Squares*.

See also FONZIE CARTOON

SHAZBOT!

Intergalactic expletive; translates most closely to "Dammit!"

See also FUCK; MORK FROM ORK SUSPENDERS; NANU-NANU

SHEEDY, ALLY

A founding member of the Brat Pack who often played a bit of a misfit: The mischievous student and bad influence on Matthew Broderick in *WarGames*; the brooding, dandruffed recluse in *The Breakfast Club*. She

sort of disappeared and then became a poet after doing *Short Circuit* and *Maid to Order*.

See also BRAT PACK, THE; BREAKFAST CLUB, THE; SHORT CIRCUIT; WARGAMES

SHEILA E.

First she was the drummer for Prince's band, the Revolution, then she struck out on her own and recorded "The Glamorous Life," then, uh, well, we're not sure.

See also PRINCE; READY FOR THE WORLD; TIME, THE; VANITY

SHE'S THE SHERIFF

Syndicated sitcom about Suzanne Somers being a sheriff. If there's anything funny or wise or significant to say about this show, we sure can't think of it.

See also HAIL TO THE CHIEF; THREE'S COMPANY

SHIELDS, BROOKE

America's Sweetheart, 1980–81 edition. Until she went to Princeton, and we all realized that our little Brooke was a big girl now, independent of her mother and able to do her own thing in life. None of which explains her *Brenda Starr* movie.

See also ATKINS, CHRISTOPHER; KLEIN, CALVIN; RETTON, MARY LOU

SHIRT TALES, THE

Ridiculous mid-'80s cartoon that featured a bunch of animals who wore T-shirts and ran a high-tech crime-fighting operation out of a hollow tree in Central Park. They also looked suspiciously like Mon Chi Chis.

See also Care Bears; Mon Chi Chis

SHIT HAPPENS

A crude statement on a bumper sticker that blossomed into a national discussion of philosophy and religion. In the late '80s, you couldn't stop at a red light and not see "Shit happens" plastered on the back of a nearby car. These stickers, which struck a common chord about the Way of the World, were then "parodied" by some unfunny Christians with "Blessings happen" and "Jesus happens."

Also, a clever list of various philosophical interpretations of "Shit happens" has been circulating around the country for years:

Buddhism: "Shit happens."

Zen: "What is the sound of shit happening?"

Hinduism: "This shit has happened before."

Judaism: "Why does shit always happen to us?"

Catholicism: "If shit happens, you deserve it."

And so on.

See also God; SubGenius, Church of the

SHOGUN

Big-time miniseries starring Richard Chamberlain as an Englishman in the world of Japanese samurai. Based on the book by James Clavell, which was about the size of a Yugo.

See also Miniseries; Teenage Mutant Ninja Turtles

SHORT CIRCUIT

The story of an intelligent and lovable robot (Number Five) that comes to life and escapes from the military, which had been training it to kill, kill, kill. Civilian Ally Sheedy finds and befriends the little guy as well as its creator (Steve Guttenberg) and an Indian geek guy (Fisher Stevens). There's also music by El DeBarge and a message: War is bad.

See also E.T.; Guttenberg, Steve; *Robocop*; Visualize World Peace; *WarGames*

SHOW BIZ PIZZA THEATER

The pizza here and at Chuck E. Cheese just wasn't very good, but they had skee ball and creatures like Chuck, Mr. Munch, and Guido so we had our birthday parties there.

See also McDonald's in Moscow

SHRINKY DINKS

Toys made from some sort of clear polymer that you painted and then put in the oven. These were cut in the shapes of familiar characters (Smurfs, Strawberry Shortcake), and they came out of the oven as smaller, harder versions of themselves.

See also E-Z Bake Oven; Small Stuff; Smurfs; Strawberry Shortcake

SIGUE SIGUE SPUTNIK

This farce of a band would have been just another one-hit wonder—if they had a single hit. With complete disregard for the "art" of European synthpop, they produced two frenetic albums without knowing how to play

Movie lines we said a lot

"Me love you long time, American Joe."

—The concept of cheap Asian prostitutes, introduced to us by movies like *Platoon* and *Full Metal Jacket*, confused our young morals so badly that the line was sure to induce nervous laughter.

any instruments. Or so it seems. To their credit, they mixed Beethoven, *Blade Runner* samples, and baroque superstar Albinoni into songs that all sounded exactly the same. Their first album, *Flaunt It*, had actual paid advertisements between songs, and the track "Love Missile F1-11" was used in *Ferris Bueller's Day Off*.

See also BUELLER, FERRIS

SILVERADO

A very underrated movie. It was strange to see a Western in 1985, and even stranger to see a good one. This gave us a glimpse (unrealistic as it may be) at life a century before the stuff in this book happened. We don't need to get into the plot, which you can guess was about pioneers and outlaws in the 1880s. It also helped the careers of Kevin Costner, Danny Glover, and Kevin Kline.

See also COSTER, KEVIN; *YOUNG GUNS*

SILVER SPOONS

A father-son (Ricky Schroeder, Joel Higgins) relationship show that had enough extraneous elements to be interesting, such as the secretary/love interest (Erin Gray), sleazy Eddie Haskell type (Jason Bateman), patriarch (John Houseman), and Dumb Guy (Freddy). Alfonso Ribiero fit in there somewhere, too.

See also *IT'S YOUR MOVE*

SIMMONS, RICHARD

Formerly obese man who became a diet and fitness guru in the go-go

'80s, with his bad hair, little shorts, and Deal-a-Meals. Then, of course, there was *Sweatin' to the Oldies* and that time Dave made him cry.

See also LETTERMAN, DAVE

SIMON

It looked like a spaceship and made noises like the score from *Close Encounters*. Then you had to duplicate its pattern, or you lost.

See also DURAN DURAN; ELECTRONIC BATTLESHIP; MERLIN; WILLIAMS, JOHN

SIMON & SIMON

Middling CBS buddy-cop show about brothers Rick and A.J. Simon (Gerald McRaney and Jameson Parker) who solved crimes while looking like a cowboy and a frat boy, respectively.

See also MATT HOUSTON

SIX MILLION DOLLAR MAN, THE

Better. Stronger. Faster. Lee Majors was Steve Austin, critically injured test pilot who got a new eye, arms, and legs, went to work for Oscar over at the OSI, and kicked ass all over the evil Fembots, Bigfoot, and assorted other commie bad guys while wearing a snappy red sweat suit.

See also WAGNER, LINDSAY

SKATEBOARDS

A simple little object that became a cultural icon for young punk aficionados in the mid-'80s listening to Dead Kennedys and Suicidal Tendencies. They got out their skateboards (which

Okay, everyone do the sound effect.

had grown substantially since their first incarnation some 10 years earlier) and thrashed, making our folks wonder yet again what the hell we were up to. Depending on where you lived, the derogatory terms were likely variations on "skate rag" or "waver."

This look didn't play so well in Hollywood as other new stereotypes like nerds and Valley Girls. The 1989 film *Gleaming the Cube*, with Christian Slater and a whole lot of rad skating, came along too late. Skaters had already begun to dissolve into more complex subgroups that eventually became snowboarders, grunge people, slackers, and stuff like that.

See also Heathers; Nerds; Punk Rock; Valley Girls; Wavers

SKID ROW

The only thing distinguishing this lightweight metal band from Warrant and Great White and Poison and Kingdom Come was that their song was called "18 and Life" and everybody else's wasn't.

See also Cinderella; Great White; Poison; Warrant

SKINNY VINYL TIES

A fashion essential for every eighth-grade guy on the make—just add a cheap sport coat with the sleeves pushed up to the elbows. All this available at Merry Go Round or down the mall corridor at Chess King, next to the Record Bar.

See also Huey Lewis and the News; Members Only

SKYLAB

Early orbiting space station that was notable mainly for the fact that it fell back to Earth after its useful time in orbit was over. Much of the world watched their weatherpersons track the plummeting metal's path across the sky, concerned that it might land in their neighborhood, before it finally crashed somewhere in Australia.

See also also Challenger; Pioneer 11

SLADE

Irish rock band that had a couple of hits in the United States: "My Oh My" and "Run, Runaway." This came after cheese-rockers Quiet Riot remade a few Slade songs, like "Cum On Feel the Noize," and found themselves with a career.

See also QUIET RIOT

SLEDGE HAMMER!

A sitcom parody of tough cop and private dick dramas. The gags usually involved hypermachismo on the part of star David Rasche and the huge .44 Magnum he talked to and called "Gun."

See also CHiPs; CRIME FIGHTING; "GO AHEAD, MAKE MY DAY"; *STARSKY & HUTCH*; ZUCKER BROTHERS

"SLEDGEHAMMER" VIDEO

You could turn on MTV at almost any time between 1986 and 1990 and see Peter Gabriel's spastic head sprout flora, spin around, and then get run over by a train.

See also SLEDGE HAMMER!; SPITTING IMAGE

SLIME

This was, as far as we know, the first bodily fluid ever marketed as a toy. It came in a little plastic garbage can, it smelled like fruity Lysol, and had no connection, technically, to the bucket of slime that doused anybody from *You Can't Do That on Television* who said, "I don't know!" *Ghostbusters* slime soon took over the plasma market, now dominated by the less viscous Nickelodeon brands Gak and Floam. The best/worst thing about slime was that it didn't come out of clothes or the carpet.

See also GARBAGE PAIL KIDS; STRETCH ARMSTRONG; *YOU CAN'T DO THAT ON TELEVISION*

SLIP 'N' SLIDE

Favorite water toy for kids without pools. Basically, this was a 40-foot strip of raincoat material that you hooked your garden hose up to and, when it got wet enough, took a running leap onto it, sliding across the slick plastic to the puddle at the end. Parents didn't like it as much because if you left it out, the grass underneath got matted down and turned brown.

See also MAGIC SAND

SMALL WONDER

A show about a little girl who acts like Spock. She did this, of course, because she was a robot. An excited producer somewhere probably said, "Hey, I know: let's have this guy build a robot for a daughter and, like, the daughter never ever acts or shows emotion or does anything interesting whatsoever! How funny would that be!" It didn't run on a network, but in syndicated 6 p.m.-Sunday-ish slots.

See also IT'S A LIVING

SMIRNOFF, YAKOV

That Russian stand-up comic who always said, "Whvat a country!" And (God bless America) he even got a sitcom in 1986 called *What a Country*, about a group of immigrants living in L.A. and taking naturalization courses at a school where Don Knotts was the principal.

See also BARYSHNIKOV, MIKHAIL; KINSKI, NASTASSJA; *THREE'S COMPANY*

SMITHS, THE

A band from Britain that competed fiercely with Depeche Mode and The Cure for the title of "Most Depressing." For the optimum Smiths listening atmosphere you needed: an all-black outfit, a dark room or basement, a pack of clove cigarettes, and feelings harbored from a recent breakup or parental dispute. Then play "Girlfriend in a Coma" repeatedly.

Rumor has it that there exists not a single photograph of frontman Morrissey smiling.

See also Clove Cigarettes; Depeche Mode

SMOKEY AND THE BANDIT

In 1977, Burt Reynolds ruled the world, so he was able to get away with (and profit hugely from) this road movie, in which he drives a black Trans Am with love-interest-of-the-moment Sally Field and outruns redneck sheriff Jackie Gleason. All this with the help of CB buddies trying to transport Coors beer (then illegal in most states) from Colorado to the South. This was also the first movie made available on video laserdisc.

See also Beerland; *Cannonball Run, The*; CB radios; Reynolds, Burt; Videodisc

SMURFBERRY CRUNCH CEREAL

This stuff lasted almost as long as the cartoon series and stayed crunchy in milk. It also suspiciously resembled Cap'n Crunch's Crunchberries.

See also Cap'n Crunch; C-3POs; G.I. Joe Cereal; Mr. T Cereal; Nerds Cereal; OJs; Smurfs; Waffle-Os

SMURFS

Most of us eventually grew to hate these impossibly precious little characters, but not until after we started to refer to everything cool as "Smurfy" and dream about marrying Hefty or Smurfette. For the record, they were three apples high and always had to look out for the evil Gargamel and his cat Azrael.

Oh, and: *La la la la la la, la la la la la.*

See also Care Bears; Strawberry Shortcake

SNAUSAGES

They were these (Snausages) little dog treats shaped (Snausages) like sausages that had this goofy ad (Snausages) campaign where a cartoon dog would poke his head (Snausages) into the screen and say the product name over (Snausages) and over again in this deadpan (Snausages) voice.

See also Meow Mix theme; Mike the dog; Morris the cat

SNIGLET

As the book jacket said, "(snig'-let): Any word that doesn't show up in the dictionary, but should."

See also Sniglets

SNIGLETS

A wildly successful idea that went from HBO's *Not Necessarily the News* to a handful of books and those 365-whatever-a-year calendars. The made-up words could be applied to actual, real-life ideas and situations, thus creating comedy.

But the whole concept was a rip-off of the British book *The Meaning of Liff* by Douglas Adams and John Lloyd (he produced *Not the Nine O'clock News*, from which *Not Necessarily the News* was itself ripped off). There should be a Sniglet for stealing great ideas from the British and making buckets of money.

See also HITCHHIKER'S GUIDE TO THE GALAXY, THE; NOT NECESSARILY THE NEWS; SNIGLET; SPITTING IMAGE; VELCRO

SNOOPY SNO-CONE MAKER

This contraption was all over the TV when we were between 6 and 10, the prime Peanuts-loving age. How it worked was you stuck some ice cubes in Snoopy's Sopwith Camel doghouse and then turned a crank. That shaved the ice, then you squirted the sugary stuff on top of it, and poof! Who needs the ice-cream man?

See also EZ-BAKE OVEN; YOGURT

SNORKS, THE

Yet another mid-'80s Saturday morning cartoon (this one on ABC) about a peaceful community of small creatures. *The Snorks* was sort of like *The Smurfs* underwater, which you could probably figure out just by the name. The creatures looked vaguely blue, they had long snouts, none of them was named Snorkette or Papa Snork and, thankfully, they never said that anything was "snorky."

See also LITTLES, THE; SMURFS; STRAWBERRY SHORTCAKE

SOCCER

Hugely popular international sport that no one in America played until we started to in the 1970s, when Pelé was kicking around for the New York Cosmos of the North American Soccer League, which was hugely popular for a few years before cannibalizing itself, since the Cosmos, about the only team in the league to make a profit, stockpiled all the best talent—Pelé, Franz Beckenbauer, Giorgio Chinaglia—and basically made games very uninteresting to watch.

See also PELÉ

SOLIDARITY

Labor movement led by Lech Walesa that helped topple communism in Poland. This started a trend in positive-sounding one-word synonyms for "anti-communism," a phrase which has sort of an angry and McCarthyist sound to it. Solid titles like Solidarity and Contra and Glasnost also sounded better than commie names like Shining Path and New Socialism.

See also GLASNOST; PERESTROIKA; REAGAN, RONALD

SOLID GOLD

This was television's input into music culture before we needed several 24-hour cable networks devoted to it. One short hour included videos, live performances, the Solid Gold Dancers, and a constantly changing host-staff. This included Dionne Warwick, Glen Campbell, Andy Gibb, Rex Smith, Rick Dees, Marilyn McCoo, and various guests.

See also DANCE FEVER; MTV; PUTTIN' ON THE HITS

SOLOFLEX

The exercise machine of The Future. It runs on rubber bands! The omnipresent TV ads and infomercials for this sold us a vision of a future lifestyle: We chisel our buff little bods on a Soloflex machine alone in our ultra-modern studio apartment, furnished with black modular furniture and a single white towel. "All it takes," the ads went, "is 30 minutes, three times a week."

See also AEROBICS; POPIEL, RON; REEBOK

SPACEBALLS

Some view this Mel Brooks space movie spoof as a work of genius, some as 96 minutes of dreck, but as with many films of this type, there are certain phrases that most of us know, even if we didn't see it. In this case it's probably "I see your Schwartz is bigger than mine." Our favorite scene is the one where the alien (from *Alien*) does a ragtime number on the lunch counter after coming out of the guy's stomach.

See also ALIEN; POLICE ACADEMY; STAR WARS; WINSLOW, MICHAEL; ZUCKER BROTHERS

SPACE GHOST

He was pale, scary, and had a deep voice . . . but he was a good guy. Traveled through space with two kids and a monkey. He later gave up the chasing-bad-guys-across-the-galaxy thing and got a talk show on the Cartoon Network.

See also GLEEK; MONKEYMANIA

SPACE INVADERS

The first truly huge video game, with its advancing hordes of evil aliens (arrayed in ascending point levels from bottom to top), its lone warrior defending all earth, and its stunning simplicity, inspired by a thought that had been the lifeblood of carnival shooting galleries for decades: Shoot the bad guys, and don't get shot yourself.

See also ATARI; MISSILE COMMAND; *V.*

SPACE SHUTTLE

The most significant advance in space travel since Neil Armstrong stepped on the moon. The launch of the first reusable spacecraft, *Columbia*, in 1981 brought back a huge wave of interest in NASA and captured a lot of our imaginations.

See also CHALLENGER; McAULIFFE, CHRISTA

SPEAK AND SPELL

Lame little talking dictionary from Texas Instruments that, once you got over the idea that it did in fact talk, went straight to the back of the closet. It wouldn't even say the cuss words when you entered them in.

See also E.T.

SPEEDBALL

A combination of cocaine and heroin, smoked or injected. What killed John Belushi.

See also LENNON, JOHN

SPELLING, AARON

Filthy rich TV tycoon who brought you such 1970s pablum as *The Love Boat*, *Fantasy Island*, *Starsky and Hutch*, and *The Mod Squad*, and who was later responsible for both his daughter, Tori, and *Beverly Hills 90210*. Also cooked up *Charlie's Angels*, *Hart to Hart*, *Melrose Place*, and *Dynasty*.

See also CHARLIE'S ANGELS; DYNASTY; FANTASY ISLAND; LOVE BOAT

SPENCER'S

One-stop mall emporium where you could get your pinup posters (male or female), edible undies, genital-shaped candy, plasma orbs, "Over the Hill" paraphernalia, and Magic 8 Balls at the same time. But they didn't like you just wandering around the store and giggling and not buying anything, so we got kicked out a lot.

See also MALLS

SPIELBERG, STEVEN

It would be impossible to overestimate the influence this one man has had on our generation's imagination and creativity. Some of the most important movies released in our lifetime had his handprints all over them: *Raiders of the Lost Ark*, *E.T.*, *Jaws* and *Close Encounters of the Third Kind*. He deals in subjects that kids (and everybody else) recognize as universally cool: aliens, sharks, adventures in foreign lands, and kids taking on the bad guys by themselves. In a Spielberg film, there's no confusing good (usually a quick-witted male

character) and evil (very often Nazis), there's no mistaking the beginning and end or when to cheer or laugh or cry. And John Williams usually does the music. Notable career low-points include *1941*, a universally panned but still pretty good John Landis-style comedy.

See also AMAZING STORIES; E.T.; GOONIES, THE; GREMLINS; LANDIS, JOHN; NIGHT OF THE COMET; RAIDERS OF THE LOST ARK

SPIES LIKE US

The Cold War inspired a vast, barren netherworld of gloomy dramas (like, oh, *The Day After* and *Amerika*) and super-earnest action movies (*Red Dawn* and *Rambo*), but not enough silly, Pez-hearted romps like this 1985 Chevy Chase-Dan Aykroyd pairing. And this wasn't even *that* silly. John Landis directed it, but the required, reverent morals dominated much of the plot about bungling spies: *Nuclear weapons are bad. The Russians are really OK. The Americans are kind of slimy, too. So why can't we all just get along?* Also, the theme song was Paul McCartney's best effort of the 1980s.

See also AMAZON WOMEN ON THE MOON; AMERIKA; CADDYSHACK; FLETCH; LANDIS, JOHN; RAMBO; RED DAWN; RUSSKIES; PRETTY MUCH THE WHOLE "R" SECTION OF THIS BOOK

SPITTING IMAGE

Another import from the mass media of Great Britain, produced by John Lloyd, the man behind *Blackadder* and *Not the Nine O'clock News*. The *Spitting Image* show featured hilarious puppets caricaturing the rich and famous, particularly the Royal Family and heads of state. During their brief popularity in the New World, the twisted heads showed up in a Genesis video and did a sketch for the Academy Awards broadcast spoofing *The Color of Money*.

See also CRUISE, TOM; HEADROOM, MAX; "LAND OF CONFUSION" VIDEO; SNIGLETS; *YOUNG ONES, THE*

SPLATTER PAINT

A design philosophy that was almost avant-garde, yet easy enough for toddlers to understand . . . or invent. All you had to do was flick small specks of paint at a surface, be it a shirt or wall or locker door. The background of choice was black, speckled all about with either primaries, fluorescents, or pastels. Some people did their whole rooms like this. Others splattered T-shirts and then adorned them with rhinestones.

See also KISS

SPOCK, DR. BENJAMIN

Although few members of our generation have read his *Common Sense Book of Baby and Child Care*, our parents used this dictionary of babydom to raise us. The most precise explanation of this book can be found in *Raising Arizona*: As two escaped convicts kidnap an infant, one of them grabs the Dr. Spock book and says, "Here's the instructions."

See also RAISING ARIZONA

SPRINGFIELD, RICK

Played Noah Drake on *General Hospital* before, after, and during his rock 'n' roll career. His big album was *Working Class Dog*, his big song was "Jessie's Girl," and his big movie (because everybody got a movie) was *Hard to Hold*.

See also LUKE AND LAURA; *RETURN OF BRUNO, THE*; WAGNER, JACK

SPRINGSTEEN, BRUCE

He had always been popular, ever since he came onto the rock scene in 1975. His live shows, we were told by older siblings, were something to behold. But we didn't really believe until 1984, when he released *Born in the USA*. After that, you couldn't swing a dead cat without hitting someone who was yelling "Bruuu-uce!" Then we believed, and we wanted to dance in the dark just like him.

See also BORN IN THE USA; COX, COURTENEY

SPY HUNTER

There wasn't a great deal that was special about this driving game except for the big weapons you could pick up and blow the bad guys off the road with. Superior to such imitators as Road Blasters.

See also ATARI; CRIME FIGHTING; POLE POSITION

SQUARE PEGS

A 1982 sitcom with Sarah Jessica Parker as a nerd, Tracy Nelson as a

You're a nerd in 1988. You have almost broken in the Wrangler jeans to the point where you can sit down without cutting yourself. Your white leather or gray vinyl sneakers stay fastened thanks to the miracle of Velcro. You're wearing an oxford shirt open over a "Surf Nicaragua" T-shirt you had printed at the mall after seeing Val Kilmer wear one just like it in *Real Genius*.

Valley Girl, and Jami Gertz as a prep. A ridiculous look at the cliques of the early '80s. A band called The Waitresses did the theme song.

See also ANNIE; NERD; PREPPIES; VALLEY GIRLS

STAND BY ME

Helped launch the careers of the Brat Pack II in 1986 with Wil Wheaton, River Phoenix, Corey Feldman, and Kiefer Sutherland. This was at once a movie about death (based on a Stephen King story), '50s nostalgia, and kids dealing with life on their own terms.

See also EXPLORERS, THE; KING, STEPHEN; NIGHT OF THE COMET

STAND-UP BOOM

It came from the fringes of the entertainment industry in the late '80s to become a major attraction on its own, with comedy clubs springing up all over the country. Comedians stopped telling straight jokes and relied instead on observations and exaggerations of real-life stuff. The master of this technique is Steven Wright, who in perfect deadpan would offer up lines like "I bought some powdered water, but I didn't know what to add to it." But he never got the '90s sitcom payoff delivered to the most successful stand-up circuitmeisters: Roseanne, Jerry, Ellen, Brett, etc.

See also CLAY, ANDREW "DICE"; *DELIRIOUS*; KINISON, SAM; MILLER, DENNIS; MURPHY, EDDIE

STAR BLAZERS

Japanese cartoon series about a spaceship that looks like an aircraft carrier. This was one of the first Japanamation shows on U.S. television (along with *Robotech* and *Speed Racer*), and introduced some of us to the art's very distinctive look, with transforming spaceships and lots of young women with enormous eyes.

See also AKIRA; ROBOTECH; TRANSFORMERS; VOLTRON

STARCADE

A syndicated game show where kids competed at popular video games for prizes, like popular video games.

See also ATARI; PAC-MAN; SATURDAY SUPERCADE

STARSKY AND HUTCH

The baddest plainclothes cops on TV during the late '70s. They drove a cool car, met lots of babes, and hung out with their street informant, Huggy Bear, in between solving crimes.

See also CHiPs; MIAMI VICE; SIMON & SIMON

STAR TREK

Although the original series was canceled before many of us were born, our generation may well have spawned the largest population of Trekkers (a term preferred over "Trekkies") in the known galaxy. Interest built with the release of motion pictures in 1979, '82, '84, '86, '89, and '91, but the increased sophistication, diversity, and acceptance/ridicule of the Trekker Nation can be attributed to *Star Trek: The Next Generation*, which debuted in 1987.

See also BATTLESTAR GALACTICA; NERD; STAR WARS

STAR TREK II: THE WRATH OF KHAN

Ask any fan. This was the only truly great *Star Trek* movie. Key moments include the brain-slugs crawling out of Chekov's ear and Capt. Kirk's sustained, tight-fisted rage as he yells, "Khhhhhhhhaaaaaaannnnn!"

See also RICH CORINTHIAN LEATHER

STAR WARS

What can we say about this? George Lucas, light sabers, the Force, Banthas, Boba Fett, Wicket, Beggar's Canyon, Luke and Leia, R2 and C-3P0, Jawas, Grand Moff Tarkin, Yavin, Yoda, Dengar, Sy Snootles, IG-88, etc., etc. This is just too significant to be capsulized here, but we'll try. In 1977, it set the standard for how outer space looks and feels in movies. The story, based on centuries of standard mythical archetypes, gave us an honest-to-goodness epic to help define ideas of heroism and that whole good-vs.-evil thing. It's also a key nostalgia point for many of us: Who didn't have some of the action figures? Who wishes they hadn't given them away ten years ago? Who doesn't get a surge of adrenaline when they hear the theme music?

See also BOBA FETT; C-3P0S; FORD, HARRISON; *JEDI MASTER'S TRIVIA QUIZ BOOK*; LUCAS, GEORGE; "MAY THE FORCE BE WITH YOU"; SDI; WEDGE; WILLIAMS, JOHN

STA-SHARP PENCIL

A form of mechanical pencil that had seven or eight little lead cartridges in it. When one wore down, you took it from the point and pushed it in the other end, and another, sharper lead came out. After you used up all the leads in one Sta-sharp, you bought a new one and made a spitball gun out of the old one.

See also MECHANICAL PENCILS

STATUE OF LIBERTY'S 100TH BIRTHDAY

Oh, we were proud to be Americans on that day in 1986, watching that amazing fireworks display on TV. Especially proud were those of us who participated in the three Stroh's Runs for Liberty in the years leading up to the big unveiling of the renovated Lady.

See also FIXX, JIM; SUSAN B. ANTHONY DOLLARS

STAYING ALIVE

Too-long-after sequel ('83) to *Saturday Night Fever*, ('77) with our boy John Travolta now trying to make it as a dancer on Broadway. The musical he's trying out for is called *Satan's Alley*, and is billed in the movie as—get this—"a musical trip through Hell." "Springtime for Hitler," anyone?

BONUS FACT: This movie was directed by Sylvester Stallone, and most of the music was by his brother, Frank.

See also PERFECT; SATURDAY NIGHT FEVER

STEALTH

Word (meaning, you know, "sneaky") that came into popular usage right around the same time a certain airplane was revealed.

See also STEALTH PLANES

STEALTH PLANES

A testament to the awesome engineering powers of both the government and toy companies. The kids over at Lockheed and the Defense Department designed and built these Stealth fighters (F-117) and bombers (B-2)—superfast and superawesome-looking aircraft that can fly through radar undetected—and they did it *mostly* in secret. The massive and expensive project was completed with only a few information leaks. These helped fuel speculation among realists and paranoids, enhancing the enthusiasm of UFO believers, JFK conspiracy theorists, and people who see significance in three-letter acronyms. But then a toy company put out a fairly accurate Stealth model kit before the planes were even revealed, which gave fuel to the argument that the military can't hide anything. Soon after this, Batmanesque T-shirts with a silhouette of the plane in a yellow oval started to show up, too.

See also FIREFOX

ST. ELMO'S FIRE

The pinnacle achievement of the Brat Pack, this 1985 ode to directionless overachievers took nostalgic ensemble movies to new lows. Significant

mostly because it put Emilio Estevez, Rob Lowe, Andrew McCarthy, Demi Moore, Judd Nelson, and Ally Sheedy on the screen at the same time.

See also OUTSIDERS, THE; YOUNG GUNS

ST. JOSEPH BABY ASPIRIN

These were orange and tiny, and you needed to eat like 10 at a time for any effect. Now we know they taste like Brass Monkey.

See also FLINTSTONES CHEWABLE VITAMINS

STEFANO DiMERA VS. ROMAN BRADY

The hottest villain vs. good guy thing going on in daytime television. Stefano was perhaps the most evil character ever on *Days of Our Lives* (Victor Kiriakus takes a close second), and he constantly toyed with the personal and professional life of Salem's finest cop, Roman Brady.

See also LUKE AND LAURA; SPRINGFIELD, RICK

STICKERS

Be they the scratch 'n' sniff or the poofy variety, they were all over our Trapper Keepers in third and fourth grade.

See also GARBAGE PAIL KIDS; TRAPPER KEEPER

STING

White-haired, Twizzler-thin, freaky-looking British crooner who somehow made himself simultaneously sexy, lovable, and downright creepy. By heading one of the best bands of all time (The Police), starring in some cult movies (*Dune*, *The Bride*), making some good solo albums and spouting off about all sorts of social issues, he emerged from the '80s as one of our culture's few everlasting superstars. The man will never truly go out of style.

BONUS FACT: As most fans know, his real name is Gordon Sumner, not to be confused with Gordon *Shumway*, aka that lovable puppet alien Alf.

See also ALF; BAND AID; BAN THE BOX; *DUNE*; "MONEY FOR NOTHING" VIDEO; POLICE, THE; RUSSIANS

STOLTZ, ERIC

One of those actors who most people, unless they're hard-core fans, will recognize but couldn't name a single movie he made. When we say he was Spicoli's surfing buddy in *Fast Times at Ridgemont High* and the disfigured guy in *Mask* and the kid from the suburban underclass in John Hughes' *Some Kind of Wonderful*, you'll go, "Oh yeah! *That* guy. He's kinda cool."

See also FAST TIMES AT RIDGEMONT HIGH; HUGHES, JOHN; MASK

STOMPERS

Self-powered 4x4 trucks considered neat because they were small (almost compatible with Hot Wheels and Matchbox) and had soft nubby tires that helped them climb over almost anything.

See also MICRO MACHINES

STONE, OLIVER

The man who taught us about the '60s.

See also CONAN THE BARBARIAN; VIETNAM-MANIA; WALL STREET

STOP! THIEF

When board games started taking a beating from video games, Milton-Bradley came up with this hybrid. You chased an invisible thief through several city blocks, using sound clues provided by a calculator-sized thing that came with the game. If you had a hunch where the bad person was, you entered the coordinates into the thing, and it would tell you if you were right.

See also ELECTRONIC BATTLESHIP; MOUSE-TRAP

STRANGE BREW

A modern retelling of Shakespeare's *Hamlet*. Bob and Doug McKenzie mirror Hamlet's comic buddies, Rosencrantz and Guildenstern, and they quest for Elsinore beer. A little too literary for us.

See also HOSER; MCKENZIE, BOB AND DOUG

STRAWBERRY SHORTCAKE

The third most annoying toy-cum-cartoon character ever invented, after My Little Pony and certain little blue characters. Each resident of her universe (including Blueberry Muffin, Lemon Meringue, and Huckleberry Pie) was supposed to smell like a different fruit or dessert product, but most of the dolls just had an overbearing plastic odor. A lot of people wished the evil Purple Pieman would just wipe her out.

See also CARE BEARS; MY LITTLE PONY; SMURFS

STRIPES

Sort of a grown-up version of *Animal House* (if there can be such a thing), set in the always-mirthful milieu of Army basic training. Bill Murray has nothing left to lose, so he joins the Army, ropes buddy Harold Ramis into signing up too, and proceeds to add volumes to the guy-movie quote lexicon ("That's a fact, Jack!," "Boom-shaka-laka-laka," etc.).

See also ANIMAL HOUSE; CADDYSHACK; GHOSTBUSTERS; MURRAY, BILL; SATURDAY NIGHT LIVE

STRETCH ARMSTRONG

A rubbery doll that you could pull and pull and pull until its limbs were three feet tall, and at least for the first month you had it, would return to its original shape. It looked like a professional wrestler and was filled inside with something that looked like grape jelly.

See also HOGAN, HULK; SLIME

STUDIO 54

A place where rich drug addicts hung out with Andy Warhol, or something.

See also DISCO; GOLDMAN, ALBERT

STUFF, THE

A campy horror flick that preyed on America's sudden faddish fascination with yogurt. In the 1985 movie, a yummy white substance marketed as The Stuff sweeps the nation. Nobody realizes that it turns those who eat it into blubbering piles of goo until it's too late! Danny Aiello and former *SNL* guy Garrett Morris starred in this cautionary tale for a troubled time.

See also RIGHT STUFF, THE; YOGURT

SUBGENIUS, CHURCH OF THE

A religion of sorts. Or rather, a collection of modern myths and pseudophilosophy revolving around popular culture, mock demon worship, and a nonexistent god called "Bob." The thing is, nobody takes the SubGenius seriously, not even its members. It's more like an ongoing science fiction series with lots of fans.

The "church" centers around two men: Rev. Ivan Stang, the guy who created and maintains it, and J.R. "Bob" Dobbs. The worship of Bob usually doesn't have to go any further than just knowing about him and his philosophy of "slack." People in the know consider themselves cool, and that's about it. Stang has put out several books on the subject: *High Weirdness by Mail*, *The Book of the SubGenius,* and *Three-Fisted Tales of Bob.* And even though this phenomenon came to being in the '80s and has a following of mostly younger folks, participants in the creation of Bob mythos include Boomer-era misfits like Timothy Leary and Robert Anton Wilson.

See also DOBBS, J.R. "BOB"; ILLUMINATI

SUCTION-CUP GARFIELD

After the "Baby on Board" boom, physical objects seen suction-cupped to car windows grew more elaborate. Thousands of Americans chose to stick Garfield plush toys, with paws splayed and eyes wide, against their car windows. And in car decor (indeed, as in life) hot trends spawn parodies. By the time the orange fur of this fad started to fade from sun exposure, crushed Garfield rear ends could be seen hanging out of trunks and gas tanks.

See also BABY ON BOARD; "GARFIELD"; SHIT HAPPENS; VISUALIZE WHIRLED PEAS

SUICIDE SLURPEES

A beverage created by mixing all the flavors of Slurpees available at 7-Eleven. Mixing all the sodas resulted in Suicide Big Gulps.

See also BIG GULP; JOLT COLA

SUMMER GAMES

A home version of the arcade game Track and Field, expanded to include other sports and reserved especially for those who had the good fortune to own an IBM computer in the early '80s. Later made for other machines, too.

See also COMMODORE 64; TRACK AND FIELD; WINTER GAMES

SUPER BOWL SHUFFLE

A really stupid rap done by the 1985 Chicago Bears, who may have become Super Bowl champions simply because of clever public relations. The best rhymes came from scrappy backup QB Steve Fuller and sweet-voiced running back Walter Payton.

See also FRIDGE, THE

SUPER DAVE OSBORNE

"Daredevil" who got his start on the syndicated comedy show *Bizarre* with John Byner. That show pretty much blew, but Super went on to become his own man, making commercials and many memorable appearances on Letterman.

See also KNEIVEL, EVIL; LETTERMAN, DAVE

SUPERFRIENDS

The seminal Saturday morning cartoon of our lives.

See also GLEEK; JUSTICE LEAGUE OF AMERICA; LEGION OF DOOM

SUPERFUDGE

Judy Blume's continuing adventures of Peter, Fudge, Sheila, Turtle the dog, and Dribble the turtle that began in *Tales of a Fourth Grade Nothing*. One of her "clean" books that didn't talk a lot about menstruation, masturbation, or sex. Others included *Otherwise Known as Sheila the Great* (about Sheila and her delusions of grandeur), *Blubber* (about being fat), *The One in the Middle Is the Green Kangaroo* (about being young and awkward), and *Deenie* (about having a back brace).

See also BLUME, JUDY; *FOREVER*

Super Dave

SUPER FUZZ

Strange little 1981 movie, seen (if at all) on cable, about a cop (Terence Hill) uncomfortable with his newfound superhuman powers. He loses the ability to fly when looking at the color red, which doesn't help much. His partner (you guessed it: Ernest Borgnine) tries to help out and (you guessed it again) comedy ensues.

See also CITY HEAT; GREATEST AMERICAN HERO, THE; SLEDGE HAMMER!; SUPERMAN: THE MOVIE

SUPERMAN: THE MOVIE

The best of the '70s live-action superheroes who fought bad guys while wearing goofy tights. In 1978, this film forever defined the Man of Steel as looking like Christopher Reeve and Lois Lane like Margot Kidder. Also, Marlon Brando played Kal-El (Superman, Sr., dead by the end of the first scene). The first sequel featured three badasses from Krypton bent on evil, plus Superman's weird ice cave. But parts III (with Richard Pryor) and IV (with an obnoxious antinuke message) effectively killed the franchise and made room for Batman.

See also BATMANIA; GREATEST AMERICAN HERO, THE; INCREDIBLE HULK, THE; JUSTICE LEAGUE OF AMERICA; NEXT; ROTH, DAVID LEE; SIX MILLION DOLLAR MAN, THE; WONDER WOMAN

SUPERPOWER

A word that applied to both the United States and the Soviet Union for decades, but became obsolete at the end of the '80s.

See also EVIL EMPIRE; GREAT SATAN; WTBS

SUSAN B. ANTHONY DOLLARS

The U.S. Treasury's weak try at replacing the big, bulky silver dollar that lasted only three years (1979–81) and resulted in the virtual elimination of all silver dollars. The Susan Bs were not different enough in size from a quarter, plus they had the same grooves on the side. Everyone was confused. But some post office stamp machines still give them as change.

See also BOSOM BUDDIES

"SUSSUDIO"

A song, the girl the song was about, a catchphrase, a bit of schtick on the Letterman show, and Phil Collins's most meaningful contribution to the 1980s.

See also "LAND OF CONFUSION" VIDEO

SUZUKI SAMURAI

The Pinto for the '80s. This cute Jeepy vehicle flipped over all the time and had to be discontinued.

See also BABY ON BOARD; YUGO

SWARM, THE

A disastrously bad 1978 disaster movie about killer bees eating a bunch of Americans, including Michael Caine, Katherine Ross, Richard Chamberlain, and Fred MacMurray.

See also FRUIT FLIES; KILLER BEES

SWATCH

Marked the fashion comeback of ana-log watches after years of domination by digitals, especially those bulky cal-culator and game watches. At last, style and class overcame functional-ity, except in the case of the Swatches with scented bands.

See also JELLIES; SWATCH GUARDS

SWATCH GUARDS

Small rubber fixtures, similar in tex-ture to Wacky Wall Walkers (but not so sticky), that fit onto Swatch watches and, theoretically, prevented the faces from getting scratched. The original guards were a small strip of rubber across the watch face, but those were discontinued in favor of a circle around the face's edge. Only hard-core nerds would put these on digital watches.

See also NERD; SWATCH; WACKY WALL WALKERS

SWEET VALLEY HIGH

A fabulously popular series of teen-girl fiction by the prolific Francine Pastal. They told the story of blond, green-eyed twins, the wild Jessica and the straitlaced Elizabeth. Usually ended with soap opera-style episodes.

See also BABYSITTER'S CLUB, THE; BLUME, JUDY; BROWN, ENCYCLOPEDIA; CLEARY, BEV-ERLY; *WRINKLE IN TIME, A*

SWITCHAROOMANIA

This is the most obvious example that one good idea in Hollywood is turned into four or five movies. The idea (originally done with females in *Freaky Friday*): *We can have a young guy switch bodies with an older guy! And wackiness will, in fact, ensue!* Within one year ('87–'88) the following did ensue: *Like Father, Like Son* (Kirk Cameron swaps with Dudley Moore), *Vice Versa* (Fred Savage becomes Judge Reinhold and, you know, vice versa), *Big* (David Moscow becomes Tom Hanks), and *18 Again* (George Burns and Charlie Schlatter).

See also BIG; CAMERON, KIRK; GOD; LIKE FATHER, LIKE SON; VICE VERSA

SYNTH-POP

Call it Euro-synth, call it New Wave, call it crap, but you couldn't escape this music in the '80s, the age of syn-thesizers. Synth-pop bands usually came from Europe and consisted of a singer or two and a couple of comput-ers. For added kicks, they might throw in a real instrument like drums or a guitar. At its peak, the craze claimed groups like Erasure, Depeche Mode, New Order, Kon Kan, Real Life . . . and on and on. And synthesizers became a staple in almost any band, even the heavy metal crowds (witness Van Halen). Synthy bands that out-lived the decade became associated with other semi-futile labels such as "house" and "alternative."

See also AEROBICS; ANYTHING BOX; ART OF NOISE, THE; BUGGLES; DEAD OR ALIVE; DEPECHE MODE; ERASURE; FALCO; NEW ORDER; NEW WAVE; SIGUE SIGUE SPUTNIK

Another big moment in our lifetimes

On July 23, 1984, Miss America Vanessa Williams was forced to give up her crown and title after naked pictures of her appeared in *Pent-house*.

TAB

Diet Coke, before it was savvy marketing to call it that.

See also *Back to the Future;* **New Coke; NutraSweet; Saccharin**

TACO

Yet another well-dressed European with only one name who stepped into the Top 40 for a few weeks and then disappeared forever. He did a synth-pop version of "Puttin' on the Ritz" that sounded as if his voice was lifted from an ancient, scratchy record.

Also a tasty Mexican treat.

See also **Falco;** *Puttin' on the Hits*

TALES OF THE GOLD MONKEY

Another 1982 *Raiders of the Lost Ark* rip-off, this one orchestrated by ABC and starring Stephen Collins as a pre-WWII danger-seeker.

See also *Bring 'Em Back Alive; Raiders of the Lost Ark*

TARTAR

Word commonly associated with condiments applied to fried fish before the 1980s, when it became better known as an evil substance—worse than gingivitis, even—attacking the teeth of America. Naturally, toothpaste companies rushed to our rescue with various tartar control dentrifices, and all was well again.

See also **Gel; Gingivitis; Plaque; Pump Toothpaste**

TARTIKOFF, BRANDON

Along with Reagan, Spielberg, and Hughes, this guy had more influence on our generation's culture than anyone. As head of NBC he was responsible for approving at least a third of the TV shows listed herein.

See also *A-Team, The;* **Glomer;** *Knight Rider; Manimal; Mr. Smith;* **Thursday night lineup**

TAURUS, FORD

The car that pretty much changed the way the American road looked. When Ford released this curvy, hyperbolic machine in 1986, it looked like something out of an EPCOT exhibit or a U.S. Department of Energy public-relations film on The Future of Human Transport. But pretty soon it began to just look like Mom's car, and then everybody's car.

See also **EPCOT; Iacocca, Lee;** *Robocop*

TAXI

One of the best sitcoms ever. Pretty much all of its stars went on to bigger and better things (especially Danny DeVito), except for Jeff Conaway, who played aspiring actor Bobby Wheeler. He did *Grease* and that was pretty much it.

See also CHEERS; NEWTON-JOHN, OLIVIA

TEARS FOR FEARS

These guys fooled a lot of people when their breakthrough album, *Songs from the Big Chair*, came out in 1985. The first single, "Everybody Wants to Rule the World," was a pretty decent, guitar-driven tune, and a bunch of rock fans went out and bought it. Then they found out that the rest of the record was just more Brit synth-poppy gunk, filled with songs like "Shout."

See also SYNTH-POP

TECHNO-

A prefix that, in decades past, added a futuristic edge to most any word. Its usage became retro with the coming of *cyber-*, which, when added to any concept, sent it at least 20 years further into the Future. (Which is more cutting-edge: Technobiology or cyberbiology? Technoids or cyberoids?) *Techno-* is clunky and mechanical; *cyber-* is sleek, portable, and outfitted with an Intel chip. *Techno-* is yet another example that words become obsolete faster and faster in the age of computers. Taking matters into its own hands, techno eventually broke off and became its own word, used to describe a variety of music involving computer-generated bass lines and very little else.

See also CYBER-; SYNTH-POP

TEDDY RUXPIN

A teddy bear that caused a Cabbage Patch-like buying crisis simply because he talked. He would mouth the words to any tape you put in the player in his back, be it the authorized fables of Ruxpin's magical world or "Straight Outta Compton."

See also CABBAGE PATCH KIDS; RAP

TEENAGE MUTANT NINJA TURTLES

Before they became the biggest thing in kiddietainment since G.I. Joe, these killer amphibians toiled for a while in the world of obscure underground comic books. Anyone who picked up a copy of the first bizarre black-and-white comic about turtles and rats in the mid-'80s could have sold it for several hundred dollars a few years later.

Of course, as often happens with crazes generated by something truly original, the turtles became oversaturated and inspired parodies, including comic book series called *Adolescent Radioactive Kung-Fu Hamsters* and *Naive Inner-Dimensional Kommando Koalas*.

See also AKIRA; DARK KNIGHT RETURNS, THE; G.I. JOE; INCREDIBLE HULK, THE

TEEN WOLF

The 1985 film that proved teenagers can do absolutely anything in '80s cinema. If killing zombies and reseeding all of mankind (*Night of the Comet*) weren't enough, if hanging with mutants in caves (*The Goonies*) weren't enough, if starting World War III (*WarGames*) wasn't

"My advice to you is to start drinking heavily."
"You should listen to him. He's pre-med."

—Sound advice from Bluto and Otter in *Animal House* to a despondent pledge with a totaled car.

enough . . . geeky teens (like, say, Michael J. Fox) could turn into werewolves and become superstars on their high school basketball team. And they can also surf on top of their scuzzy buddy's van. The sequel, *Teen Wolf, Too*, took this lame idea to college with a furry Jason Bateman.

See also EXPLORERS, THE; FOX, MICHAEL J.; GOONIES, THE; IT'S YOUR MOVE; NIGHT OF THE COMET; SILVER SPOONS; WARGAMES

TEMPEST

The thinking person's video game, featuring fancy geometric shapes and a title cribbed from the Bard his own self.

See also ATARI; STRANGE BREW

TERMINATOR, THE

The *Conan* movies might have made him recognizable to many folks, but it was the role of the unstoppable cyborg sent from the future to kill the mother of the future leader of the Resistance (Linda Hamilton, beauty from *Beauty and the Beast*) that defined Arnold Schwarzenegger as a Hollywood badass. The movie made the most of its basically one-note story by packing lots of cool explosions and, for the time and the budget, pretty good special effects. And "I'll be back" became one of the most quoted movie lines in eons.

See also BEAUTY AND THE BEAST; CONAN THE BARBARIAN; "GO AHEAD, MAKE MY DAY"; "I'LL BE BACK"; SCHWARZENEGGER, ARNOLD

TEST-TUBE BABY, THE

Born in August of 1978, ushering in a new era of post-human existence and TV movie plotlines.

See also BABY M; CLARK, BARNEY

TEXAS

Admitted into the union in 1845, the state became the center of the universe in the late 1970s, boasting the setting of the No. 1 show on TV, *Dallas*; America's Team, the Cowboys; the Cowboys' cheerleaders; and a mechanical bull at Gilley's.

See also DALLAS; DALLAS COWBOY CHEERLEADERS; MECHANICAL BULL

THAT "HEY VERN" GUY

Also known as Jim Varney. Perhaps no one better represents the American Dream than he does. He started out doing commercials for anyone who would have him, telling his off-camera buddy Vern about the great financing available for a limited time or the freshness of this great dairy's milk. And from there, he made four feature films with his character, Ernest.

See also BLU-BLOCKERS GUY, THE; HERB

THAT'S INCREDIBLE!

Look at what humans can do! This one can bend himself into a ball and fit into a 1-foot glass cube! This one lifted a trash dumpster off his wife! This kid with no arms writes and plays piano with his feet! With your hosts John Davidson, Fran Tarkenton and Kathie Lee Crosby! Wow! Neat-*o!*

See also KNEIVEL, EVIL; REAL PEOPLE; THOSE AMAZING ANIMALS

Why is this man famous?

THIRTYSOMETHING

A show distinctly and vehemently not about us, although many of us know all the plotlines and characters. It got almost as much attention for gripping script writing as it did for focusing on introspective, whiny Boomers caught in a deadly dull cycle of money-making and self-realization. Lots of people remember the episodes when a gay couple kissed and when that long-haired Gary guy died. The show also coined the word "thirtysomething," which has fallen into common usage and spawned offspring like twentysomething, fiftysomething, etcetarsomething. These words are now a permanent part of our language, appearing in newspapers and books like this one.

See also DAYS AND NIGHTS OF MOLLY DODD, THE; POINDEXTER

THIS IS YOUR BRAIN ON DRUGS AD

Omnipotent TV spot sponsored by the National Council for a Drug-Free America in which we were informed that an egg was our brain, and that the egg—when cracked open and sizzling in a frying pan—was our brain on drugs. "Any questions?" the narrator would ask.

Yeah. *What are you talking about?*

Needless to say, this was endlessly parodied on T-shirts for spring break–type places, ski resorts, and on posters like "This is your brain. This is your brain on drugs. This is your brain on drugs with a side of sausage and hash browns."

See also COCAINE; JUST SAY NO; WATCHMEN

THOMPSON TWINS

They weren't twins and they weren't named Thompson, but this band did have several hits, including "Hold Me Now" and "Lay Your Hands on Me."

See also DOUBLE TROUBLE

THORN BIRDS, THE

Weepy, epic miniseries that was something like 100 hours long and about a priest (Richard Chamberlain) who falls in love with a woman (Rachel Ward) and has a hard time dealing with that.

See also AMERIKA; ROOTS; SHOGUN; V.

THOSE AMAZING ANIMALS

Creatures that move about the planet all by themselves! Wow! Look at them go! With your hosts Burgess Meredith and Priscilla Presley! Super!

See also KIDS ARE PEOPLE, TOO; REAL PEOPLE; THAT'S INCREDIBLE!

THOSE THINGS IN THE CAR THAT MAKE BOMB NOISES

Small black boxes with four buttons, each with the power to make a noise simulating a method of destruction: machine gun, laser, falling and then exploding bomb, death ray. Popular as '80s car accessories and key chains.

See also BABY ON BOARD; MEAN PEOPLE SUCK; SUCTION-CUP GARFIELD

3-D MOVIES

For some reason, these things enjoyed a comeback around 1983. Key players were *Jaws 3-D*, *Friday the 13th Part 3-D*, *Amityville 3-D*, *Space Hunter: Adventures in the Hidden Zone*, and *Maelstrom*. Even a few movies on TV, like *House of Wax*, the original 3-D film, were shown that way (glasses available at your local 7-Eleven). Could it be our parents were wistful for the good old days of Hollywood?

See also EMMANUELLE

THREE-MILE ISLAND

A piece of bum uranium in this Harrisburg, Pa., reactor caused a little "accident" in 1979 and became the war hero of antinuke folks. A wave of panic spread across America: *Could this—or worse!—happen in our town?* The most tangible example of how dangerous nuclear power can be . . . until Chernobyl and *The Toxic Avenger.*

See also CHERNOBYL; MANHATTAN PROJECT, THE; SALT II; TOXIC AVENGER, THE; WARGAMES

THREE O'CLOCK HIGH

Underrated teenage movie about a kid (Casey Siemaszko of *Amazing Stories* and *Young Guns*) who works for the school paper and is assigned to do a story about a psycho student who just transferred in. Of course, he makes the bully mad and gets called out, and must then spend the rest of the day figuring out how not to get killed in the after-school rumble.

See also AMAZING STORIES; FAST TIMES AT RIDGEMONT HIGH; YOUNG GUNS

3 ROBOTIC STOOGES, THE

Saturday morning cartoon of the late '70s that took Larry, Curly, and Moe and made them into Dynomutt-like, crime-fighting androids, but retained the wacky eye-gouging and noggin-knocking of the real Stooges.

See also BLUE FALCON; DYNOMUTT; GLOBE-TROTTERS; INSPECTOR GADGET

THREE'S COMPANY

The 1970s show. It set women's and gay rights movements back about 10 years each, and most of our parents wouldn't let us watch it until it and its two crappy spin-offs, *The Ropers* and *Three's a Crowd,* were canceled and the original was in syndication.

See also AMERICATHON; ROPERS, THE

3-2-1 CONTACT

Kiddie science show on PBS, usually on before or after *The Electric Company.* The mock network news–style show taught us about stuff like hurricanes and square roots, and featured a mock–Sherlock Holmes segment about science-minded sleuths called "The Bloodhound Gang."

See also ELECTRIC COMPANY, THE; MR. WIZARD

THRILLER

Still the best-selling album ever. Michael Jackson owned the Top 40 in the early '80s, with no fewer than five singles reaching the Top 10. Also, the John Landis-directed video for the title song is considered by many to be the greatest of all time.

See also LANDIS, JOHN; MTV

THUNDARR THE BARBARIAN

Bad rip-off of *Star Wars* in the form of a Saturday morning cartoon.

See also OOKLA THE MOK

THUNDERCATS

Yet another mid-1980s, toy line-cum-cartoon series, this time featuring a bunch of remarkably human-like cats battling the forces of evil on a planet vaguely resembling some postapocalyptic version of our own. The cats also had a "pet" called Snarf.

See also G.I. JOE; GOBOTS; *M.A.S.K.*; MASTERS OF THE UNIVERSE; TRANSFORMERS; VOLTRON

THURSDAY NIGHT LINEUP

The best night on television. Ever. From '84 to '86, it was *The Cosby Show*, *Family Ties*, *Cheers*, *Night Court*, and *Hill Street Blues*. It was still almost as good when *L.A. Law* replaced *Hill Street*, but the whole thing began falling apart when *Family Ties* moved to Sunday and *A Different World* took over. All stability vanished when *Night Court* ended a year later and a series of lesser shows, like *Wings*, *Dear John*, and *Grand*, tried to fill the air.

See also CHEERS; COSBY SHOW, THE; FAMILY TIES; HILL STREET BLUES; L.A. LAW; SEPT. 22–OCT. 3, 1982; TARTIKOFF, BRANDON

The Huxtables, rulers of prime time.

THX 1138

George Lucas' first movie. It takes place in some sort of Orwellian future where people wear white jumpsuits, live in white boxes, and have names like "THX 1138." The title is also on a license plate in Lucas' second film, *American Graffiti*.

See also HOWARD THE DUCK; LIVING IN A BOX; LUCAS, GEORGE; ORWELL, GEORGE; STAR WARS

TIANANMEN SQUARE

The mysterious East didn't have as much positive influence in our pop culture as it did on that of the Boomer Era. The harsher aspects of Asian life had a higher profile than things like Zen and Buddha: The Japanese were outdoing us in every aspect of business and also exporting some great television and cartoons. The ancient Chinese general Sun Tzu had become a strategic hero to '80s American business types. A rash of Vietnam movies had nothing nice to say about the place. And the June '89 Tiananmen Square incident, in which young anti-communist protesters were shot and run over with tanks, reminded us again of how much it sucks to live in a less-than-free society.

See also AKIRA; EVIL EMPIRE; GUNG HO; HOLLYWOOD SQUARES, THE; SQUARE PEGS; TRANSFORMERS; TZU, SUN; VIETNAM-MANIA

TIC TAC DOUGH

Game show hosted by giant-toothed, helmet-coifed emcee Wink Martindale, in which two contestants answered trivia questions and placed their Xs and Os on a giant tic-tac-toe board. The final round featured a prize-killing dragon, and all games featured Wink's "You block!" call on defensive maneuvers.

See also FAMILY FEUD; WHAMMY

TIEGS, CHERYL

After Farrah, Ms. Tiegs sold more pinup posters than anyone else had at the time and pretty much was famous for being beautiful, a harbinger of things to come.

See also FARRAH POSTER, THE; KINSKI, NASTASSJA

TIFFANY

Not too attractive, no voice, did mostly cover tunes, did a tour of malls across America. Had several Top 10 hits in 1987–88. End career, end entry.

See also GIBSON, DEBBIE; MARTIKA; NEW KIDS ON THE BLOCK

TIMBUK 3

A group that stepped into our lives for a few minutes to let us know that the future's so bright, we gotta wear shades.

See also BALTIMORA

TIME, THE

Quasi-funk band led by Prince-wanna-be Morris Day. Had a few hits like "Jungle Love" and "The Bird," but lacked the staying power of their *Purple Rain* costar.

See also PRINCE; READY FOR THE WORLD; SHEILA E.; VANITY

TIME-LIFE OPERATOR, THE

She wore a headset and a smile. She invited you to dial the 800 number on your screen and order one of the Time-Life books series on the Old West, WWII, Vietnam, outer space, or handyman techniques for around the house. One would arrive every other month for only $9.95, and you'd get a free desk reference set, too! Call her. Now.

See also KRAZY GLUE; K-TEL; MR. MICROPHONE; POPIEL, RON

TIMELORDS

A British band that you couldn't exactly call a one-hit wonder. That would be giving their song too much credit. In 1988, they did an eerie, synth-pop ditty called "Doctorin' the Tardis" (a takeoff on that "Rock And Roll Part 2" song by Gary Glitter that, in the 1990s, has become a trendy thing to chant at sporting events: "Rock 'n' ro-oll . . . hey! Rock 'n' roll.

Duh-duuh . . . hey!"). The Timelords tune sampled theme music from the classic British sci-fi show *Dr. Who* and went a little like this: "Dr. Who-oo . . . hey! Dr. Who. Dr. Who-oo . . . hey!"

See also DR. AND THE MEDICS; *HITCH-HIKER'S GUIDE TO THE GALAXY, THE*

TOGETHER FOREVER TOUR

Run-D.M.C., rap's first true superstars, got together with the obnoxious, white Beastie Boys and hit the road to show that everybody could share the hip-hop spotlight, and, oh yeah, to promote *Tougher than Leather* and *Licensed to Ill*, respectively.

See also BEASTIE BOYS; RUBIN, RICK; RUN-D.M.C.

TOMMY TUTONE

A rock group, not a guy. They knew Jenny pretty well and were good at math.

See also 867-5309

TOOTSIE

People older than us seemed to think this movie was the funniest thing since rubber chickens, but all we really wanted to know was why Dustin Hoffman was dressing up as a woman.

See also ISHTAR

TOP GUN

The ultimate date movie. Perhaps even the ultimate '80s movie. Unlike *Dirty Dancing*, this was fun for both halves of a couple. For guys, this had fighter jets, anti-communism machismo, Navy

Probably working in a mall now.

lingo, Kelly McGillis, motorcycles, great one-liners, lots of high fives, bad guys in black, and cool (at the time) music. For girls: Tom Cruise playing volleyball shirtless and Berlin's mega-ballad, "Take My Breath Away."

BONUS FACT: *Top Gun* did so much to boost the image of the military that Navy recruiters set up tables outside movie theaters.

See also BE ALL YOU CAN BE; *COCKTAIL;* CRUISE, TOM; GOOSE; *RIGHT STUFF, THE*

TOTALLY

A multipurpose word that fit into Valley Girl, surfer, skater, and Bill&Ted-speak slang categories. *Totally* has two meanings:

1) It signifies agreement, in much the same way as "Right on" and "You know it." Witness the following conversation, which (statistically speaking) probably took place several times in the 1980s:

"*That* Death Wish *movie was rad.*"

"*Totally.*"

2) It can also be used as an adverb, as in: "*Charles Bronson totally rocks my world*" or "*That* Death Wish *movie was totally rad.*"

See also BILL&TEDSPEAK; LIKE; SKATE-BOARDS; VALLEY GIRLS

TOWER COMMISSION REPORT, THE

The '80s version of 'Nam-era government-document classics *The Pentagon Papers* and *The Warren Commission Report.* Only more popular. With the publication of the *Tower Commission* paperback, the Iran-Contra affair/scandal/deal/thingy reached a pitch of popularity that movie studios pay millions in advertising to achieve. Not only did the hearings make for great television, but the congressional investigation read like a Tom Clancy novel. Or so you might suspect from their best-seller status. But did anybody actually tear through this while lounging on the beach? We didn't think so.

See also IRAN-CONTRA THING; NORTH, OLIVER

TOXIC AVENGER, THE

The best known of the Troma cult films. A janitor gets doused in poorly disposed nuclear waste, turns into a goofy-looking mutant (Toxie), and then takes revenge on the greedy corporate and government types responsible. Any sort of serious antinuke message is overshadowed by gratuitous breast shots and very disgusting, very cheap gore effects. They made three of these, one being *The Last Temptation of Toxie.*

See also CHERNOBYL; *DAY AFTER, THE;* *LAST TEMPTATION OF CHRIST, THE;* THREE-MILE ISLAND; TROMAVILLE; *WARGAMES*

TRACEY ULLMAN SHOW

Best known as the birthplace of Bart, Homer, Marge, Lisa, and Maggie Simpson, this maybe-a-little-too-British-for-the-States sketch variety show died despite being terribly bloody funny.

See also ULLMAN, TRACEY

TRACK AND FIELD

Video game from Atari that featured several events from the sport for which it was named. Great for getting out aggression, because you had to pound the two "run" buttons really hard to make your guy go fast. Players gunning for a high score sometimes used a pen held in one hand to hit the buttons extra fast, but soon Atari was making the game with shields around the buttons to prevent such chicanery.

See also ATARI; SUMMER GAMES; WINTER GAMES

TRANSFORMERS

Both the cartoon and the toys were better than Gobots. Players in the Autobot/Decepticon wars on Planet Cybertron included Optimus Prime, Galvatron, and Megatron. A key sortie in the invasion of techno-heavy Japanese animation.

See also AKIRA; GOBOTS; *STAR BLAZERS*

TRAPPER

Perhaps the only major advance in folder design this century. In the early '80s, scientists at Mead discovered how to put pockets on the side edges of folders, instead of the bottom. This had a few advantages, namely: Paper could no longer escape out the top of the folder. But, on the downside: You had to open a Trapper all the way to get inside. You couldn't just peek inside and grab those notes. And did anyone really have a problem with paper escaping anyway?

At first, these came only in pri-

mary colors, but later they had designs resembling posters found in the back of mall record stores or Spencer's, stuff like pictures of cars, heartthrobs, bands, and cartoon characters.

See also MALLS; PEE-CHEE FOLDERS; SPENCER'S; TRAPPER KEEPER

TRAPPER KEEPER

The ultimate in school-time organization (from Mead!). You could put doodles in the three-ring binder parts, along with folders (they had to be Trappers, unless you punched holes in the sides of Pee-Chees and other "traditional" models) for handouts. You could cover the outside with stickers, and write your name all over with outliner pens. The early models had a primitive metal snap on the closing flap, but the design quickly progressed into the age of Velcro.

See also OUTLINER PENS; PEE-CHEE FOLDERS; STICKERS; TRAPPERS; VELCRO

TRAVELING WILBURYS, THE

Late 1980s supergroup made up of four rock legends: Roy Orbison, Bob Dylan, George Harrison, and Tom Petty. Then they realized they needed someone who could play the drums. So they called Jeff Lynne, who used to be in ELO and had nothing but time on his hands.

See also ASIA; PETTY, TOM; POWER STATION

TRIVIAL PURSUIT

The game, the description of which was fully contained in its title, that brought the adult board-game industry back from oblivion when it was introduced in 1981 by two guys from Canada who had taken the time to compile a lot of little facts in the blue (geography), pink (entertainment), yellow (history), brown (arts and literature), green (science and nature), and orange (sports and leisure) colors of knowledge. Followed by countless other trivia-word-knowledge games with catchy names and premises that could easily be adapted by college students to facilitate drinking.

See also PICTIONARY

TROLL/SCHOLASTIC PRESS

We got order forms for these books every month in elementary school. In addition to all the latest Hardy Boys/ Nancy Drew titles, you could also get those precious posters of puppies and kittens hanging from tree branches overprinted with phrases like "I hate Mondays!" and "Why Me?"

See also BLUME, JUDY; CLEARY, BEVERLY; DREW, NANCY; HARDY BOYS; SWEET VALLEY HIGH; *WRINKLE IN TIME, A*

TROMA

Production company behind a series of masterfully schlocky cult films, including *Class of Nuke 'Em High* (parts 1 and 2), *The Toxic Avenger* (parts 1, 2 and 3), and *Surf Nazis Must Die*. The overriding theme usually involved environmental issues, like disposal of nuclear waste. But you wouldn't exactly call these cautionary, eco-films. Other themes played much more heavily, like half-naked women and drooling mutants.

See also CHERNOBYL; THREE-MILE ISLAND; *TOXIC AVENGER, THE*

TRON (THE MOVIE)

Released in 1982, this Disney film was fascinating in that it was the first one to use a lot of computer graphics (the light-cycle and tank scenes were especially cool), and it played on our early fascination/fear with the power of computers. Unfortunately, the story of a programmer (Jeff Bridges) who gets digitized by an evil master program (the MCP) and sent inside the computer world, where he joins forces with a program called Tron (Bruce Boxleitner) to fight the MCP, was pretty lame.

See also ELECTRIC DREAMS; HEADROOM, MAX; TRON (THE VIDEO GAME)

TRON (THE VIDEO GAME)

By all accounts superior to the movie.

See also ATARI; *TRON* (THE MOVIE)

TRS 80

Another in the first generation of home computers. Some of these by Tandy–Radio Shack had a major advantage over the early Apple and Texas Instrument machines: color, hence the nickname "Color Computer." This, and the fact that it was easier to take apart, made it popular with early computer types who weren't lucky enough to have IBMs. Disparaged by snobs as the "Trash 80."

See also APPLE IIE; ATARI 400; COMMODORE 64; MS-DOS

TRUE STORIES

Off-center 1987 film made by the Talking Heads' David Byrne about a small town in Texas and the people who live there, including a woman who refused to get out of bed, ever. One of John Goodman's first starring roles, too.

See also Raising Arizona; Texas

TRULY TASTELESS JOKES-MANIA

In the early '80s, somebody decided to anthologize all the dead-puppy, quadriplegic, Polish, black, Jewish, gay, and Helen Keller jokes that everybody already knew in a book called *Truly Tasteless Jokes*. This became a franchise, with countless sequels and copycats (*Totally Gross Jokes*). This took place, of course, before something called Political Correctness. Whoever had the guts to go and buy one of these books and bring it to school knew how to get attention.

See also Clay, Andrew "Dice"; Garbage Pail Kids; Stand-up boom

TRUMP, DONALD

If there is a man who better symbolized the 1980s, we don't know who it is. He bought and sold about half of Manhattan and pretty much all of Atlantic City, then got poor after his divorce from Ivana, then got rich again. A hero to many B-school grads and best-selling author of *The Art of the Deal*.

See also Boesky, Ivan; Tzu, Sun; Wall Street

TUBULAR

Valley slang describing something with desirable qualities. Anything rad may also be considered tubular. The word is rarely used without the "totally" modifier, as in: *"Totally tubular!"*

See also Totally; Valley Girls

TURBO

Early road-racing video game that set the standard for all others to follow.

See also Atari; Pole Position; Spy Hunter

TURNER, TED

Round about 1970, he bought himself a little UHF station down in Atlanta. Ten years later, he had the first of cable television's "superstations," feeding us a diet of cartoons, cheesy old movies, and Atlanta Braves games. A few years after that, he started up a little fly-by-night venture called the Cable News Network.

Now, as we understand it, he owns 17 percent of the free world and goes to bed next to Jane Fonda every night. You gotta love this country.

See also Cable; CNN; Fonda, Jane; Spielberg, Steven; Tartikoff, Brandon; WTBS

TUTANKHAMEN

Ancient Egyptian king who caused a sensation and a Steve Martin bit in 1977–78, when his remains and the accompanying treasures and trinkets toured U.S. museums.

See also Tzu, Sun

TUTU, DESMOND

Black Anglican bishop in South Africa who led the 1980s fight against apartheid while Nelson Mandela was still imprisoned. For a lot of Americans, he was the one who made us understand what was going on over there. He won the Nobel Peace Prize in 1985 for his efforts.

See also APARTHEID; NELSON, MANDELA

21 JUMP STREET

Depp! Grieco! Holly Robinson! Beautiful people with guns! This was the first big show over there on Fox, about a troupe of cops who go undercover in high school to bust all the kids who stick gum to the bottom of their desks.

See also FOX

TWINKIE THE KID

Oblong cowboy who, along with the Fruit Pie Magician, adorned Hostess snack packages and was animated for the company's ad campaigns. Never really caught on as icons of the product the way Peanuts characters did for Dolly Madison.

See also DOLLY MADISON; FRUIT PIE MAGICIAN

TWISTED SISTER

Phenomenally ugly, cartoonish metal band fronted by the phenomenally ugly, cartoonish Dee Snyder. They would have gone unnoticed, except their videos for "We're Not Gonna Take It" and "I Wanna Rock" appealed to the rebellious headbanger in all of us. They, along with Mr. T cereal, had a cameo in *Pee-wee's Big Adventure*. The band's videos also featured that ROTC guy from *Animal House* yelling, "You're all worthless and weak!!!"

See also HEAVY METAL BOOM; JUDAS PRIEST; QUIET RIOT

2 LIVE CREW

Depending on your point of view, this rap group from Miami was either: 1) a heroic band of artists crusading against censorship, 2) a sick crowd of perverts selling exploitative pornography to kids, or 3) just a crappy band that got lucky and thus famous by embroiling themselves in a huge legal controversy. Some Florida record store owners were arrested under anti-obscenity laws for selling the album *Nasty as They Wanna Be*, which had a lot of songs about naked people and what they do to each other. (Who among us has never sang along to, "He-e-ey, we want some pu-u-ssy!") Lead singer Luther "Luke Skywalker" Campbell went to jail for simply performing concerts, and the whole mess was instrumental in the creation of the now-standard Parental Advisory label.

See also FUCK; GORE, TIPPER; MAPPLETHORPE, ROBERT; PARENTAL ADVISORY LABEL

TWO-TONE JEANS

In the heady jeans-designing days of the mid-1980s, just before acid-washing gained supremacy, it was considered the height of style to make and wear blue jeans that were not, in fact, entirely blue. The trend contained itself mostly to women's jeans, and the most common second color was gray, and it was usually found adorning extra pockets on the legs or, sometimes, an entire leg. Looked especially cool with a nice neon sweatshirt.

See also Acid wash; Chic; 501 Blues; Neon Clothing

TYLENOL SCARE

Some guy in Chicago laced some tablets with cyanide in 1982, and the nation refused to take painkillers for months afterward. Responsible for all medicine now being packaged in annoying shrink-wrap and impossible childproof caps.

See also Ibuprofen; St. Joseph Baby Aspirin

TYLER, BONNIE

The raspy, sexy voice behind "Total Eclipse of the Heart," one of the longest, slowest-building songs allowed on the radio during the height of the Top-40 era. She also did "Holding Out for a Hero" from the *Footloose* soundtrack, which was shorter.

See also Footloose

TYSON, MIKE

When he won his first heavyweight title at age 19, he was seen as the man who could restore boxing to the glory it enjoyed when Muhammad Ali was in his prime. But after his mentor Cus D'Amato died, Tyson fell into slimy promoter Don King's lap, and while he beat the bejesus out of just about everybody he faced, there was always a sense of impending doom surrounding him. We saw glimpses of it in his short marriage to actress Robin Givens, a whole bunch of it in his loss to Buster Douglas, and the end of it with his rape conviction.

Bonus pop music tie-in: D.J. Jazzy Jeff and the Fresh Prince had a song about how they thought they could beat Mike Tyson, which, as we all know, they couldn't.

See also D.J. Jazzy Jeff and the Fresh Prince; Givens, Robin

TZU, SUN

A Chinese military strategist who died 2,400 years ago but made a huge comeback in the '80s. It became trendy in business circles to study Tzu's book, *The Art of War*, and apply the principles to the corporate world. Advice like "Know the enemy, know yourself; your victory will never be endangered" made for great inspirational posters. However, wisdom like "Generally, operations of war require one thousand fast four-horse chariots, one thousand four-horse wagons covered in leather, and one hundred thousand mailed troops" did not. Also, a hot video game for PCs called The Ancient Art of War took a cue from Master Tzu.

See also Iacocca, Lee; Trump, Donald

Another big moment in our lifetimes

On December 22, 1984, Bernhard Goetz shoots four teens on a New York subway train who were, depending on who you listened to, either trying to rob him or asking for some spare change. The uproar surrounding the case made Goetz a folk hero to some and the embodiment of crude, racist vigilantism to others.

ÜBER-

Prefix used to elevate a person or concept to a height of almost god-like prowess. An über-anything is usually definitive in its class. Pee-wee Herman could arguably be called an übernerd, and some might refer to Alan Dershowitz as an überlawyer. The use of this prefix has been proliferated by writers at magazines like *Rolling Stone*, who use it almost indiscriminately.

See also CYBER-; HYPER-; MEGA-; PEE-WEE HERMAN

UEBERROTH, PETER

The man who brought the Olympics to Los Angeles, then made sure that not a single athlete was shot during the competition. Later had a less successful turn as commissioner of baseball.

See also LEWIS, CARL; RETTON, MARY LOU

ULLMAN, TRACEY

She had a song once, before having a TV show. One-hit thing. "They Don't Know." Top 10 even. She had green hair in the video and sounded like Cyndi Lauper.

See also BALTIMORA; LAUPER, CYNDI; *TRACEY ULLMAN SHOW*

UNDEROOS

Theme-oriented underwear and T-shirts. These came in everything from Strawberry Shortcake to Batman to Darth Vader. The point was lost on us because we were too young to enjoy being seen in our underwear, and wearing the T-shirts in public was considered dorky.

See also JUSTICE LEAGUE OF AMERICA; *STAR WARS*; STRAWBERRY SHORTCAKE

UNION CARBIDE

Giant chemical company that accidentally gassed Bhopal, India, in 1984, killing about 3,500 people.

See also CHERNOBYL; EXXON *VALDEZ*; MOUNT ST. HELENS

UNITED STATES FOOTBALL LEAGUE

Jim Kelly, Steve Young, Herschel Walker, a team owned by Donald Trump. This short-lived attempt at competition for the NFL had all that going for it but one big problem: it moved its games to the fall, and most Americans still liked the NFL. Then the USFL sued the NFL for antitrust and won, and received the triple damage award that is the law in such cases—

$3, triple the $1 a judge awarded the league.

See also JACKSON, BO; TRUMP, DONALD

UNO

Multihued card game that was pretty much like playing hearts, only more fun because the cards were so brightly colored and styled in that inimitable way that veritably screamed "1981."

See also ELECTRONIC BATTLESHIP; TRIVIAL PURSUIT

USA FOR AFRICA

The biggest of the musical cause projects around 1985. This one featured 45 artists, including Michael Jackson, Stevie Wonder, Bruce Springsteen, Bette Midler, Ray Charles, Billy Joel, Huey Lewis, Cyndi Lauper, Kenny Rogers, Harry Belafonte, and on and on. If you listened carefully, you could distinguish who sang what part. They recorded one of the biggest-selling (and most overplayed) singles ever, "We Are the World," which, on April 5, 1985, was played on thousands of radio stations at the *exact same time*.

See also BAND AID; FARM AID; HANDS ACROSS AMERICA; HEAR'N AID; LIVE AID; NORTHERN LIGHTS

USA TODAY

Launched in 1982, this was supposed to be newspapers' response to the short-attention-span style of television. With cutesy, primary-color graphics and stories no longer than this entry, *USA Today* tried to redefine the role of pulp products in American life. The thing is still around, so maybe it did.

See also CABLE; MC-; MTV

V

V.

Or *The epic saga of V.*, as NBC called it. This colossally bad miniseries starring Marc Singer (of *Beastmaster* fame) was revived for a second run, then became a series. It was a forerunner to *Alien Nation* in that supposedly friendly aliens wanted to take over the planet and we mated with them and stuff like that. The most memorable scene from the series involved a woman giving birth to a big lizard-alien.

BONUS FACT: Robert "Freddy Krueger" Englund was in this.

***See also* MINISERIES**

VALLEY GIRL

In 1983, the title of this movie turned a lot of people off, and probably rightfully so. But for what it was, a typical boy-from-the-wrong-side-of-the-tracks-chases-upper-middle-class-girl story, it was pretty good. Nicolas Cage got his first starring role as the punker who falls in love with the Valley Girl, much to the disdain of both their circles of friends. Also featured a soundtrack of New Wave nuggets, the most famous being Modern English's "I'll Melt with You."

See also* MODERN ENGLISH; *PRETTY IN PINK*; PUNK ROCK; *VALLEY GIRL DICTIONARY

The cast of V.

VALLEY GIRL DICTIONARY

Released in 1982, at the height of the national craze imitating the culture and dialect of females from Los Angeles' San Fernando Valley, this novelty reference book caused controversy by being too racy for the young girls who wanted to read it.

***See also* VALLEY GIRLS**

VALLEY GIRLS

A complete culture—with its own language, dress, and other societal norms—that many teenage girls adopted in the early '80s. The Valley Girl's natural habitat was Southern California, particularly in the San Fernando Valley, specifically in a mall, most likely the Sherman Oaks Galleria. But they were spotted in every mall and high school in '80s America saying things like "Oh mah gawd!" and "Like, totally gag me with a spoon!" and meaning it. Their existence generated a small industry of reverence and parody including the movie *Valley Girl*, the show *Square Pegs*, the *Valley Girl Dictionary*, and almost anything comedienne Julie Brown did.

See also Bill&Tedspeak; For sure; Gag me with a Spoon; Gnarly; Go; Grody; Like; Oh my gawd; Omigod; *Square Pegs*; Totally; Tubular; *Valley Girl*; *Valley Girl Dictionary*; Was all; Was like; Zappa, Moon

VAN HALEN

Four guys from Southern California who, thanks to innovative guitar-playing, bawdy lyrics, MTV, and the ultimate rock-star lifestyle, singlehandedly brought heavy metal music into the mainstream, especially with *1984*. And we all remember where we were when David Lee Roth left the band and was replaced by Sammy Hagar.

See also Bon Jovi; Heavy Metal Boom; Mötley Crüe; Orwell, George; Roth, David Lee

VANS (THE SHOES)

These shoes had two advantages over other cheap sneakers: no laces, and you could play chess on them. They peaked in popularity around 1985, but fit in with so many subcultures (break-dancing, surfers, skaters, nerds) that they didn't vanish entirely with parachute pants and sequined gloves.

See also Breakdancing; Parachute Pants; Skateboards

VANS (THE VEHICLES)

Mode of transportation that fell out of fashion just as we were becoming old enough to drive. In the '70s and early '80s, nothing screamed "smooth, sexy, hip, kinda sleazy, with-it guy who gets a lot of action" more than a customized van, especially one with velvet interior or maybe even a mural on the side. Witness Damone in *Fast Times* and Michael J. Fox's buddy Styles in *Teen Wolf* and, to a lesser degree, the gang in the Mystery Machine from *Scooby Doo*. There was also a movie called *The Van* (1976) in which a teenage guy lures in honeys with his wheels.

But the van's decline can be marked by two symbolic moments: 1) The introduction of the Dodge Caravan, the first true minivan (a very unhip machine incapable of displaying a mural; pretty much the anti-VW microbus), and 2) The scene in *Silence of the Lambs* where a psychopath lures a woman into his van and then kills and skins her. Bad PR for guys in vans.

See also Fast Times at Ridgemont High; Fox, Michael J.; Minivans; *Scooby Doo*

VARNEY, JIM

That "Hey Vern" guy.

See also That "Hey Vern" guy

VCR

Machine that first signaled the end of television networks controlling the lives of millions. People could tape *L.A. Law* or *Manimal* and watch them any time they wanted. The movie industry also made noise about the VCR killing theaters and so forth, but that never happened. If anything, the VCR (along with HBO) has increased the endurance level of human beings, allowing them to watch a movie over and over again until they can quote every line.

See also BETAMAX; BLOCKBUSTER; CABLE; CADDYSHACK; FLETCH; HBO; MONTY PYTHON AND THE HOLY GRAIL

VELCRO

Unquestionably the most important fastener of our time. First developed by NASA (or so it was rumored) as an alternative to buttons or snaps. The Army came up with a silent version so as not to give away a unit's position when someone opens his pack, and David Letterman leaped into television history when he trampolined onto a Velcro wall in a Velcro suit. Also, there were necessary Sniglets defining the fuzzy side (negacro) and the prickly side (posicro).

See also LETTERMAN, DAVE; SNIGLETS

VELOUR

The fabric of choice for a few years. Soft and fuzzy like the fur of a short-haired cat, velour could be found on sweaters, vests, and even pants.

See also MORRIS THE CAT

VENUS BUTTERFLY

Very few people know how to perform this imagined sexual maneuver, as mythologized on *L.A. Law.*

See also CARROT TRICK; *L.A. LAW*

VICE VERSA

Dad Judge Reinhold and son Fred Savage touch an ancient skull from Thailand and inhabit each other's bodies for a while. About all we remember of this movie is the poster, which was Reinhold in suit and tie, carrying a briefcase, riding a skateboard.

See also BIG; FREAKY FRIDAY; LIKE FATHER, LIKE SON; SKATEBOARDS; SWITCHAROOMANIA

VICTORY TOUR

The most anticipated, and most disappointing, music tour in history at the time of its staging in 1984. Michael Jackson was fresh off the success of *Thriller*, and he was rejoining forces with Tito, Jermaine, and the rest of the family for a megatour. It turned out to be a gigantic bust, plagued by technical problems all the way. The highlight of the whole ordeal was the single, "State of Shock," featuring Mick Jagger.

See also JACKSON, MICHAEL; *THRILLER*

VIC 20

Cheesy-but-cheap little home computer put out by Commodore in the early '80s. William Shatner did the TV commercials.

See also COMMODORE 64; *STAR TREK*

VIDEODISC

RCA's attempt at honing in on the burgeoning video market, introduced in late 1981, was a player that worked only with album-sized platters. But you had to get up halfway through the movie and turn the disc over, just like a record, and the picture wasn't that great, so they are now relegated to the trash heap of technological history.

See also BETAMAX; COMPACT DISCS; *SMOKEY AND THE BANDIT*; VCRs

VIETNAM-MANIA

While the 1980s was one of only three decades this century in which the U.S. wasn't involved in a major war, we made up for it with 'Nam films. In 1986 Oliver Stone set the gruesome visual standard for this, the third-wave of Vietnam movies, with *Platoon*. He was followed in 1987 by Stanley Kubrick's *Full Metal Jacket*; *Hamburger Hill*; *Hanoi Hilton*; *Good Morning, Vietnam;* and *Gardens of Stone*. This barrage was preceded by *Missing in Action* and *Rambo: First Blood Part II,* and followed by ABC's *China Beach* and CBS's *Tour of Duty*.

See also APOCALYPSE NOW; LAST EPISODE OF *M*A*S*H*; *PLATOON*; *RAMBO*; STONE, OLIVER

VIOLENT FEMMES

One of few bands to survive punk, hop past synth-pop, and emerge as elder statespeople in the fairly popular New Wave movement. "Blister in the Sun" is part of any standard repertoire of rebellious and/or angstful music.

See also PUNK ROCK; SMITHS, THE

VISUALIZE WHIRLED PEAS

This well-deserved counter to the popular granola-culture "Visualize World Peace" bumper sticker showed up a few years after its progenitor, proving that even the most sacred of causes can be effectively skewered.

See also MEAN PEOPLE SUCK; SHIT HAPPENS; VISUALIZE WORLD PEACE

VISUALIZE WORLD PEACE

Popular, leftist bumper sticker that emerged during the Reagan Years.

See also REAGAN, RONALD; VISUALIZE WHIRLED PEAS

VOLTRON

Technically *Voltron: Defender of the Universe*, this was *the* definitive big-transforming-Japanese-robot cartoon, usually on in the afternoons when we got home from school. There's this galactic bad guy named Zarkon who always tries to take over the universe, and only the invincible robot Voltron can stop him. The thing is: Voltron got busted up a while back and split into five pieces, each one a spaceship type thing that turns into a robotic lion. So five members of the galactic defense force (Lance, Keith, Sven, Pidge, and Hunk) fly around in the lions and, when it comes time to really kick the shit out of whatever bad guy Zarkon sent on evil errands that day, they say "Ready to form Voltron!" During the stock animated montage, the five lions combine together into the big biped robot and easily dispense of any trouble. The question is: Why did they wait until the end of the show? Why not just be Voltron and be invincible all the time? Silly big transforming Japanese robot.

See also AKIRA; ROBOTECH; STAR BLAZERS; TRANSFORMERS

VOYAGERS!

Jon Erik-Hexum (may he rest in peace) and Meeno Peluce use hand-held time travel devices called Omnis to jump through time and correct historical screwups. This was taken off the air after complaints about too much violence.

See also EXPLORERS

VUARNET

Faddishly popular sunglasses that made people look like they had two giant pools of black paint oozing from their eyes. These shades (*fabrique à France*) also cost way too much for most high school kids who bought them.

See also CROAKIES

W

WACKY WALL WALKERS

Created by a Japanese inventor, these jelly-like spiders and other creatures slithered down a wall when slung against them. The biggest drawback was that they got dirty easily and lost their stickiness. Wendy's included them in kids' meals for a while.

See also PELLER, CLARA; SLIME; STRETCH ARMSTRONG

WAFFLE-OS

A short-lived cereal that looked liked waffles (both plain and blueberry) but tasted like Cap'n Crunch. A tiny cartoon cowboy pitched these to us while herding crowds of little Waffle-Os across the Great Plains. Through a stroke of literary luck, these crunchy buddies achieved immortality by being mentioned on the first page of Don DeLillo's novel *White Noise*.

See also CAP'N CRUNCH; COOKIE CRISP; OJS; SMURFBERRY CRUNCH

WAGNER, JACK

Heavily moussed *General Hospital* hunk who, in 1984, did lots of public brooding and crooning with a hit song and video, "All I Need."

See also LUKE AND LAURA; SPRINGFIELD, RICK

WAGNER, LINDSAY

You might know her better as Jamie Summers, the only woman ever on TV who could rip a phone book in half. That's because she was *The Bionic Woman*, kids. She battled fembots and other evildoers for Oscar and the OSI, occasionally teaming up with Col. Steve Austin, usually during sweeps.

See also SIX MILLION DOLLAR MAN, THE

WAITRESSES, THE

Minor New Wave band notable for two songs: "I Know What Boys Like" and the theme song to the TV show *Square Pegs*.

See also NEW WAVE; *SQUARE PEGS*

WALKMAN

One of the most successful brand names to assimilate into the English language as a real word. Like Kleenex and Frisbee and Nintendo. This was also revolutionary in the never-ending chain of cheap technologies we can wear on our bodies. When Sony revealed this hip-pocket wonder in 1979, America seemed to change into a place where such things have always existed and always would. The Walkman also has a couple of strange properties: 1) There is no comfortable plural (Is it Walkmen? Walkmans?), and 2) it becomes waterproof simply by being colored bright yellow.

See also BOOM BOX; *IRON EAGLE*; -MAN; POLAROID; VELCRO

WALL, THE

Pink Floyd album and movie that is basically a monument to self-destruction and going crazy. Both the album and the film sold like mad in the early '80s.

See also BAND AID

WALL OF VOODOO

Truly weird band fronted by Stan Ridgway, responsible for the song "Mexican Radio."

See also BALTIMORA

WALL STREET

A film that, in its scope and tone and direction, tried to be the definitive movie of the decade. Oliver Stone took all the cultural buzz concepts surrounding '80s business—greed, white males, individualism, sex, dark suits—and personified each one as someone like Daryl Hannah or Michael "Mr. Hot Social Issue" Douglas or son Charlie "Mr. Whatever Work I Can Get" Sheen. But the self-important breadth of the film dates it, and something like *WarGames* still beats it out in capturing terms like "definitive" and "quintessential."

See also BACK TO THE FUTURE; *BONFIRE OF THE VANITIES, THE*; COCKTAIL; MILKEN,

MICHAEL; OCTOBER 19, 1987; VIETNAM-MANIA; *WARGAMES*

WARGAMES

Matthew Broderick's first big role introduced most of us to the concept of computer hacking in 1983. While filled with familiar antinuclear buildup messages, this also had a lot of cool military acronyms like DEF-CON and NORAD and featured Ally Sheedy and Slap Maxwell himself, Dabney Coleman.

The mixture of computer paranoia, teen mischief, and Cold War moralizing makes this a good candidate for the most quintessentially '80s movie ever made. Director John Badham also holds a similar title for the previous decade with his *Saturday Night Fever*.

See also BACK TO THE FUTURE; COCKTAIL; COMMODORE 64; *DAY AFTER, THE*; *NIGHT OF THE COMET*; *SATURDAY NIGHT FEVER*

WARRANT

One of the last cheap '80s metal bands to make it big, they sang about the pain of being a woman in "Cherry Pie" and "I Saw Red." (OK, maybe those songs weren't about the pain of being a woman. Maybe they were about sex. Maybe we lied.)

See also POISON; RATT

WAS ALL

Another synonym for "said." For example: *She was all, "We are the knights that go ni!" and I was like, "Enough with the Monty Python," and she was all, "Ni! Ni! Ni!"*

See also Go; Like; *Monty Python and the Holy Grail*; Was like

WAS LIKE

A synonym for "said." As in: *I was like, "Shut up! Mikey did too die!"*

See also Go; Like; Mikey; Was all

WATCHMEN

Violent, grim, and very cool mid-'80s comic book series responsible for the "Have a nice day" smiley face with a bleeding bullet hole in its forehead, which was used on pins, T-shirts, and ads for the comic.

See also Akira; Dark Knight Returns, The; Have a nice day; Teenage Mutant Ninja Turtles

WAVERS

A social stereotype for people who got into New Wave music and style before they became mainstream.

See also Nerd; New Wave; Skateboards; Valley Girls

WEAVER, SIGOURNEY

Tough enough to be the hero in the *Alien* pictures, funny enough to play the possessed love interest in *Ghostbusters*, and almost sexy enough to woo Harrison Ford away from Melanie Griffith in *Working Girl*, Ms. Weaver was one of the better and more versatile, not to mention taller, actresses to make a name for herself in the 1980s.

See also Alien; Ford, Harrison; Ghostbusters; Working Girl

WEBSTER

ABC's answer to *Diff'rent Strokes*, with Emmanuel Lewis starring as the diminutive young black child adopted by a white couple, played by Alex Karras (George) and Susan Clark (Ma'am). From the outset, the show was a little too cute for its own good.

See also Diff'rent Strokes; Emmanuelle

WEDGE

The only Rebel fighter besides Luke Skywalker to fly in all three *Star Wars* movies. Sort of the anti-"Goose."

See also Boba Fett; Goose; *Jedi Master's Trivia Quiz Book*; Star Wars

WEEBLES

They wobbled and wobbled, but dammit, they just wouldn't fall down. The Weeble treehouse was the coolest playset.

See also Adventure People

WEEKLY READER

Nationwide magazine distributed to elementary-school kids that gave us a little introduction into what was going on in the world. Plus it had some really neat puzzles in the back.

See also Dynamite magazine; Troll/Scholastic Press

WE GOT IT MADE

OK, so two guys live together in New York, one's neat and straight and a lawyer, and the other's free-'n'-easy and kind of messy. Sound familiar?

Sound like a sitcom? Oh, but wait: Throw in a saucy young maid (Teri Copley) who hangs out in their place an awful lot, and then you've got a sitcom. This was so bad NBC canceled it after less than a season in 1984, but it mysteriously resurfaced in syndication three years later with new episodes.

See also SHEEDY, ALLY; *SMALL WONDER*

WEIRD SCIENCE

Teenage male nerd fantasy film about teenage male nerds (Anthony Michael Hall and Ilan Mitchell-Smith) who create a woman (Kelly LeBrock) with their computer. Another insightful journey into the mind of suburban kids from John Hughes.

See also BREAKFAST CLUB, *THE*; HUGHES, JOHN; *ZAPPED!*

WELCOME BACK, KOTTER

Probably the only show ever to combine juvenile delinquency and Borscht-Belt comedy and make the whole shebang worth watching. In the process, it made John Travolta a star. What else can you say about a show so pervasive, omnipresent, and everlasting? Except maybe: "Ooo! Ooo! Mistah Kottah! Mistah Kottah!" Oh, yeah, and those jokes Gabe Kaplan always told to his wife in bed at the end of every show.

See also CARE BEARS; *PERFECT*; *SATURDAY NIGHT FEVER*

WESTHEIMER, DR. RUTH

For no apparent reason, this woman was everywhere in the 1980s, dispensing frank-but-not-too-frank sexual advice on television, on the radio, in books, and in magazines. She filled in where Dr. Joyce Brothers left off. But couldn't our national sex therapist be just a little more, you know, sexier?

See also BROTHERS, DR. JOYCE; CARROT TRICK; *FOREVER*

WGN

Part of a small family of TV channels known as "superstations," on which we watched tons of cartoons and reruns. This station out of Chicago earned its prefix because it could be picked up without cable some places and popped up on services across the country. And also because it carried Bozo the Clown's show.

See also CABLE; WTBS

WHAM!

More universally hated by the males of our generation than even Duran Duran, the duo of George Michael and Andrew Ridgeley (where have you gone, Andrew?) wore a lot of white and Frankie-style "message" T-shirts and recorded a string of ballads and little poppy numbers that gave you cavities just listening to them. Oh, yeah, and George always had that too-perfect two-day growth under his duotoned mop.

See also DURAN DURAN; FRANKIE GOES TO HOLLYWOOD; HALL AND OATES; *MIAMI VICE*; MICHAEL, GEORGE

WHAMMY

Ugly cartoon creature who tried to take all your money if you happened to be a contestant on *Press Your Luck*. Several chants were used to ward him off, including, "Big money. Big money. No Whammy."

See also NOID, THE; PAT SAJAK SHOW, THE; REMOTE CONTROL; WIN, LOSE OR DRAW

WHATCHAMACALLIT

The best new candy bar to be introduced in the last two decades. In its original form, it was the rice-krispy type stuff held together by peanut butter and surrounded by chocolate. An added bonus was you could eat them cold without breaking your teeth. But then some Hershey's exec decided that, because it was a candy bar, it had to have caramel in it, and the magic was gone.

See also FUN DIP; JACKSON, REGGIE

"WHATCHOOTALKINBOUT"

Adorable catchphrase spoken in every episode of *Diff'rent Strokes* by that adorable sprite, Arnold. Funny, funny, *funny* to the very end.

See also DIFF'RENT STROKES; "I PITY THE FOOL"

WHAT'S HAPPENING!!

Essentially a black *Happy Days*, with Re-Run, Rag, Shirley, Dwayne, Mabel, and Dee—all hanging out at Rob's Place. Most everybody returned a few seasons later for *What's Happening Now!!*

See also FAT ALBERT AND THE COSBY KIDS; GOOD TIMES

WHEN IN ROME

Forgettable synth-pop band that had a hit with "The Promise." So why didn't we forget them?

See also BALTIMORA; SYNTH-POP

WHERE'S THE BEEF?

Along with "I'll be back" and "Go ahead, make my day," one of the most overused catchphrases from the 1980s. What was genuinely funny at first—the Wendy's ads featuring old ladies looking for the burger part of their hamburgers at other fast-food places—soon devolved into something out of a joke book for 11-year-olds, to wit:

Q. What did Wendy say when Ronald McDonald pulled down his pants?

A. Where's the beef?

See also "CAN WE TALK?"; "GO AHEAD, MAKE MY DAY"; "I'LL BE BACK"; "MAY THE FORCE BE WITH YOU"; PELLER, CLARA; "WHATCHOOTALKINBOUT"

WHITE, RYAN

The most famous noncelebrity to have AIDS. And he was our age, too. After he got infected from a blood transfusion in 1984, the Kokomo, Ind., school board tried to ban him from middle school and people pretty much ran him and his family out of town. They moved to Cicero, Ind., and attracted lots of media attention. Ryan died in 1990.

See also AIDS; HUDSON, ROCK; PATIENT ZERO

WHITE, VANNA

Letter-turner on *Wheel of Fortune* who put the *Price Is Right* models to shame with her wholesome good looks and sparkly clothes. Everybody loved Vanna (who couldn't, the girl was so sweet), even after her semi-nude picture (taken years earlier) appeared in *Playboy*.

See also L.A. LAW; PAT SAJAK SHOW, THE

WHITE NIGHTS

Cold War flick from 1985 about a Russian and an American (Mikhail Baryshnikov and Gregory Hines) who dance their way out of a Soviet prison camp. Soundtrack featured Lionel Richie's "Say You, Say Me."

See also BARYSHNIKOV, MIKHAIL; PELÉ; RAMBO; RICHIE, LIONEL

WHITESNAKE

British semi-metal band that had lots and lots and lots of hair and one hit: "Here I Go Again."

See also BON JOVI; GREAT WHITE; MOUSSE

WHIZ KIDS

During the height of the Geek Era, this 1983 CBS series pitted smart kids against wrongdoers of the world. A squad of L.A. high school students, with help from a newspaper reporter and a talking, know-it-all computer named Ralf, ran a mini-detective agency.

See also CRIME FIGHTING; GEEK ERA; MIS-FITS OF SCIENCE

Vanna, who could sell vowels to the Webster people.

WHO FRAMED ROGER RABBIT

Before *The Little Mermaid*, this film proved that people would go to the theaters to see a cartoon. The plot was not the greatest, but the integration of the animated and human characters was so good, most of us didn't notice. Director Robert Zemeckis and, of course, Steven Spielberg were behind this.

See also BLACK CAULDRON, THE; SPIELBERG, STEVEN

"WHO SHOT J.R.?"

His sister-in-law, Kristin Shepard, who was pregnant with his baby. You'd know this if you were one of the millions who tuned in on November 21, 1980.

See also DALLAS

WHO'S THE BOSS

For many guys, there was only one reason to watch this show: Alyssa

Milano. A budding, fair seraph among the ugliness of prime time. A Clearasil-perfect vision of teendom, with hair like Jane Seymour and skin like Cheryl Ladd. She played the daughter of a maid (Tony Danza, who had hair and skin like . . . well, Tony Danza), and the show got better as the years went on. But anyone not impressed by Alyssa probably didn't have any reason to watch this show.

See also CHARLES IN CHARGE

WILDING

The act of running around in a group of guys looking for trouble, especially if you're so adrenal and full of anger that you commit random violent acts. The term came to popular usage after the horrific Central Park Jogger incident, in which about 30 New York punks went out wilding and bludgeoned and raped a woman who was just out for a run. The term caught on, as a concise example of how bored, violent, and degenerate the Youth of Today have become. And TV news teams across the nation did similar stories: "Are kids wilding in your neighborhood? We find out for you . . . "

See also CENTRAL PARK JOGGER

WILLIAMS, DENIECE

Pop singer who rode the *Footloose* wave until it crashed with her song "Let's Hear It for the Boy."

See also BALTIMORA; *FOOTLOOSE*

WILLIAMS, JOHN

The most prolific composer of our time. He wrote the music for the biggest movies ever (and a few duds): *Star Wars*, *Raiders of the Lost Ark*, *E.T.*, *Jaws*, *Close Encounters of the Third Kind*, *1941*, and *Superman*. He also did the intro music for *NBC Nightly News* and scored one season's version of *The Cosby Show* theme. Anyone who can't hum at least one of Williams' ditties simply didn't pay attention during the last 20 years.

See also COSBY SHOW, THE; *E.T.*; McFERRIN, BOBBY; *RAIDERS OF THE LOST ARK*; SPIELBERG, STEVEN; *STAR WARS*; *SUPERMAN: THE MOVIE*

WILLIAMS, VANESSA

She achieved two firsts in the history of the Miss America pageant: She became the first black woman to win the title, and then became the first to have the crown taken away after nude photos of her appeared in *Penthouse*.

WILLIAMS, WAYNE

Better known as the Atlanta Child Murderer. He was convicted of killing some 30 kids in and around the Peachtree City in the early '80s and was one of the first infamous serial killers of the decade.

See also BUNDY, TED; GACY, JOHN WAYNE

WILSON, JUSTIN

Cajun chef who became famous in the latter part of the 1980s, first for doing a few Ruffles commercials and later when Cajun cooking became all the rage and he had his own show on PBS. Catchphrase, phonetically

Another big moment in our lifetimes

In March 1985, following the death of Constantin Chernenko, a 54-year-old man with a splotch on his head took over as leader of the Soviet Union. Mikhail Gorbachev would soon be talking to avowed Cold Warrior Ronald Reagan like an old football buddy. For pushing the bloated Soviet Union toward its demise and opening up Russian society, he would be named *Time* magazine's Man of the Decade.

spelled: "I gare-AWN-tee."

See also "IKO IKO"

WIN, LOSE OR DRAW

Pictionary rip-off that became a game show where B-list celebrities competed for cash and prizes in teams of three that included one regular schmo. Hosted by Mark DeCarlo, who was also the host of *Studs* and the basketball coach in *Buffy the Vampire Slayer*.

See also PICTIONARY; REMOTE CONTROL; STARCADE

WINSLOW, MICHAEL

Better known as "the sound effects guy," who played Jones in all the *Police Academy* movies and one of Dark Helmet's soldiers in *Spaceballs*.

See also POLICE ACADEMY; SPACEBALLS; THAT "HEY VERN" GUY

WINTER GAMES

Kinda like Summer Games, except this time you used the arrow keys and space bar to ski jump, skate, and slalom.

See also SUMMER GAMES; TRACK AND FIELD

WITNESS

The movie that proved wrong anybody who ever said that the Amish can never be a nationwide pop culture rage. This Harrison Ford/Kelly McGillis film combined tough cops and thugs with the simple Amish of rural America and somehow became a huge hit. Burger King didn't sell churn-your-own-milk toys with kids

meals, but that probably wouldn't have come as a surprise.

See also FORD, HARRISON; STAR WARS; TOP GUN

WKRP IN CINCINNATI

Baby, we've been wondering what ever became of this sitcom about a radio station in the Queen City that starred Gary Sandy, Howard Hesseman, Loni Anderson, Jan Smithers, Gordon Jump, and Tim Reid.

See also HEAD OF THE CLASS; REYNOLDS, BURT

WOMAN WHO KEPT BREAKING INTO DAVID LETTERMAN'S HOUSE, THE

That about sums her up.

See also LETTERMAN, DAVE

WONDER WOMAN

The best attempt by a TV network to build a series on a comic-book character and stay true to the stories while using live actors. Lynda Carter played the woman from Paradise Island, with Debra Winger as her sidekick. Far less campy than the *Batman* of Adam West, and well above the short-lived *Spiderman* series. It probably didn't hurt the show's rating among men that Carter was basically in a bikini for half the show.

See also INCREDIBLE HULK, THE; LIVE-ACTION SUPERHERO SHOWS

WOO-YEAH! SAMPLE

One of the most frequently sampled

noises in the rap, house, and hip-hop tunes of the last decade. After it drove the beat of Rob Base and D.J. E-Z Rock's "It Takes Two," this sound of somebody screaming, "Woo! Yeah! Woo! Yeah! Woo! Yeah!" turned up in dozens of extended dance mixes for almost any kind of music.

See also CLINTON, GEORGE; RAP; ROB BASE AND D.J. E-Z ROCK; SAMPLING

WORD

A brilliantly conceived '80s slang word that can be used as an exclamation, a space filler, or just when no other utterance will fit. Usage includes: 1) "Word" 2) "Word!" 3) "Word word word"

See also D.J. JAZZY JEFF AND THE FRESH PRINCE; FUCK; GAG ME WITH A SPOON; SHAZBOT!

WRINKLE IN TIME, A

By Madeleine L'Engle, one of the more intellectual books we read in elementary school. It touched on obtuse subjects like folding space ("tesseracting," she called it), time travel, explaining sight to alien species with no eyes, Jesus Christ, and the nature of the entire universe. Similar math-and-weirdness books included the sequels, *A Wind in the Door* and *A Swiftly Tilting Planet*, and Norton Juster's *The Phantom Tollbooth*.

See also BLUME, JUDY; CHOOSE YOUR OWN ADVENTURE; CLEARY, BEVERLY; *PHANTOM TOLLBOOTH, THE*

WTBS

One of the few so-called "superstations," whose sole purpose, it seems, was to broadcast old episodes of *The Flintstones*, *The Brady Bunch*, and *Gilligan's Island* and some game shows. Households across the country received this Ted Turner-owned, Atlanta-based anomaly, some without even having cable.

The big question remains: Is there something wrong with the space-time continuum in Georgia? Why do shows *always* start five minutes later on WTBS, like at 11:05 or 2:35?

See also ATHENS, GA.; TURNER, TED; WGN

X Y

XANADU

Arguably, this is the film that put the roller-skating boom over the top in 1980. It starred Michael Beck as the roller-entrepreneur/dreamer, Gene Kelly as his mentor (musta needed the cash), and Olivia Newton-John as the friendly apparition who inspired them.

See also NEWTON-JOHN, OLIVIA; ROLLER SKATING

YAHTZEE!

Dice game from Milton Bradley (in regular and travel versions) that challenged players to risk their current roll of five dice for a roll that might turn up more of the same face on top. Of course, if you got the same number on all five dice, you were allowed to scream the magic word.

See also ELECTRONIC BATTLESHIP; UNO

YANKOVIC, "WEIRD" AL

He didn't really catch on until he started making fun of Michael Jackson with "Eat It" from his album *Dare to Be Stupid*. Other notable parodies included "Ricky" and "I Lost on Jeopardy" and "Yoda," a takeoff on the Kinks' "Lola."

See also BASIL, TONI; JACKSON, MICHAEL; KIHN, GREG; *STAR WARS*

YEAGER, CHUCK

In a strange twist of fickle American hero worship, this WWII fighter pilot, who was widely regarded as the greatest aviator ever to live, resurfaced in the 1980s. Tom Wolfe's book *The Right Stuff* (and the 1983 movie) told of how Yeager was the first man to travel faster than the speed of sound, of how he, more than anyone, possessed the undeniable "right stuff" that makes a good pilot. The aged Yeager had a cameo in the movie as a bartender and then put out his best-selling autobiography. But this new public excitement about the space race–era pilots died down as Tom Cruise showed up and took over as aviator of the hour.

See also BONFIRE OF THE VANITIES, THE; CRUISE, TOM; GOOSE; *RIGHT STUFF, THE*

YELLO

Rare is the person who owns any album by this music group. Rarer still is the person who doesn't recognize the mechanized, guttural "Oh yeah" and "Chk, chka-chk-aahh" from its one known song, featured in *Ferris Bueller's Day Off*, *The Secret of My Success*, Twix commercials, and uncountable sporting events.

See also BUELLER, FERRIS

YELLOW RIBBONS

What we tied around our trees when the Iran hostages were freed on the very same day that Ronald Reagan was inaugurated for his first term.

See also IRANIAN HOSTAGE CRISIS; REAGAN, RONALD

YO-BALLS

Yo-yos for uncoordinated people. The glow-in-the-dark, plastic ball always came back, but what's the fun in that?

See also GLO-WORM; KOOSH

YOGURT

Mysterious dairy product rife with live enzymes that became hugely popular in the '80s, particularly when served in big frozen mounds. We saw the birth of two chains fond of negative contractions: This Can't Be Yogurt (later changed to The Country's Best Yogurt and then shortened to simply TCBY) and I Can't Believe This Is Yogurt (later changed to I Can't Believe We Didn't Stay In Business), and ice cream shops had to install yogurt machines to keep up. All this because the stuff tastes kind of like ice cream, but has less fat and calories and can thus be called "healthy." Imagine what would happen if scientists discover that chocolate reduces the risk of heart disease.

See also OAT BRAN; RICE CAKES; *STUFF, THE*

YOU CAN'T DO THAT ON TELEVISION

Canadian kid sketch-comedy show seen on Nickelodeon. It didn't have any cussing or nudity, so we never quite understood the name.

BONUS FACT: Alanis Morrisette got her show-biz start here.

See also SLIME

YOUNG, PAUL

English balladeer with lots of hair who sang sensitive love songs, like "Every Time You Go Away," that were slow-dance staples at high school proms. Appeared in London at Live Aid.

See also BILLY VERA AND THE BEATERS; HART, COREY; MARX, RICHARD

YOUNG GUNS

The Brat Pack takes a break from the trials of modern-day suburban high school life to do a Western. But this 1988 bore would have been halfway entertaining had stars Emilio Estevez, Lou Diamond Phillips, Charlie Sheen and Kiefer Sutherland grabbed some guns and hats and run around the halls of Ridgemont High instead of 19th-century Kansas. The sequel (that would be *Young Guns II*) surpassed the first one simply because it had some kind of a plot.

See also BRAT PACK, THE; *BREAKFAST CLUB, THE*; *OUTSIDERS, THE*; *SILVERADO*; *ST. ELMO'S FIRE*; *THREE O'CLOCK HIGH*

YOUNG MC

Also known as Marvin Young, he had a knack for the plain-English "anecdotal rap" pioneered by the Fresh Prince and Tone Loc. After studying architecture at USC, he busted a move, hung out in the principal's office, and then disappeared.

See also D.J. JAZZY JEFF AND THE FRESH PRINCE; LOC, TONE; RAP

YOUNG ONES, THE

British sitcom about a bunch of punk-rock, counterculture types with really weird hair. Countless reruns of this made it into our brains thanks to MTV.

See also MOHAWKS; MTV; PUNK ROCK

"YOU'RE NO JACK KENNEDY"

Political catchphrase coined in 1988 during a vice-presidential debate between Lloyd Bentsen and Dan Quayle. Lloyd says to Dan: "I knew Jack Kennedy. You're no Jack Kennedy."

See also HORTON, WILLIE; "I'LL BE BACK"; "READ MY LIPS"

YUGO

From behind the tattered Iron Curtain in the late 1980s came this car, priced under $4,000, and you got what you paid for. One Cadillac dealer in Centerville, Ohio, ran a promotion whereby if you bought a new Caddy, they would give you a Yugo for free.

See also BERLIN WALL; DELOREAN; SUZUKI SAMURAI

YUPPIES

A stereotype born from the dual-income lifestyle of upper-middle-class Boomer couples who worked and lived in cool places and bought stuff they liked. The term, an ironic twist on hippies, which a lot of yuppies were before they became yuppies, stands for Young Urban Professionals and will probably apply to many of us when we get jobs and start buying stuff we like.

See also BABY ON BOARD; SALT II; *THIRTYSOMETHING*; YUPPIE PUPPIES

YUPPIE PUPPIES

One of the first catchall terms for our generation that failed to stick. A series of 1985 ads referred to Nickelodeon's target audience as Yuppie Puppies. This, of course, didn't last long. We outgrew Nickelodeon and culture marketers found plenty of other terms for us.

See also CABLE; GENERATION X; MTV GENERATION

Z

ZAMFIR

Master of the pan flute and the not-sold-in-stores recorder album.

See also K-Tel; Popiel, Ron; Time-Life operator, The

ZAPPA, MOON

If anybody tells you that the language, culture, and look of the Valley Girl evolved naturally as a biological reaction to being female and in Los Angeles, they are lying to you. *Duh!* The persona was invented and propagated by Moon Zappa, daughter of punk hero Frank.

See also Duh; Valley Girls

ZAPPED!

Teenage male nerd fantasy film about a teenage male nerd (Scott Baio) who creates a potion to give himself supernatural powers, which he and his buddy (Willie Aames) use to look up girls' skirts.

See also Charles in Charge; Weird Science

ZAXXON

The 3-D look of this game and the somewhat angular movements of your spaceship made it really, really hard the first few times you played it.

See also Atari; 3-D movies

ZORK

The first in a series of "text adventure" games for home computers. The Infocom company existed solely on a diet of Zork-style games, in which the computer describes your surroundings and you issue instructions.

For example:

Computer: **You emerge from the burning castle and into a clearing. A trail to the East is littered with what appears to be Pop Tart crumbs, and deep moans can be heard from behind a door to the West.**

You: Touch door.

Computer: **The door feels warm and wet, as if alive.**

You: Open door with magic key.

Computer: **As you slide the key into the door, the moaning becomes a shrill scream and the door turns into a 20-foot dragon drooling fire all over the place.**

You: Kill dragon with key.

Computer: **No use. The dragon eats you. You emerge from the dragon's esophagus into a large stomach. Deep moans can be heard from an intestine to the West . . .**

And so on. Zork took place in a magic underground kingdom of the same name. Other popular titles included Planetfall, Enchanter, and

The Hitchhiker's Guide to the Galaxy. If you got stuck, you could always buy the official clue books, which were written in invisible ink and had to be rubbed with a special pen to reveal hints.

See also ATARI; DUNGEONS & DRAGONS; HITCHHIKER'S GUIDE TO THE GALAXY, THE

ZUCKER BROTHERS

Common name for a trio of cinematic comedy geniuses, only two of which are named Zucker (Dave and Jerry). Along with Jim Abrahams, these guys from Milwaukee are responsible for some of the funniest movies made in our lifetime. They collaborated with John Landis on *Kentucky Fried Movie*, then went on to skewer disaster movies in *Airplane!*, war pictures and Elvis films in *Top Secret!*, and every conceivable type of cop movie in *Naked Gun*, which was based on their short-lived TV series *Police Squad*. They also did a one-time spoof of TV newsmagazines called *Our Planet Tonight*, which ran on NBC. No one was safe from their over-the-top, ridiculous, laugh-till-you-pee humor.

See also AIRPLANE!; KENTUCKY FRIED MOVIE; LANDIS, JOHN

Sex Romp 101:

A RECIPE FOR THE PERFECT '80S HIGH SCHOOL-STYLE HIJINKS MOVIE

Ask any historian. The '80s were the Golden Sexual Age of Nerds, a time of kinky freedom and lewd expression for the skinny, for the weird, and for the geeky. It was an era of wacky shenanigans, of so-called "brewskies" and elaborate practical jokes enjoyed among friends, of casual sex, or at least "brief nudity." One art form in particular (aside from beer commercials) most accurately captured this lifestyle: the sexual hijinks movie. And for those who want to relive the era of *Bikini Car Wash* and *Revenge of the Nerds*, a few key ingredients are all you need for 85 minutes of adolescent entertainment worthy of any 11:30 P.M. slot on Cinemax! Stir and enjoy . . .

1. THE PERFECT SETTING. Of course, the movie should fit the classic Aristotelian ideal of drama, of a single time and place, if for no other reason than budget. This means one, maybe two, sets. If your characters are kids or students, they need to travel somewhere away from home to explore their sexual rumblings, where they can create and destroy their own intercourse-based social structures. You can use camp (as in the almost-perfect *Meatballs*), a summer resort (as they did in *Hot Resort*), a backwoods race of some sort (*Up the Creek*), spring break (*Hardbodies*)

or, classically, any high school (*Porky's*) or college (*Revenge of the Nerds*, *H.O.T.S.*). But if your heroes are adults, panty-raid-style fun requires a framework of authority, something against which they can rebel. So choose a setting of imposed order such as boot camp (*Stripes*), police academy (*Police Academy*) or even traffic school (*Speed Zone*).

2. HERO (AND HIS BUDDIES). The movie's protagonist should be the most "normal" member of an off-beat band of misfits and/or geeks that, by the end of the movie, have warmed the hearts of not only the viewer, but all the babes. This posse must also include a fat guy, a dumb guy, a super-smart guy, and some sort of danger-seeking sex fiend played by Tim Matheson.

3. LOVE. (OR AT LEAST ONE MAN'S DESPERATE URGE TO HAVE SEX WITH ONE WOMAN.) Achieve this by having the everyguy hero imediately fall for the film's object of desire (see No. 5), a woman who should swiftly rebuff his advances simply because he's a dork.

4. VILLAINS. Create a rival band of guys—they need to be blond, bronze, toned, and well financed—who just happen to be doing exactly what the hero and his buddies are doing (going to camp, joining the Army, working as waiters at a ski resort so they can

have sex all winter long, whatever). Except only better. They come from the same social group as the OBJECT OF DESIRE, and, thus, she likes them best. Their presence creates not only tension, but makes the film *seem* less pointless, as if there were a plot.

5. OBJECT OF DESIRE. When she first meets our hero, she is moving in slow motion and soon disses him for one of the villains, a total dick (usually wealthy and Aryan) who more fits into her social strata. Toward the middle of the film, she must somehow fall for the hero's boyish charm and, when he beats the pants off the villains in the impending SPORTING COMPETITION, she's in love.

6. HER FRIENDS. And a lot of them. They want nothing more than to have sex with anybody (except the fat guy) and to wear shorts and T-shirts that almost—but not quite—reveal their tender parts.

7. ONE OR TWO GRATUITOUS BREAST SHOTS. For the entire sex romp, use no more than two seconds total of exposed breasts. This will qualify you for the "brief nudity" description necessary to get viewers. The nakedness should appear no sooner than two-thirds of the way into the film, as a sort of payoff, preluded by an hour of teasing bikini shots and aborted intercourse opportunities. (EXAMPLE: Have a couple try to "do it," as they say, in a tree and then fall right onto the head of an authority figure.) The exposed breasts shouldn't belong to the OBJECT OF DESIRE but instead to a supporting female character who, arguably, is better-looking but has less screen time.

8. SUPPORTING CHARACTER WHO SPENDS THE ENTIRE MOVIE TRYING TO HAVE SEX WITH AN OUT-OF-HIS-LEAGUE FEMALE. This needs to be Tim Matheson.

9. WACKY AUTHORITY FIGURE WHO TAKES HIMSELF TOO SERIOUSLY. A whip-cracking sergeant or camp counselor or restaurant owner can provide the perfect foil around which the hero-villain rivalry revolves. The villians suck up to the authority figure, thus gaining the endorsement of The Man in their pursuit of pussy. If at all possible, the figure should be played by Bruce McGill, who created the WACKY AUTHORITY FIGURE WHO TAKES HIMSELF TOO SERIOUSLY role in the bible of all sex romps, *Animal House*. Also, he needs a sidekick who can be tormented by the hero's buddies throughout.

10. SPORTING COMPETITION. You say you can't think of a climax for these complex relationships? Simply pit the heroes and villians against each other in an obvious and overdone sport. If they're at a ski resort, let it be a hotdogging competition. If they're spring-breaking in Daytona, let it be a long-board competition. Easy. Throughout the movie, the misfits must annoy the villains to the point that head-to-head competition becomes an allegory for war, be it a river-raft race, a talent contest or a topless flag football game. While the stronger villains may have the advantage, a series of clever pranks (pulled off during a peppy rock 'n' roll–enhanced montage of clever misfits at work) derails the evildoers and delivers victory—and the beautiful woman—to your hero. The villains scowl, the wet T-shirt contest begins, and the credits roll.